KURT
&WOLFF

Kurt Wolff in 1963

KURT & WOLFF

A PORTRAIT IN

ESSAYS & LETTERS

EDITED WITH A FOREWORD BY

MICHAEL ERMARTH

Translated by Deborah Lucas Schneider

The University of Chicago Press

CHICAGO & LONDON

9200002846

Some of the essays and letters in this book
were first published in Germany as *Autoren, Bücher,
Abenteuer*, Klaus Wagenbach Verlag,
© 1965 Helen Wolff, and *Briefwechsel eines
Verlegers*, edited by Bernard Zeller and
Helen Otten, © Scheffler Verlag 1966.

The University of Chicago Press, Chicago 60637
The University of Chicago Press, Ltd., London
© 1991 by The University of Chicago
All rights reserved. Published 1991
Printed in the United States of America
00 99 98 97 96 95 94 93 92 91   5 4 3 2 1

ISBN 0-226-90551-9 (cl.)

Library of Congress Cataloging-in-Publication Data

Kurt Wolff : a portrait in essays and letters / edited with a foreword
by Michael Ermarth ; translated by Deborah Lucas Schneider.
     p.   cm.
   Includes bibliographical references and index.
   1. Wolff, Kurt, 1887–1963.   2. Wolff, Kurt, 1887–1963—
Correspondence.   3. Authors and publishers—Germany—Frankfurt am
Main—History—20th century.   4. Literature publishing—Germany—
Frankfurt am Main—History—20th century.   5. Publishers and
publishing—Germany—Correspondence.   6. Publishers and publishing—
Germany—Biography.   I. Ermarth, Michael.
Z315.W72K875   1991
070.5'092—dc20
   [B]   91-16490
                                                            CIP

CONTENTS

CONTENTS

FOREWORD

If ever a publisher could be invested with Goethe's idea of "world literature," it would be Kurt Wolff. His life spanned a period of drastic changes in his native Germany, in the world at large, and in publishing in particular. Yet for all the effects these upheavals worked upon his aspirations, he remained intent upon a vision of publishing as true calling and craft. Today, amidst continuing structural changes in what is less and less often called the "book world," it is rewarding to ponder a chapter that is in a sense closed—or better, enclosed—by the career of this dedicated man. It is also a chapter that remains open by the force of his singular presence. This collection of essays and letters allows that person to speak in his own eloquent, gently resolute voice: its aim is to show something of the man, his sense of literary calling, and his milieu.

The Kurt Wolff Verlag, along with its antecedents and offshoots in Germany and the United States, established a reputation for publishing works of unmatched literary quality. Under the imprint of these firms Wolff published an astonishing number of authors who rose to world renown—Franz Kafka, Georg Heym, Franz Werfel, Georg Trakl, Romain Rolland, Martin Buber, Rabindranath Tagore, Robert Walser, Boris Pasternak, Günter Grass, among others. The letters to these writers—to Wolff himself and to others—testify emphatically to their devotion to his unique style of publishing, one that remained in almost contrapuntal relation with their own way of thinking and writing. He observed that a publisher should so fully identify with the author and his work that their relation becomes "not anonymous but synonymous." Fostering such a close relationship with this variety of powerful talents became an alter-art in its own right. It might be called the art of publishing with a human face—

paradoxically, with an inimitable personal stamp of selfless fidelity, one as indelible as the signet of the firm itself.

His life showed a pattern of energetic renewal around a core commitment: the vocation of bringing forth books that would serve as resources of the human spirit. Along with the original Kurt Wolff Verlag, he founded, acquired, or guided the Verlag der Weissen Bücher, Hyperion Verlag, Der Neue Geist Verlag, Pantheon Casa Editrice, Pantheon Books, and Helen and Kurt Wolff Books. He enjoyed nothing so much as moving in a new direction with an animating purpose. If there is one "secret" of success for this man who disliked all pat formulas and labels, it was that he had an elective affinity for writers, thinkers, and artists who were capable of the same kinetic feats of continual renewal.

The affinities and ruptures in his life were more pronounced than those of most Central European intellectuals of this turbulent time. He was born in Bonn in 1887, into a highly cultured family—perhaps familiar imaginatively to some readers through the works of Thomas Mann set in Imperial Germany. His father was a professor of music history and academic music director at the university; the son's lifelong love of music and poetry was rooted in generations of family experience. His Jewish mother, from an old, assimilated family of Bonn, died when he was seventeen. Already as a youth he devoted himself to cultivation of the "spirit" in that peculiarly German sense of *Geist*. His notion of culture, however, remained free of the sort of sclerotic idolatry mocked by Friedrich Nietzsche as "bowing backwards" toward the greats of the past.

Wolff attended the *Gymnasium* in Bonn and Marburg, but spent the year of 1906 abroad in São Paolo, Brazil, in the overseas training program of a German banking institute. The following year he returned to Germany to fulfill his military service, at which time he became acquainted with members of the literary circle around the poet Stefan George. This circle included the professor and pedagogue Friedrich Gundolf, who commented upon the young Wolff's acute intelligence and literary taste. Very early on Wolff became a systematic collector of German books of different periods and stylistic directions. Showing no inclination for military or financial matters, he decided upon university studies in German literature, enrolling at

Marburg, Darmstadt, and Leipzig. During his period of Leipzig study, he edited and published scholarly texts at Anton Kippenberg's Insel Verlag, one of the most famous German publishing houses of the day. This experience intensified his literary leanings in a way that projected them beyond personal enjoyment.

Belletristic publishing was long and well established in Germany, associated with the names Samuel Fischer, Reinhard Piper, Eugen Diederichs, Albert Langen, and others. Each house was known for a certain cultural tendency—concentrating upon certain styles or genres, such as Classicism, Naturalism, drama, poetry, the plastic arts, translation, and so on. But despite the flurry of cultural revival and talk of the "rejuvenation of the spirit" before the First World War, these established publishing houses were less than receptive to the new generation of defiant writers and artists who came to maturity after 1910. Wolff set about finding and nurturing the best work of his own generation. After an initial partnership with Ernst Rowohlt, the independent Kurt Wolff Verlag was founded in 1913. In a letter to Karl Kraus from this period he compared the role of publisher to that of a seismograph registering the tremors of the times. Such tremors would soon build to major quakes that would change the face of the world.

Like others of his rebellious generation, Wolff harbored no great awe for the pillars of the Wilhelmine establishment—the prominent professors, literary lions, and official custodians of Imperial culture. In addition to music and books, Wolff's zeal was reserved for the new European writers and artists of urgent originality—those who could address this age from a point beyond its own complacent self-images. After befriending author-students Walter Hasenclever, Franz Werfel, and Kurt Pinthus, he enlisted them as readers in his new firm; they would later emerge as major forces in the Expressionist movement. In these early years, Wolff displayed an uncanny sense for discerning and fostering writers of utmost talent. This sense was sharpened rather than blunted by the passage of time—and by Wolff's gradual passage from outsider to insider in the German publishing world.

His foremost criterion for a publisher was, as he put it emphatically, "enthusiasm, enthusiasm, enthusiasm." This manifold personal passion on the part of the publisher was, so to speak, raised to the third power, but it was a far cry from the self-aggrandizing "hype" that often permeates modern publishing. Wolff meant rather a compound enthusiasm that grows naturally out of the work itself: first and foremost, for the quality of work at hand; second, for bringing the work to a wider audience; and third, for eliciting a corresponding response from the public. But this final enthusiasm was only to be hoped for, not to be curried. In Wolff's writings there is discussion of the reading public and of public taste, but remarkably little attention given to the "market" as such. Not that a book market did not exist or was not solicited, but it did not supervene as the preeminent consideration. If Wolff did not go so far as Nietzsche in saying that in matters of the spirit "success is the great liar," he nevertheless saw success as the happy side effect of good judgment regarding the quality of the work at hand. Such judgment might not find instant corroboration by the public. (Thus, he risked publishing unknown authors like Franz Kafka, Robert Walser, and Joseph Roth—all of whom emerged to fame decades later.)

After World War I Wolff moved his firm from Leipzig to Munich, and rededicated himself to publishing books that became bridges of cultural communication between reading publics that had been former enemies—prize-winning German translations of Emile Zola, Henri Barbusse, Anatole France, Paul Claudel, Maxim Gorky, Anton Chekov, and Sinclair Lewis. Kafka's *Amerika* and *Das Schloss* [The Castle] were published after the author's death in 1924; Lewis's *Babbitt* and *Arrowsmith* followed the next year. Wolff emerged as an innovative but respected publisher, operating under harrowing conditions of astronomical inflation and staggering fluctuations of credit, of availability of paper, and of other vital resources. Despite enormous practical difficulties, Wolff remained firm in his belief in the creative promise of the generation of Weimar writers who gave such luster to the period. He was the engine behind several different, smaller houses, with distinct offerings in contemporary fiction, the fine arts, and illustrated classics. International connections were made with houses abroad (Pegasus in Paris, Harcourt Brace in New York, and Gili in Barcelona) in connection with the founding of Pantheon Casa Editrice S. A. in 1924 in Florence, for the publication of a comprehensive international history of art, to be written and published in German, French, English, and Spanish. This venture was the forerunner of the many international coproductions of later years.

Wolff pioneered editions of high quality but relatively low cost which went into large printings. It is doubly ironic that in his youth he was criticized by competing German firms for introducing "American methods" and unseemly "commercialization" into the sacrosanct German book guild. (Later he would become renowned in American publishing circles for following impossibly exacting German standards of quality!) He favored bold and colorful jackets, newspaper and kiosk advertising with striking designs, and other innovations held by his staider colleagues to be more suitable to newspaper and magazine publishing. He initiated several new thematic series with open-ended lists: "The New Novel," "The European Novel," "Modern Poetry in Translation." He enlisted the contemporary artists Frans Masereel, George Grosz, Alfred Kubin, Ernst Ludwig Kirchner, and Paul Klee for book design, dust jackets, and illustrations.

The Kurt Wolff Verlag rapidly gained fame throughout Germany and Europe as the "House of Expressionism," for its dedication to bringing out the works of major writers grouped under this umbrella term. These would include Werfel, Hasenclever, Kafka, as well as Carl Sternheim, Oskar Kokoschka, and many others. The common denominator for this new poetic "pandemonium" was an ethos of reformist, even revolutionary inner spirituality. With many different shadings and tendencies, it called for an inner reformation of the human soul through the transfigurative power of art. Wolff would later try to distance himself from his reputation as "publisher of the Expressionists," for he did not put much credence in cultural coverlets or collective slogans, just as he did not believe in tradition and fame as votive talismans. He cannot be snared in the usual dichotomy of traditionalist or avant gardist, for he continued to publish fine editions of the classics in very "modern" format. Voltaire's *Candide*, for example, was accompanied with drawings by Paul Klee. His catholic tastes did not, moreover, amount to a taste for everything. He had little patience for the Dada movement, calling it "totally imbecile gobbledygook." He acknowledged that he was blessed not only in his authors, but also in his readers and editorial advisors, who, in addition to Werfel and Pinthus, also came to include Willy Haas, Hans (later Giovanni) Mardersteig, and Carl Georg Heise, the art historian and museum director. As his letters indicate, the closest rapport of author to publisher remained his central and abiding concern.

But these innovations and allegiances were not enough to save his firm from the rising tide of economic depression and political radicalization in Germany. With rapidly deteriorating conditions, he was forced to disband Kurt Wolff Verlag in 1930 and to retire altogether from publishing in Germany. The Nazi book burnings of the spring of 1933 included many Wolff titles and authors. Sharing the fate of many of his authors, he emigrated from Germany. The ten-year period 1931–41 he spent in France and Italy with his second wife Helen and their son Christian. During this time he was repeatedly propelled in new directions by changing outer forces and conditions.

The family emigrated to the United States in May, 1941. Within a year Wolff had founded Pantheon Books, Incorporated, after spending long hours reading and researching in New York Public Library to determine what literary lacunae might be filled by his new venture. Like the earlier Wolff Verlag of 1913 in Leipzig, it began humbly in a single multipurpose room, but with the whole world as its horizon. One of the early Pantheon catalogues repeated Wolff's lifelong quest through the words of a writer he cherished: "Pantheon Books, Inc. hopes to bring to discerning readers only such books as deserve Stendhal's praise: 'They widen the horizon, abolish barriers, and lead men to understand and love more and more.' Our field is world literature, poetry, history, philosophy, and art."

Pantheon published about forty titles a year, primarily in the humanities and humane disciplines. Contemporary authors in translation included Hermann Broch, Karl Jaspers, Romano Guardini, Julien Green, Jacques Maritain, Paul Valéry, and Robert Musil—along with the "classics" of Pascal, Dante, Goethe, Tolstoy, Jacob Burckhardt, and the Grimm brothers. As in the Weimar era, Pantheon books were known for their fine type and striking visual format, with drawings by Alexander Calder, Ben Shahn, and other artists. Under the direction of Jacques Schiffrin, the French publisher and also a refugee, the firm published a French language series with such authors as André Gide, Albert Camus, Vercors, and Denis de Rougemont. A truly native American best seller came in 1955 with Anne Morrow Lindbergh's *Gift from the Sea*, which sold well over 600,000 copies as a hardcover and two million as a paperback. Outstanding successes followed with the publication of Boris Pasternak's *Doctor Zhivago* (1958) and Giuseppe di Lampedusa's *The Leopard* (1960). To Pasternak, who was forced to decline the Nobel Prize in 1958 by the Soviet authorities, Wolff expressed his unflagging conviction that "being a publisher is not a 'job' but a passion and obsession."

Wolff's reputation for quality was reflected in his being chosen as publisher of the Bollingen Series. This ambitious and distinguished series published complete editions of major thinkers and writers, such as Carl Jung, Paul Valéry, and Hugo von Hofmannsthal, along with individual titles. Over the years, books under the Wolff imprint garnered prizes too numerous to mention here. He himself was awarded the Medal of Honor of the German Booksellers Association in 1960. The laudation for this occasion appears as a fitting conclusion to this volume.

In 1960 Kurt Wolff, then living in Switzerland for reasons of health, resigned from Pantheon Books, which was subsequently acquired by Random House and placed under the management of André Schiffrin, the son of Jacques.

In 1961 the seventy-four-year-old publisher was offered yet another avenue for his unflagging enthusiasm: to publish, in association with William Jovanovich, the young president of Harcourt, Brace and World (later Harcourt Brace Jovanovich) under his own personal imprint, Helen and Kurt Wolff Books, a list of his own selection— fully "synonymous, not anonymous." Imprint publishing, now a widely practiced form of affinitive publishing, was then invented, by William Jovanovich, to accommodate a celebrated elder colleague who had always been a founder and, as Jovanovich realized, would not fit into the mold of subordinate. The relationship was fruitful up to Wolff's death, and continued to be so with his surviving partner Helen Wolff.

The essays in this volume were prepared and read by Kurt Wolff in the years 1962 and 1963 for broadcasting over the following German stations: Norddeutscher, Westdeutscher, and Bayerischer Rundfunk.

Kurt Wolff was killed in a traffic accident in the fall of 1963. He

was in the midst of a strenuous trip which included, characteristically, a visit to the Frankfurt Book Fair, participation at the
annual gathering of the fresh and fiercely independent German literary Gruppe 47, and a visit to the Schiller National Museum, the
German state literary archive. He is buried in Marbach, Schiller's
birthplace.

His credo was at once simple and demanding: "We must remain
as open to the present as the past." He lived these words with remarkable fidelity. Is it possible that, in the emerging era of "world-
publishing" on a truly global scale, we can retain something of his
individual yet ecumenical spirit of world-literature? Of publishing
with an indelibly human face?

It is obvious that Kurt Wolff published translations of the highest
literary merit—and that he too must be served in a similar fashion.
The skilled efforts of Deborah Schneider convey his pithiness and
gentle directness. Professor Walter Arndt has rendered the verses of
Karl Kraus and Franz Werfel into spirited, even sprightly English.

The role of Frau Helen Wolff in this volume—and in Kurt
Wolff's endeavor as a whole—was gracefully "synonymous," but by
that very token must not be allowed thereby to remain "anonymous."
She should be recognized as prime mover and thanked as prime
nurturer in the genial alter art of publishing, as practiced by Kurt
Wolff.

The Wolff papers are at Yale University Library. A short bibliography of works by and about him is included in this volume, along with
a brief biographical glossary elaborating upon the names appearing in
the text.

Michael Ermarth
Dartmouth College

TRANSLATOR'S NOTE

All translations in this book are my own, with the exception of the Kraus and Werfel poems translated by Walter Arndt and portions of the Kafka correspondence translated by Richard and Clara Winston, as noted. Following Mrs. Wolff's example, the abbreviation KW is used for Kurt Wolff and KWV for Kurt Wolff Verlag [Kurt Wolff Publishing House]. English versions of German titles are given in brackets following the originals; they are given in italics when the work in question has been published in English and otherwise in my own ad hoc translation in roman type. I wish to thank Mrs. Wolff for her invaluable help in preparing the translation.

Portrait of Kurt Wolff by Felice Casorati, 1925

KURT WOLFF:
A BIOGRAPHICAL SKETCH

Compiled by Helen Wolff
from diaries, notes,
correspondence, and lectures

"I, Kurt August Paul Wolff, was born in Bonn on March 3, 1887 to Leonhard Wolff, a university professor, and his wife Maria, née Marx. I received the one-year volunteers' certificate and passed the *Abitur* examination at the Königliches Gymnasium in 1906. I attended the universities of Bonn, Munich, Marburg, and Leipzig and served for a year with the Field Artillery Regiment of the Grand Duchy of Hesse in Darmstadt. On September 2, 1909, I married Elisabeth Merck of Darmstadt.

"Bonn—the town where I was born on a March evening in 1887 as my father, the university music director, was conducting a performance of the 'Messiah' in the old Beethoven Hall—had little appeal to me. Still, it was the town where I spent a happy childhood and received my first impressions of great music. It was where my mother's family had lived for generations, while the home of my father's family was not far away in Krefeld . . . The most profound impression of beauty was made by the chamber music played at home, and I became familiar with the entire literature from Bach to Brahms."

Kurt Wolff recalled how he spent the year 1905 at the University of Marburg to Boris Pasternak in 1958: "I was a student in Marburg about a year before your time and spent an unforgettable semester reading Plato in Cohen's seminar . . . What pleasure it would give me to talk about Cohen, Natorp, and the others with you! (Perhaps you remember Theodor Birt, the professor of Latin, Johannes Weiss, the theologian and excellent pianist, Jenner, the musicologist who was also a pupil of Brahms, the Germanist Professor Vogt, and Elster.) I was on friendly terms with all of them, not because I was a brilliant student (I certainly wasn't), but because I always took my cello along when I went to call on them, and in those days I was the only decent amateur cellist in Marburg . . . "

Besides music, Kurt Wolff's interest in literature and literary history was evident from early on. A diary entry from December 1908 runs: "Have begun sending proofs for the Merck edition to Insel Verlag" (see Bibliography). In June 1909 he writes: "Signed contract with Insel Verlag for Adele Schopenhauer's diaries." 1910: "Have written a small essay on editions of *Werther.*"

He had also begun collecting books: "I laid the foundations for a large collection during my school days, but most of my library was acquired between 1907 and 1911. In the summer of 1912 I owned a total of about 12,000 volumes." His bibliophile interests are reflected in his contributions to the journal *Zeitschrift für Bücherfreunde* (see Bibliography).

Kurt Wolff entered the field of publishing during the winter of 1908, when he was a twenty-one-year-old student of German literature in Leipzig. His first step was to join Ernst Rowohlt's firm as a silent partner. His diary for July 30, 1910 reads: "The firm of Ernst Rowohlt Verlag is now listed in the Leipzig commercial register. Goethe's *Tasso* being printed." *Tasso* was the first volume of the first series created by Kurt Wolff: ". . . the Drugulin editions were the first to be in large format and printed on the highest quality paper . . . The idea of luxury editions that were still low in price was combined with a carefully thought-out plan for a series of widely varying content: Our aim was to publish masterpieces of world literature in single volumes, in the original language, with a scrupulously correct text."

The diary for 1910 reports: "First letter written to Heym," and soon thereafter, "Have asked Heym for poems." The names Eulenberg, Hasenclever, Pinthus, and Dauthendey appear in 1911–12. KW later wrote about this period: "The personal friendship which developed with Walter Hasenclever meant far more to both of us than our relationship as author and publisher. The beginnings of this friendship go back to the year 1909. We sat next to each other at the University of Leipzig in the classes of Albert Köster, Georg Witkowski, and Karl Lamprecht. When I began to work in publishing about that time, Walter was the friend who advised me, along with Franz Werfel and Kurt Pinthus. We worked out the announcements and program for the series *Der Jüngste Tag* [The Last Judgment] and many other projects at the Café Merkur or Wilhelm's Wine Bar." June 29, 1912: "Kafka and Brod at the office." September 1, 1912: "Have become a partner in Rowohlt Verlag with 35,000 marks capital and a loan of about 55,000 marks (I was a silent partner before)." From the same year: "Contract signed with Kafka for *Betrachtung* [Meditation]." "Werfel's first visit." "Negotiating with Werfel Senior about contract for Franz as a reader." "Sent first manuscript to 'Reader' Werfel."

On October 24, 1912 the diary reports: "Discussion has begun about disagreements with Rowohlt," and on November 2, "Signed agreement with Rowohlt dissolving the partnership."

The Kurt Wolff Verlag was entered in the Leipzig commercial register on February 15, 1913. From the same month: "Negotiating through Werfel with Kraus-Kokoschka about the *Chinesische Mauer* [The Great Wall of China]." In March KW acquired *Die Weißen Blätter*, a magazine that was edited during the war by René Schickele. April, 1913: "Wrote first letter to Trakl." August: "Poetry manuscripts Stadler and Schickele." October: "Hyperion Verlag founded as a limited company." Talking of this expansion in 1963, KW said: "I wanted to do more and more—that was due to my youth. And then, too, there weren't all that many authors for a literary publishing house. Adding others would have altered the image of the original Kurt Wolff Verlag, however, and watered it down, shifted the emphasis. This was why I began to look for other names, or another profile, you might say. And when the Hyperion Verlag came up for sale . . . I acquired it, so I could produce beautiful books to my heart's content: Luxury editions, illustrated books, translations, and also a series called *Die Romantischen Taschenbücher* [Romantic Pocket Editions]."

October 28, 1913: "*Jüngster Tag* 7–12 published." The aims of this series with the subtitle "New Writing" were described in the firm's catalogue for 1910–13: "*Der Jüngste Tag* is intended to be more than a book and less than a series; it will contain works by the newest authors, inspired by the shared experience of our time. These works, informed in both substance and form by this new spirit, will appear in single volumes at irregular intervals and carry a brief but powerful summary of their ideas to the widest possible audience at a very low price. Each volume will cost 80 pfennigs in paper and 1.50 marks in cloth." Here, as in the Drugulin editions, we find his intention to make works of the highest quality available to broad sections of the public by keeping prices low.

In 1914 the diary reports: "Vienna with Karl Kraus," "Sternheim in Leipzig, a reading from *Napoleon*," "Have accepted Trakl's *Sebastian*," and the further entry, "Am acquiring the Leipzig Theater." July: "Corrected proofs of *Golem* ready." On August 2 KW is sent to the front as a lieutenant; in his absence Georg Heinrich Meyer takes over the management of the business. "During the First World War I was able to arrange for Walter Hasenclever to join my unit as soon as he was called up, so we were together as long as he was in uniform, first in Belgium, and later in Russia and the Balkans." In September 1916, Kurt Wolff is given indefinite leave from the army on the instructions of the Grand Duke of Hesse, in order to continue his publishing activities. 1916: "Private printing of *Untertan* [*The Patrioteer*] finished"—this was Heinrich Mann's novel, of which only ten copies were printed. In that same year the "Verlag der Schriften von Karl Kraus" (Press for the Writings of Karl Kraus) was founded, followed by a series named "Der Neue Roman—Sammlung zeitgenössischer Erzähler" [The New Novel—Contemporary Fiction]. A year later, 400,000 volumes of this series were in circulation. The diary for 1917 mentions two people who were to steer the firm in an important new direction: Hans Mardersteig and Carl Georg Heise. They contributed greatly to making the Kurt Wolff Verlag the leading publishing house for modern art. Diary entries from 1917 read: "Sent contract for portfolio work to Kirchner." "Mardersteig seeing Kollwitz in Berlin." "K. Kollwitz sent drawing 'The Poor.'" In the same year yet another series was begun: "Ten volumes of the Dionysus Library printed—ask Preetorius for cover drawings." 1918: "Seven volumes in the Dionysus Library published." "Kraus, *Worte in Versen* III [Words in Verse III] published." "'Der neue Geist Verlag' [The New Spirit Press] founded." "Contract for Schmidt-Rottluff's portfolio work." "Heinrich Mann, novels and stories in ten volumes." From the diary for 1919: "Twenty-seven hours to get from Darmstadt to Leipzig." "General strike in Leipzig, plus a railroad strike." "Martial law in Leipzig." Nevertheless thirteen volumes of the new *Jedermannsbücherei* [Everyman's Library] go into production—a charming miniature library of world literature, with cover silhouettes by Emil Preetorius. May, 1919: "Paula Becker-Modersohn book published; Pacquet, *Geist der russischen Revolution* [Spirit of the Russian Revolution]; Hofmannsthal, *Gespräch* [Conversation] and *Genius* I finished; five volumes Strindberg in production." September: "Played trio with Klee." In October the firm moved from Leipzig to new headquarters at Luisenstraße 13 in Munich.

Book prices mentioned in the diary reflected mounting inflation. 1920: "*Der neue Roman* [The New Novel], original price 3.50 marks, now priced at 9 marks." Hausenstein's *Kairuan, oder die Geschichte vom Maler Klee und von der Kunst dieses Zeitalters* [Kairuan, or the History of Klee the Painter and the Art of this Era] appears. In 1921 the Kurt Wolff Verlag became a corporation, since it had grown beyond the scope of KW's personal means. February, 1921: "*der neue Roman* now priced at 12 marks." November, 1921: "*der neue Roman* priced at 18 marks."

Catalogue titles for 1922 reflect the larger proportion of art books in the firm's output; from now on they read *Die Bücher und Graphischen Publikationen des Kurt Wolff Verlags* [Books and Art Publications] of the Kurt Wolff Verlags and *Bücher und Graphik—Almanach für Kunst und Dichtung* [Books and Prints—Almanac for Art and Literature]. From the diary for 1923: "A KWV novel now priced at 5 million marks."

Kurt Wolff's inclination for publishing books in series led to the creation of a new type of book: the art book with separate illustrations in full-page format. The first six-volume series, *Deutsche Plastik* [German Sculpture], was begun in 1924 and completed in 1926. In order to carry out the same idea on a larger scale, KW founded another publishing house, the last of his ventures in Germany. In 1924 the Pantheon Casa Editrice was established to create a corpus of international art history in five languages. The economic crisis and foreign currency regulations in Germany, however, made it impossible to continue running the business from there.

In the summer of 1930 Kurt Wolff began closing down his various

Monogram by Walter Tiemann, 1912

Variation of a colophon by
Emil Preetorius, 1916 (first produced by
Walter Tiemann, 1914)

Colophon by Emil Preetorius, 1918

Monogram of Drugulin Press by
Walter Tiemann, 1911

Colophon by Emil Preetorius, 1919

Colophon for Pantheon Casa Editrice
by Lucian Bernhard, 1924
(used again in 1942
for Pantheon Books, Inc.)

publishing ventures. In a letter of June 23, 1930 he wrote: "I cannot, I will not keep the Kurt Wolff Verlag going . . . It is a fact that the firm has exhausted me, both physically and materially; for the past six years I have been slowly bleeding to death. When the inflation ended and the mark became stable again, I was left with no cash assets, of course, like so many others, but I did have an immense stockpile of books, most of them printed on paper of poor quality. At first sales continued to be good, and this misled me to believe, like so many others, that I had a large operation requiring a large staff. And obviously I also felt that employees who had stood by me during the hard times of inflation should be kept on as long as possible . . . There was no cash; the vast majority of the books we had in stock were not selling well, since the public's taste had changed so thoroughly . . . New production did not even bring a return on our investment (not even Schickele), while we were losing money on an author like Joseph Roth . . . I refuse to declare bankruptcy, even though these days that is not considered a dishonorable step, nor am I inclined to do what so many of my colleagues have done and become a front man for the manipulations of my creditors, printers, and bookbinders. What money I had of my own is gone . . . I will sell out enough to get us out of debt (that, actually, is the case already, since we never failed to pay what we owed and do not intend to do so now)."

A brief entry in KW's notes: "Why did I stop? There was nothing new in sight. No sign of anything new." The word "new" was significant. The table of contents for the 1917 KW Almanac lists "The New Novel—New Narrations—The Last Judgment (Collection of New Writing)—New Poetry—New Drama." Later the section "New Art" was added. In the last year of his life Kurt Wolff recalled, "I have *great* respect for the Ellermann Verlag and the pains they took with [reissuing] Heym . . . but if I were a German publisher today, I would not like to invest in such projects, and I am not at all convinced that five hundred poems are more than fifty. When in my time I published a pristine original work that was fresh and vital, I am particularly reluctant to view the corpse."

In 1925 Carl Georg Heise, in the KWV Almanac, commented on the public's changing tastes: "There can be no doubt: at the current time all intellectual activity is taking place under the sign of deep resignation." About the forces of opposition he said, "They love to claim that art is dying—and that it is a good thing. A new age will dawn, they say, an age not of art but of great deeds."

This new age was to dawn without the participation of Kurt Wolff. In 1930 he closed down his publishing enterprises with the same energetic determination he had applied to their founding. At the same time his first marriage ended; he remained on friendly terms with Elisabeth Merck and maintained a close relationship with their two children, Maria and Nikolaus, who stayed with their father whenever they had vacations. KW spent most of 1931 and 1932 outside of Germany, traveling in England and France. "I rest, swim, go for walks; when I am fully rested I may think about what I can do next."

In the winter of 1932 KW went to Berlin to sound out some new possibilities; among them a position as director of a radio station was under discussion. The diary entry for February 10, 1933: "Speech by Hitler." During the night of February 27, 1933 the *Reichstag* burned down. February 28th: "Packing [until] 1:30 A.M." On the night of March 1–2 KW left Germany.

His second marriage, to Helen Wolff (née Mosel), took place in London on March 27, 1933. In the fall they rented a house in the hills above Nice, where they were joined by Walter Hasenclever at the end of the year. For KW this was the beginning of eight years of resignation and leave of absence from his profession. Christian Wolff, his son from his second marriage, was born in Nice in March 1934. In the spring of 1935 KW moved to Italy, at the time when Mussolini was mobilizing against Hitler at the Brenner Pass. Il Moro, a country house in Lastra a Signa near Florence, became the family's new home. By 1938 the politics of the Axis were beginning to threaten this refuge, too. Diary entries from August of that year read: "Newspaper depressing." "Rain, sad, many letters; afternoon: packing and cemetery." August 27: "Departure for Nice." September 9: "With Schickele. Worried about war." September 10 and 11: "Worries about war." September 12–18: "Danger of war." September 29: "Les 4 à Munich—accord."

KW's passport had expired; the German authorities refused to renew it, and he could not return home to Italy. On November 10 the diary records the suicide of close friends, the Kraemers, a Jewish couple who had stayed in Munich. On November 14 and 15: "To American Consulate with H. to apply for visa." On May 1, 1939 the family moved from Nice to Paris and on August 9 into an apartment on the Quai des Grands Augustins. September 14, 1939: "Read the decree this morning. Started packing; made will; to bed at 12." September 16: "Finished packing in morning; Colombes [internment camp for German nationals] at 4 o'clock." On October 5 KW was released through the efforts of French friends. On May 14, 1940: "Germans assembled, Stade de Buffalo." May 16: "Up all night, putting things in order." May 17: "With H. taxi to Buffalo—H. is refused entry." From May 16 to July 28, 1940 the diary laconically lists several internment camps.

In August the family was reunited in still unoccupied Nice. August 22 and 31: "American Consulate with H." September 20: "Mass for Walter." Hasenclever had taken his own life in an internment camp. December 27: "Received visa American Consulate." January 10, 1941: "[Received] safe-conduct in afternoon." January 31 and February 1: "Nervous." February 6: "Exit visa [necessary in order to leave France]." February 7: "Packed." February 8: "Luggage to station." February 9: "Nice–Marseilles–Toulouse." February 10: "Toulouse-Confranc" [on the Spanish frontier].

March 30, 1941: "New York. Disembarked 10 o'clock, glorious weather."

By December 1941 there is mention already of new plans: "Discussed publishing venture with Faber du Faur."

Curt von Faber du Faur, a friend from the Munich days, and his stepson Kyrill Schabert, who had also been a frequent visitor at the Wolff's house there, placed the sum of $7,500 at KW's disposal to found a publishing house on the following terms: first, KW was to find other backers willing to match these funds; second, no salary would be paid to him until the firm was showing a profit. Only then would KW receive a modest salary and have a share in the profits.

Circumstances being as they were—America had entered the war and KW was technically an enemy alien—Kurt Wolff did not use his own name for the firm, nor did he figure officially as its head. The business was incorporated with the imprint "Pantheon Books, Inc.," in 1942. In this same year KW wrote: "If I wish that these efforts might find some material reward in the not-too-distant future (out of the question for the time being), I do not say this because we want to get rich. All I wish for is improvement of our working conditions—an additional room, and some professional assistance. At the moment everything is done in a single room (admittedly a large one by local standards): it functions as our living-dining-bedroom and office." The first person to join the staff was Wolfgang Sauerländer, a friend of Hermann Broch's whose hatred of Nazism had led him to leave Germany. He began by "writing addresses and licking stamps," and stayed on, soon becoming indispensable.

On April 8, 1944 *Publishers' Weekly* reported from New York: "This January Pantheon Books, Inc. celebrated its first birthday. The firm has a list of fifteen books and is known throughout the trade for high quality and outstanding production . . . Pantheon Books began very modestly in the Wolffs' apartment in Washington Square." At about the same time KW wrote: "Pantheon was funded on a extremely small amount of initial capital to give me the chance to earn a living. It was an experiment—and since no matter what the balance sheet says on April 30, 1944, a profit is now unavoidable—the experiment is a success."

Talking about the firm's list in the early New York years, KW later commented, "I was in my 50s, when it is quite difficult to adapt to a foreign country if you are not fluent in the language. Acquiring authors doesn't come easily. My American publishing career really started when I realized, 'You are here in a country where you can be a pioneer.'" Such pioneering work included translations of Stefan George, Charles Péguy, Jacob Burckhardt, of Paul Valéry, Charles de Coster, Hermann Broch, and the firm's first big success: a complete edition of Grimms' Fairy Tales, with illustrations by the Bavarian artist Josef Scharl.

Right at the start in the United States KW had the good fortune to become publisher to the Bollingen Foundation established by Paul and Mary Mellon. "We published a splendid long list of books, including the Collected Works of C. G. Jung and the extensive and important work of the late Indologist Heinrich Zimmer. But I or we cannot take credit for that; it was the work of a foundation." The cordial relationship existing with John D. Barrett, head of the Bollingen Foundation, made it possible to broaden the firm's scope and collaborate on beautiful and lavishly produced books without financial constraints. Jacques Schiffrin joined the firm as a partner, having emigrated from Paris to New York in 1941. He remained associated with Pantheon until his death in 1950.

Although the firm was highly respected, substantial financial success did not materialize until 1955, when Anne Morrow Lindbergh's *Gift from the Sea* became a best seller. Pantheon's offices at 333 Sixth Avenue in New York remained quite modest.

1958 was an eventful year. In the spring KW began showing the first symptoms of heart disease. Diary for March 9, 1958: "Sick." March 31: "To office for the first time." October 23: "10 A.M.: Pasternak Nobel Prize." In November of that year disagreements arose within the firm, and in 1959 KW decided to move to Switzerland. A year later, in July of 1960, he withdrew entirely from Pantheon Books, and his career as a publisher seemed to be over.

Then in February, 1961—when KW was almost seventy-three years old—he wrote to several friends and colleagues: "Since you know what happened to us last year, I would like to inform you of recent developments, which we confidently expect to come to fruition soon. When we resigned from Pantheon Books, we had no intention of entering into a new association. But then, to our surprise, we received some attractive proposals from various large American publishing houses—firms whose heads were completely unknown to us personally.

"We have now decided to join the firm of Harcourt, Brace and World. We liked the company's young president, who has visited us twice in Locarno and impressed us with his intelligence and integrity. He offered us terms that are extremely fair in every respect; they leave us a great deal of independence and identify us by name with all the books we will publish . . . In short, we are returning to our beloved profession, and I feel rejuvenated."

It was the first time KW had collaborated with a firm which he had not helped to build himself, but the experiment succeeded all the same. He worked tirelessly in the years remaining to him. Among his projects were editions of Bernard Berenson's and Julien Green's diaries, which appeared after his death. He was in contact with authors and publishers from all over the world; he traveled to a great many places, including New York in 1963, and undertook projects outside the sphere of publishing as well. Between 1961 and 1963 he gave a series of radio talks that led to publication of a book. From October 7–12, 1963 he attended the Frankfurt Book Fair, as he had so often before. He sent the contract for Günter Grass's *Hundejahre* [*Dog Years*] to his American partner William Jovanovich. On October 21 he was once again en route to a meeting, this time a "Gruppe 47" conference, full of curiosity and anticipating new discoveries. He took a detour by way of Marbach, to see some documents from the early years of his publishing career. The exhibition catalogue of the Schiller-Nationalmuseum in Marbach was on his bedside table when he stopped in Ludwigsburg, seven kilometers short of his destination, to take a walk on the afternoon of October 21. There he was hit by a backing truck and died soon afterwards. He was buried in Marbach on October 24, 1963. "His friends came to his funeral: every German publisher—not one was missing—and many authors."

"If another person's good qualities far outshine our own, there is no recourse but love."–Goethe

*In Kurt Wolff's hand.

KURT
&WOLFF

Essays
on
Publishing

The Publisher's Profession

THE IMPRESSION laymen have of what a publisher does is amazingly primitive: they seem to think he reads manuscripts or has other people read them—manuscripts that apparently arrive automatically in great quantities—and then sends what he likes best to the printer's. Since the book is also supposed to be attractive in appearance, he hires an artist to design the cover and dust jacket. Success or failure is a matter of luck.

The reality is somewhat different, but it is hard to convey a clear sense of how immensely complicated this profession is, how many elements must come together to give the term "publisher" a truly legitimate and positive meaning, how some irrational event will come along to upset every rational plan and decision, over and over again, creating a situation of permanent uncertainty and tension, a constant source of joys and disappointments.

Before I continue speaking about publishers, their calling, and their profession, however, I should say that I personally am able to envision the genuine publisher only within certain limits of size. A publishing house that produces between one hundred and four hundred new titles each year (and the world contains a number of them) may be a very respectable business enterprise, and some of its many books will also be good ones—but naturally it can never bear the individual stamp of a publisher's personality. As a general rule it can be said, although the exception does exist, that the books of great writers have not been published by giant companies, and that important literary movements were supported and developed by small firms, that is to say by individual publishers. Stefan George and his circle were in the hands of the outsider Bondi; S. Fischer founded a house for the Naturalist movement at the beginning of the century, and Expressionism found a home in the Kurt Wolff Verlag. Outside Germany the situation is similar: Proust, Gide, and Valéry were not published by Hachette, nor did Hemingway and Ezra Pound have American publishers at first.

An author entrusts himself to a person he thinks understands him, not to the board of directors of the kind of company which in France goes by the very appropriate name of "Société Anonyme." The publisher is not anonymous, but rather synonymous with his work. It is only this individual type of publisher I am concerned with here. Whether or not he distinguishes himself; whether he is able, in however modest a way, to make a contribution to the cultural life of his times; whether he produces significant accomplishments or merely reduces the value of paper by printing on it—all this depends on an endless number of conditions, only a few of which can be sketched here.

Luck is an indispensable ingredient: fate determines the literary sterility or fruitfulness of the period in which a publisher works; if the times do not produce creative writers, he is condemned to inactivity.

In my view the essential tools a publisher must bring to his work are a level of education beyond that of a good secondary school; familiarity with world literature and not just the literature of one's own country; a sound and independent sense of intellectual and literary values, combined with the ability to distinguish between genuine and counterfeit, between what is original and what is imitation; and intuition for the meaningful currents of the times, those which will shape the future. A publisher must also be able to write clearly, not only in correspondence. The right form must be found to present authors and books to critics, readers, and book sellers; even the few words with which a book is described in advertisements can be decisive for triumph or defeat.

And finally there is the author, who cannot be seduced by good meals, cocktail parties, and a large advance alone. What he seeks is a human being, in whom he finds an echo and a subtle feeling of fellowship; someone who pays attention to his work, whose word of praise or criticism has weight for him, someone whose genuine interest in his creative future (and also in the material needs of the present, obviously) makes itself felt. Authors have sharp ears and cannot be fooled: in the first minute they know whether the publisher to whom they are speaking is really familiar with their work, or whether he has taken only a superficial glance at it, or even seen nothing at all except a reader's report.

Publishers can always find some plausible reason to hand an author over to an editor, of course. If an editor has the right sort of personality, and the author gets along with him, there is nothing wrong with it. It is even common practice nowadays. But then the publisher becomes merely a front in the author's eyes and also in reality—an administrator, the person who signs contracts and checks. A working partnership and intimacy come to exist between the author and his real collaborator; the author's loyalty will belong to him and to him alone.

Publishing important works from the past in new editions and works from other languages in translation can be rewarding and meaningful tasks—but at the center of every genuine publisher's wishes and hopes stands the goal of acquiring the best contemporary writers in his own country and if possible other countries as well—and keeping them.

The author is a difficult person to handle, of course, and there are no rules for it, for how could all authors be the same, or even similar to one another? It is a great mistake to try to "use psychology" on them. We should remain entirely natural and human, but we should also never forget one thing: the creative artist is never balanced—he becomes creative only by enduring the tragic conflict between reality and the imagination.

A publisher's relationship with his author must be like a love affair in which he asks nothing and has already forgiven every failing in advance: both small lapses and—as is always possible—unfaithfulness on a large scale.

On Publishing in General
and the Question
How Do an Author and Publisher
Come Together?

THE QUESTION WHERE did you learn your profession? is one I have been hearing for the last fifty-five years. The answer is always the same: nowhere.

It seems to me that a particular attraction of our profession is that it cannot be learned. People respond, wouldn't it be useful to have worked at a printer's and a bindery? Why? I want neither to print books nor to bind them. Or, they say, it would at least be desirable to have worked in a book store for a short time. Why? Since the age of twelve I have spent hours and hours in book stores almost daily, at home and while traveling. Whether I stand behind or in front of the counter, whether I am the clerk or the customer, makes no difference. If someone has a passion for books and the publishing trade, he is at home in book stores. Nor do I believe in the importance of a Ph.D. To be well read in world literature is of course desirable, just as is knowledge of three or four living languages, so as to be able to read foreign literature yourself and not have to rely on the recommendations of others. But all this is no more than a so-called "general education." And that will not take you far in our profession.

One day I moved out of the German Department of the University of Leipzig and into the building at Königstraße 10 in the city, the premises of the Drugulin Printing Company and the two-room office of Ernst Rowohlt, who had a similar nature and obsession with books, and who had invited me to join him. I brought nothing with me except for the main thing, which cannot be learned but must be brought to the task in large quantities: enthusiasm. Naturally this enthusiasm must be combined with taste. Everything else is secondary and can be learned rapidly on the job.

To start with, you must of course be clear about the field in which you want to publish. In principle, however, this has already been determined by an individual's own taste and enthusiasms. By taste I mean not only judgment and a feeling for quality and literary values. Taste should also include a sure sense for the form—format, type area, type face, binding, dust jacket—in which a specific book should be presented. Literary taste, on the other hand, must be combined with an instinct for whether a particular book will interest only a small group of readers, or whether the subject and form make it suitable for a larger audience. This will have a decisive influence on the size of the edition and advertising, and care must be taken that personal enthusiasm does not entice us into false and over-optimistic expectations.

When I moved into Rowohlt's two-room office that day—the third room was Rowohlt's living quarters—my enthusiasm knew no bounds; my taste in typography, however, was limited to knowing whether the type area, title page, binding, and so forth were nice or hideous. It took quite a while before I was able to say to the printer: 2 points more leading, put the headings in italics, etc. In such matters Ernst Rowohlt was far ahead of me. He had worked at Drugulin's and learned a great deal. On matters of literary taste we got along extremely well: his idols at the time were Scheerbart and Dauthendey, and it was not hard for him to infect me with enthusiasm for both of them. Let it also be said without false modesty that we shared a love and admiration for the playwright Eulenberg. And when he received the Schiller Prize for his *Belinde,* we seemed to have some justification.

BUT HOW DO MANUSCRIPTS reach a publisher, and where do they come from? How does the encounter between writer and publisher come about? And above all, what are the decisive criteria in choosing what you are going to publish?

Either you publish books you think people *ought* to read, or books you think people *want* to read. Publishers in the second category, publishers, that is to say, who slavishly cater to the public's tastes, do not count in our scheme of things—wouldn't you agree? They belong to another "order," to use the nice Catholic term. For publishing activity of this kind you need neither enthusiasm nor taste. You simply supply the products for which there is a demand. You need to know what activates the tear glands, the sex glands, or any other glands, what makes the sportsman's heart beat faster, what makes the flesh crawl in horror, and so on.

Those of us publishers who belong to the other category make an effort—even though it is certainly of the most modest scope—to be creative; we try to win readers for works which appear to us to be original, of literary merit, and important for the future, no matter whether they are easily understood or not. This applies both to nonfiction and to fiction. It goes without saying that we can make mistakes, and we make mistakes very often. Sometimes we think we see future promise in the personality or the manuscript of an author, and this promise is not realized. The effort is what counts; success is not the determining factor—often it is an accident. Indeed, acquiring a good author is actually more a matter of chance than of merit—but let us leave the realm of the theoretical.

It so happened, because I had accepted a manuscript of Max Brod's and he felt he had found in Kurt Wolff a publisher for all his writings, that he sent to me a young fellow-countryman and friend named Franz Werfel, and one day brought along with him another friend and countryman named Franz Kafka. Whoever had ears to hear could not resist the magical tone of Werfel's early poems, could not help falling immediately under the spell of Kafka's prose.

At that time, when I was still a student and already a publisher, I was taking Albert Köster's seminar at the University of Leipzig and sat next to a young man I took a liking to; we began to talk, and over the course of time he became a close friend. He was Walter Hasenclever. And one day after Walter had written a play, he brought it to me for publication. It was *Der Sohn* [The Son], and its literary qualities are not at issue here. In any event it offered more than mere entertainment, and the father-son conflict it dealt with had an explosive effect on the generation born around 1890. It was performed at a number of German theaters, but the excitement it caused then must be incomprehensible in our time and in our world.

Kafka, Brod, Werfel, Hasenclever—these were the first authors of the Kurt Wolff Verlag, and it was, as you can see, more accident than our merit that brought them. Of course one did have to have a sense that each, in his own way, was worthy of a publisher's efforts.

In the Innsbruck magazine *Der Brenner* I read the poems of an unknown writer named Georg Trakl. So immediate was the sense of a great poet's voice that I wrote him at once—it was April 1, 1913—proposing the publication of a volume of poetry. In the same year *Gedichte* [Poems] appeared in the series *Der jüngste Tag* [The Last Judgment], and only eleven months later, in March 1914, Trakl sent the manuscript of a new book, which he called *Sebastian im Traum* [Sebastian Dreaming] and which is perhaps the purest, most beautiful book of poetry of that era. What great expectations we had for the future of this young poet! Then on October 9 a telegram arrived from Trakl from the military hospital in Cracow, where he had been taken when he proved unequal to the horrors of the war. The famous telegram reads:

> YOU WOULD DO ME A GREAT FAVOR IF YOU WOULD SEND ME A COPY OF MY
> NEW BOOK SEBASTIAN DREAMING. AM ILL HERE IN THE MILITARY HOSPITAL
> CRACOW.
>
> GEORG TRAKL

We were unable to do him this favor. The book was not yet ready. And the poet committed suicide three weeks later. With poison.

From a Swiss by the name of Robert Walser there arrived, also in the spring of 1913, the first letters in a delicate hand straight out of the eighteenth century, letters whose contents could not have been simpler and whose tone was recognizably unique. The first letters have been lost, but listen to a few lines from a later one:

> I have just completed a new book . . . in which I have bound together twenty-seven pieces . . . All the pieces have been given a new form, every single one, so as to make them as good as possible. Choosing them and deciding on their order has been done with thought and care, in a conscious effort. I believe I can say that the book makes a solid, round, and pleasing whole. There are shifts in it from landscapes to concrete humor, from comedy to complete seriousness, even now and then to tragic form . . . It contains some older pieces and some quite new ones as well, ones that have only just occurred to me . . . I see the work as a kind of modest but quite cozy and livable house . . .

That was the tone of the letters—who could have resisted it? And still there could be no doubt that the pieces of prose bound together would find fewer than a hundred readers. I published three volumes of Walser's stories for these one hundred readers, with illustrations by his famous brother; in appearance, too, they were most attractive books. And yet the stories were not as simple as they might seem on first reading. Walter Benjamin wrote an intelligent essay on them, and in the *Neue Rundschau* in August 1914 Robert Musil wrote:

> Walser makes his characters suddenly fall silent and lets the story speak as if it were a character. An atmosphere of marionettes, romantic irony; but also something in this joke that reminds one faintly of Morgenstern's poems, where the gravity of real circumstances suddenly begins to slide along a train of verbal associations; only with Walser the association is never purely verbal, but always one of meaning as well, so that the emotional tack he happens to be on at the moment suddenly appears to be about to take a great leap, veers, and then goes on contentedly rocking in the direction of a new enticement. I would not actually want to claim that this is not playfulness, but it is no mere writer's game—despite the way one could fall in love with his uncommon command of language; it is a very human kind of playfulness, gentle, dreamy, and free, with the moral richness of one of those lazy, apparently useless days when our most firmly held convictions relax into a pleasant indifference.

Walser's prose would be virtually unknown today, however, if Suhrkamp Verlag had not published a lovely selection in an edition of a thousand copies.

Other authors did not introduce themselves by letter, but by appearing in person, suddenly and without warning. Who or what prompted Gustav Meyrink, who lived on the Starnberger Lake, to appear in the office in Leipzig one day, I do not know. At the time Meyrink had written nothing more than some short pieces that had appeared in the magazine *Simplicissimus* and not been particularly successful in book form. He had also translated twenty volumes of Dickens, where the lunatic notion had occurred to him to put Dickens's slang and local idiom into Bavarian dialect. The Dickens edition was a complete flop. Nevertheless, Meyrink's fantastically grotesque stories and parodies, successful or not, had great charm and a highly characteristic flavor.

I remember Meyrink's visit well: a gentleman of aristocratic appearance and impeccable manners, with a slight limp. He had the honor, he said, of proposing that the firm accept his first novel, although no typescript of it was available yet. He had recorded it on a dictating machine, he reported (highly unusual at the time, in the winter of 1913/14, indeed scarcely credible), and while he would be unable to send us a copy of his novel *Der ewige Jude* [The Wandering Jew], he had brought along a handwritten copy of the first chapter.[1] He wished to reach an agreement on the novel at once, before returning to Munich the following day. He would not demand the usual royalties, but instead desired immediate payment of ten thousand marks as a lump sum, in return for all rights and editions in all languages. Would I be so kind, he asked, as to read the pages he was now pleased to present to me and to make a decision? This extraordinary proposal was put forward with great formality and utmost seriousness—and I had imagined the author of *Des deutschen Spießers Wunderhorn* [The German Philistine's Magic Horn] to be a humorist!

Taken aback and embarrassed, I read the folio pages of the manuscript—which I still have today—and was then expected, after perusing them for no more than fifteen minutes, to say yes or no. I liked the few pages I had seen; of the book as a whole I knew nothing, and ten thousand gold marks was a great deal of money. I found the situation absurd, wanted to show that I was equal to it—and said yes. This is no doubt the sort of thing a young man of twenty-six likes to do. The title of the novel was later changed to *Der Golem* [The Golem], and it sold in the hundreds of thousands of copies. Nonetheless, it was not a bad book at all; in fact it is Meyrink's only good novel. (I was never able to convince C. G. Jung that *Das grüne Gesicht* [The Green Face] was a bad novel—Jung thought very highly of it.)

To quell any moral doubts I would like to note that, in spite of the lump sum agreed upon for world rights, the author did have a considerable share in the profits. Incidentally, I was interested to read recently that Meyrink, who was born in 1868, was an Expressionist. This statement is to be found in *Knaur's Kleines Lexikon* [Knaur's

---

1. Such "parlograph" machines had then been in existence for several years, in fact: Tolstoy used them in the last few years of his life, so that the sound of his voice has been preserved for us, and Kafka's fiancée, Felice Bauer, was employed at that time by a "parlograph" company. [Author's note]

Concise Dictionary], a work whose accuracy I hold in high regard. But perhaps we should save a discussion of that hot potato called "Expressionism" until later, and stay with our topic: how do manuscripts and writers reach a publisher's office?

The case of *The Golem* offers a good occasion to mention that if a publishing house is fortunate to have a very great success with a title, even though it has literary merits, there are pleasant consequences: it attracts other authors. In less successful years the flow of new authors was a mere trickle, in successful years a flood. This was our experience at that time with *The Golem*, and somewhat later with Heinrich Mann and Tagore. (No, Tagore should not be rated in the way you think: André Gide, William Butler Yeats, Rilke, Ezra Pound, and other writers of high standing knew better than the German littérateurs of the twenties, for whom success was always identical with inferior quality—but this traditional snobbery in German literary attitudes is a broad topic . . .)

Even if it cannot be proved in single instances, still there can be no doubt that the notable successes the Kurt Wolff Verlag achieved with Meyrink, Heinrich Mann, Tagore, and also with Werfel's early poems and his play *Die Troerinnen* [The Trojan Women] brought in a wealth of manuscripts and publishing proposals that would not have been offered otherwise. The existence of a new publishing house open to the younger generation, that printed the works of Kafka, Werfel, and Hasenclever, led countless talented and untalented young writers to send us their work. However, the successes just mentioned, which suggested that we were a dynamic firm, presumably also brought the Kurt Wolff Verlag a number of nonfiction books, in which I saw a felicitous complement to belles lettres and which I hoped—in many cases correctly—would be titles of lasting merit. Some examples are the letters and diaries of Paula Modersohn-Becker, Anselm Feuerbach's *Vermächtnis* [Legacy] and *Briefe an seine Mutter* [Letters to His Mother], Mechthilde Lichnowsky's book on Egypt, Georg Simmel's *Rembrandt*, the works of Buber, and others.

Friends should also not be forgotten, to whom the firm was indebted, friends who were colleagues or authors. First among them is Kurt Pinthus, the most faithful of our literary advisers, on whose good judgment we could rely. For a short time there was also Willy Haas, while Franz Werfel was an editor more in name only—we did not want to interfere with his creative work. Subsequently there was my friend Hans, later Giovanni, Mardersteig, today the famous printer of the Officina Bodoni and Valdonega in Verona, and in those days the person to whom the Kurt Wolff Verlag owed the distinction of its book design. It was Mardersteig who established the connection with Frans Masereel. When we first published his *Stundenbuch* [Book of Hours] in 167 woodcuts, the Belgian's name was completely unknown in Germany. Within a few years Masereel's series of woodcuts—*Stundenbuch, Sonne* [Sun], *Passion eines Menschen* [A Human Passion], *Die Idee* [The Idea], *Geschichte ohne Worte* [Story without Words]—produced in inexpensive editions with introductions by Thomas Mann, Hermann Hesse, and others, won a surprisingly large circle of admirers and attained a number of printings we had never expected, given the uncompromising quality and character of these books. Thanks for the increased inclusion of art books in the Kurt Wolff Verlag list are also due to Hans Mardersteig and his friend Carl Georg Heise, the art historian who at the time was director of the Lübeck Museum and later of the Kunsthalle in Hamburg.

I had risked a few amateurish ventures in the field of art books earlier and am proud to have published in 1913 the first book on and by Kokoschka: *Dramen und Bilder* [Plays and Pictures]. I had also gone to Paris, where I called on Rodin and acquired two of his books: the highly successful volume entitled *Die Kunst* [Art], and the far more beautiful work on the cathedrals of France. But the firm had the friends named above to thank for essential works of historical significance, among them Will Grohmann's outstanding work on Kirchner, Sauerlandt's book on Emil Nolde, Gustav Pauli's book on Modersohn-Becker, *Kunst und Religion* [Art and Religion] by Gustav Hartlaub, and many others. Above all I should mention *Genius*, the most handsome and truly representative modern art journal to appear in Germany after *Pan* and *Insel*, which owed its conception and realization to Mardersteig and Heise. Their names figure as editors of this journal of ancient and modern art over its three rich years of publication from 1919 to 1921.

Finally, it should not be underestimated how often authors bring other authors to their publisher: a writer who feels he is supported and in good hands at his publisher will tend to encourage his fellow artists to submit their manuscripts to the same house. Sometimes, of course, this may be due not so much to a conviction of outstanding quality as to a spirit of camaraderie, but now and again it calls forth the deepest sense of obligation. I am thinking here of Max Brod, who occasionally made me feel he was sending me all of his compatriots who ever put pen to paper at all, though he must have been aware that apart from Kafka and Werfel, or Czechs such as Brežina and Bežruc, most of them were puny, insignificant figures.

AFTER THESE EXAMPLES of how a writer and publisher come together, let me cite an instance of how a publishing house and authors failed to come together, a Dadaistic instance. From time to time, when I surveyed the firm's production as a whole, one element very appealing to me struck me as underrepresented: humor, comedy, the absurd, the amusing, the grotesque. A few small volumes of Mynona, Mehring, Reimann, funny as they were, did not seem to me enough. And so I showed keen interest when the Dadaists approached me with some publishing proposals in 1917.

At the time I knew little or nothing about Dada, but I did know that Hugo Ball, a likable man I had encountered as a dramaturge at the Munich Kammerspiele [Chamber Theater], was one of the movement's founders. I had published Ball's rather conventional tragicomedy *Die Nase des Michelangelo* [Michelangelo's Nose] and also, at Werfel's urging, a volume of poetry by Ball's friend Emmy Hennings. If Ball had such close ties to Dada, I thought, then the movement must have some merit. However, the letters regarding a large work to be called *Dadaco* or *Dadaglobe* and to be published by the Kurt Wolff Verlag came not from Ball, but from [Richard] Huelsenbeck and Tristan Tzara. Even before I became aware that what was performed and deformed in the name of Dada was utter drivel, the pedantry, tedium, and sheer dreariness of their correspondence had cured me of the delusion that they might be the source of any creative fun. On rereading the letters I do not find a single sentence it would be interesting or amusing to quote. I put an end to the correspondence, which had dragged on from September 19 to April 21, and decided to do without Dada and *Dadaco*. I much preferred to publish *Kuttel Daddeldu* and *Turngedichte* (Gymnastic Poems) by Joachim Ringelnatz. All the Dada manifestos and Dada babble were not worth a single verse of Ringelnatz, much less one of Morgenstern's *Galgenlieder* [Gallows Songs].

The Dadaists soon vanished into thin air, only to land again as solid burghers: one acquired a lucrative psychoanalytic practice in the USA; another married a rich woman, and so on. Only poor old Tristan Tzara sits sad and lonely over a *café crème* on the terrace of the Café des Deux Magots. Hugo Ball converted to Catholicism and wrote a book on Hermann Hesse, who was hardly a Dadaist himself. It seems astonishing that at least six publications have disinterred the defunct Dada movement again in recent years, unless one wants to interpret it as a warning to the present generation. The most widely distributed of them, from the Deutscher Taschenbuch Verlag, contains as an illustration a never-published prospectus for our old Dada project that never appeared. I saw this prospectus, of which the Kurt Wolff Verlag was entirely innocent, for the first time in this paperback, and finding that it named the Kurt Wolff Verlag in large letters as publisher of the nonexistent Dada book did not please Kurt Wolff. Even for Dadaists, I would think, the words of the poet Hölty should apply: "Make loyalty and honesty your watchwords."

The sole real events to occur on the fringes of the Dada connection were the publication of a non-Dadaistic short story, "Doctor Billig am Ende" [Doctor Billig's Bad End], referred to by its author, Huelsenbeck, as a novel, with illustrations by George Grosz, and a talk given to an audience of about 150 people by the selfsame Huelsenbeck one evening in Munich in February 1920, in the library of the Kurt Wolff Verlag. The topic was "The Nature and Aims of Dadaism." The next morning the local newspaper *Münchner Neueste Nachrichten* reported:

> Although pressed by members of the audience, the speaker would not or could not do more than respond to questions about this newest trend with a few clichés, some of which were directed against Expressionism, some against philistines, and some against the life of the mind in the broadest sense. He could only stress, again and again, that through its

cabaret scandals, through bluffing, publicity stunts, and brawls, Dadaism had achieved much success and spread throughout the world.

Forty years later, Richard Seewald recalled the evening in a "brief anecdote, the scene of which was the auditorium of the Kurt Wolff Verlag in the Hirth Building in Munich":

> The poet Huelsenbeck was to speak on Dadaism to a select group of invited guests. And speak he did. After a quarter of an hour an atmosphere of paralyzing boredom enveloped the room, and I expressed the general mood when I called out to the podium, "Mr. Huelsenbeck, is what is coming just as boring as what we have already heard? After all, people can't just get up here and read from their doctoral dissertations." Applause and laughter greeted my Dadaistic remark, which was the only one of its kind to have been voiced thus far. The unfortunate speaker began to stammer an apology, saying that it was not supposed to be an evening of Dada but rather a talk on the history(!) of Dada, etc. He wanted to lead up to a reading of his own poems, but he did not have much luck with this. The evening had developed into a Dadaistic happening despite him. Soon from one corner of the room came a shout of "Goethe!" and from another, "Rilke!"

Thus for Seewald, too, the only memorable aspect of this evening of Dada was boredom.

But—you may perhaps object—the Kurt Wolff Verlag did publish the poetry of Johannes R. Becher, who is barely distinguishable from the Dadaists. Now I do happen to believe that there is a difference between babbling and stammering, though I am certainly not proud to have been Becher's publisher. Becher was not a Dadaist but rather, as the literary historians write, an Expressionist. And here the tiresome word crops up again which dogs my steps like a shadow; I referred to it in passing when speaking of Meyrink.

The subject of Expressionism has become almost an obsession with me, and a brief and very personal comment on it seems in order with regard to authors of the Kurt Wolff Verlag, both those named here and others:

For years I took myself to be a publisher of young writers and older authors I considered, correctly or incorrectly, to have merit. Never did I place myself at the service of a slogan or a trend—but over the years this has been more and more contested. It became my detested, indeed accursed claim to fame that I had been the publisher of the Expressionist movement. Even today, in fact now more than ever, attempts are made to attach the label of Expressionism to a group of writers whose work appeared between 1910 and 1925, to force on them a shared identity they never acknowledged. For thirty-five years now I have been protesting against such labels in conversation with friends and foes. In vain. Allow me, therefore, to make a public statement of my

CREDO

"Expressionism" is a term applicable to a collective. A collective never produces a poem, not a single line. Creative achievement is always the work of an individual. The term and what are taken to be typical Expressionist features do not apply to the *great* creative writers of those years. Poets and writers of stature, whom I am proud to have published at the time, had *nothing* to do with so-called "Expressionism," even if they are exhibited as Expressionists today and so classified in histories of literature. They are:

Kafka, who as a writer is closer to Johann Peter Hebel and as a thinker closer to Kierkegaard than any other author of the twentieth century.

Heym, Baudelaire's brother in the German language.

Trakl, who carries on the great tradition of Hölderlin.

Stadler, from Alsace, who loved Francis Jammes and Péguy, not Johannes R. Becher.

Werfel, whose *Weltfreund* [Lover of All the World] was inspired by his love of Walt Whitman.

Ernst Blass, who does not really belong in such exalted company but is named here because this "Expressionist" wrote to me in 1915: "[Stefan] George and I jointly are carrying on the lofty tradition in German letters."

Sternheim, whose ambition it was to become a German Molière.

Schickele, the nature lover, who paints landscapes and women like Renoir, not Kirchner.

Heinrich Mann, who to my uncomprehending amazement continues to be ranked by many above his brother Thomas.

Karl Kraus, who made the Expressionists victims of his satire and la-
mented, in an elegy addressed to Kurt Wolff, that I put them in
print.

Enough. These are, more or less, the vital, living presences
among the authors of the Kurt Wolff Verlag. I believe only very few
others might have a claim to join this list. May the dead—whether
below or still above ground—forgive me.

In any event, none of those named ever wanted to be considered
an Expressionist, so why speak of Expressionism, if the rest is silence?
(My remarks here have omitted mention of Alfred Döblin, Georg
Kaiser, and some others because I have been concerned solely with
the activities of the Kurt Wolff Verlag.)

Benn is missing, you say? But isn't it the Benn of the late years
who was the great poet? He did say (in print!) that he did not know
what Expressionism was, and I find a letter Benn wrote me in 1917
concerning a poem from an early cycle called "Morgue"; I had inquired about it, and he answered, "It is a very inferior poem."
Unfortunately I was Benn's publisher only for *Gehirne* [Brains], an
early collection of short stories, and it would not be appropriate for
me to list Benn here alongside Kafka and Trakl.

Ehrenstein is missing? "Slimy growth of arse and powder?" I am
unable to consider him a living presence, even though efforts are un-
derway to resurrect him in reprint. [2]

With these comments and strictures on Expressionism, so-
called, whose accomplice and chief perpetrator I became, the publisher takes his leave of you, a publisher whose responsibility for far
worse books—Expressionist and non-Expressionist—will consign
him to purgatory at the very least, if not to Hell. Think kindly of him
for the sake of the few good ones, until the day comes when even the
good ones will have become distant strangers to your children and
grandchildren and lie buried in the graveyard of literary history.

2. In the meantime these efforts have been successful: Albert Ehrenstein, *Gedichte und
Prosa* [Poems and Prose], edited and with an introduction by Karl Otten (Neuwied: Luchterhand, 1961). [Author's note]

On "Luring Away" Authors, or How Authors and Publishers Part Company

EVERY COUNTRY in the world has strict laws about white-slave traffic. Authors, on the other hand, are an unprotected species and must look after themselves. They can be bought and sold, like girls for the white-slave trade—except that in the case of authors it is not illegal.

The problem is as old as the profession of book publishing, but in the last few years a new term for it has come into existence. It is called "luring away" authors.

"What do you say to this," publisher A tells me, "B is trying to take *my* author C from me. But thank heaven I have a firm option for C's next three books . . ."

Whenever I hear something like this—and I hear it often—I remain silent and at a loss for words. In my experience it is useless to get into a discussion. I happen not to believe in options; in dealings between an author and publisher I consider them immoral (although dealings between a publisher and an agent are a different matter).

A brewery salesman has a perfect right to make a pitch to a tavern owner to stop selling brand X beer, and to keep brand Y on tap instead. A human being, however, particularly a creative artist, should and must never become the object of such horse trading. Any limitation of his freedom seems to me to be both insulting and demeaning. A writer should be able to change publishers as he sees fit, according to whim, for an advance of a thousand dollars if he feels like it. He ought to be free. But whenever I aired such heretical views to a colleague, I used to sense that he didn't believe me, and that he was convinced I did not practice what I preached.

I will admit that a publisher may occasionally feel bitter. When you have launched an author because his books showed promise for the future, when he will have matured as a writer; when you have made the sacrifices necessary in such a case—and then this author takes his first truly successful effort to another publisher, it is hard to accept it with equanimity. But still I would insist every time on the author's right to freedom of choice. In my view this takes priority over all other considerations.

And now I would like to tell you about a few instances of how I lost authors, or how they were "lured away" from me. The cases vary considerably as I found them in going through old correspondence and notes. I have chosen to mention a few writers by name because they are still of interest today, or because interest in them is beginning to revive.

NOT LONG AGO I came across some very nice letters from Carl Zuckmayer, dating back to 1920–24. I also found a letter of mine to him. I had published Zuckmayer's first and not very exciting drama *Kreuzweg* [Way of the Cross] in expectation of better plays to come, and had done much more for the author financially than was the norm for generally unprofitable book versions of unstaged plays. Zuckmayer had been very appreciative. When I sent the contract to him, I enclosed a letter (dated October 25, 1920):

> We have now read your work and been most favorably and positively impressed by it. We hope that this play will prove to be the beginning of a long association, since we do not believe in publishing isolated works. If, on the other hand, we have not tried to tie you to us by the contract clauses that are current in the publishing business concerning rights to your future work, it is out of fundamental considerations. As a matter of principle we do not wish to create obligations on an author's part with regard to his future work, for we believe that free will is the only possible basis for a cordial association . . .

Over the next few years the author sent us detailed reports about his work on two new plays, including excerpts from them, etc. And what happened? Without consulting me, Zuckmayer published his next play, *Der fröhliche Weinberg* [The Happy Vineyard] with Ullstein Verlag.

One has to learn to take experiences like this in one's stride. They did not change my aversion to option clauses, and I describe them here without the least resentment. To bear a grudge for more than forty years would in any event be somewhat ridiculous.

One embarrassing incident did occur right at the outset of my publishing career, but at least it remained the only one of its kind. I had signed a contract with a writer after seeing a few handwritten pages, the beginning of his first novel, since it seemed promising. In the contract I agreed to pay the young and completely penniless author a monthly sum over a considerable period of time, so that he could concentrate on his writing and not have to take part-time jobs. The time agreed on for this subsidy expired, and was extended; I never saw a single page, or received word of any kind. Finally we stopped the monthly stipend. Years went by. Since my letters went systematically unanswered, I had our attorney write him in legal terms. At long last we received a reply, a friendly and cheerful little note to say I shouldn't waste good money on lost causes. His contract was invalid and not worth the paper it was written on, since he, the writer, was in possession of a so-called "yellow certificate," popularly known as a "hunting license." For those unfamiliar with this term, let me explain that a "yellow certificate" was a document certifying that its owner was mentally incompetent or unsound and therefore, under Paragraph 51 of the German Criminal Code, not legally responsible for his actions.

I take the view that the author was incompetent morally, but not mentally so. In any case the novel whose opening I had read and for which the firm had paid a subsidy it never recovered was brought out by another publisher (no, it wasn't Fischer); it was excellent, it was a success, and its author was and is widely known and admired.

I know that the publisher of that first novel did not intentionally try to "lure" my author away. Instead, as it turned out, he too had been paying the writer a monthly stipend over the same period as I had.

Now a very different case: I was on friendly terms with Rilke, but our contacts were of a purely personal and not professional nature. I was never his publisher, and I don't think the fact that Rilke once wrote an introduction to a Lotte Pritzel book I published contradicts this. [1]

In late 1917 I received two long letters from Rilke that were later

---

1. Lotte Pritzel (1887–1952) was a well-known Munich artist and puppeteer. Hyperion Verlag published her work *Puppen* [Puppets] in 1921, with a foreword by Rilke. [Editor's note]

lost (or, like so many, many others, stolen). I remember them clearly, because they were so unlike Rilke in character: embarrassed, awkward, and obviously written at someone else's instigation. The instigator in this instance had been Kippenberg, the head of Insel Verlag and Rilke's publisher, a man extremely sensitive to attempts to "lure away" his authors. Poor Rilke had been given the assignment of reproaching me in a matter that it would be boring to go into here. I felt sorry for the awkward role Rilke had been forced to play, and with regard to Kippenberg, with whom I was basically on good terms and who had also been my own publisher, I was annoyed. So I answered Rilke with a letter that was also quite different in tone and content from the rest of our correspondence. Since my letter went beyond the specific occasion and in fact virtually formulates my fundamental creed as a publisher, I am including the crucial part of it here. I ask you to remember that the writer was very young. However, in the decades that have passed since it was written, very little has changed in my practices or in my attitude:

> For some time now I have noticed (not without amusement) that annoyance over another person's successes tends to be vented (understandably) in accusations that this person is guilty of practicing vicious and brutal American business methods. In reading your last two letters I did not find this accusation in or between the lines, but I did find certain assumptions I wish to contradict most emphatically: not out of stubbornness, and certainly not out of any need to justify my actions, but rather because it will give me pleasure to tell you, a creative artist for whom I have great admiration, about the joys possible in my profession, granted that they may be slight and meager compared to those of creativity itself.
>
> When I became dissatisfied with the limitations of academic pursuits and literary scholarship and abruptly decided to devote myself to publishing with all the passionate energy of my twenty-odd years, the impulse came not solely from my interest in current writing. It was this and more. It was the wish to become involved in what seemed to me important, timely, and genuine, to put my most fervent convictions to use, to join the struggle against the Moloch of human stupidity. Need it concern me that a great many publishers already existed—perhaps too many (although their activities seemed to me almost without exception unsatisfactory)? And wasn't I entitled to hope, on joining their ranks as a

foot soldier, that I might be a future field marshal? After laboring in the profession myself for a few years, I was in a better position to appreciate the real value of my competitors' work and saw more clearly the frightening number of my own mistakes, but I was able to maintain the conviction that had supported me from the start, namely that my publishing house could be a mirror of the age, giving the truest reflection of its heart and spirit in all their varied manifestations: its hysteria and bizarre distortions, its longing for brotherhood and kindness, its love of humanity, and its hatred of philistines. The truest reflection—although still incomplete and imperfect, even more imperfect than the imperfect age itself.

We publishers live only a few short years, if we have ever been truly alive at all. Cotta, Göschen, and many others are examples. Thus our task is to remain alert and youthful, so that the mirror does not grow tarnished too quickly. I am still young, these are my own years; I take pleasure in using my powers and seeing them grow with the tasks to be done, seeing them doubled by struggle and obstacles. I enjoy the give and take, the opportunity to make a difference, and although I may be mistaken, I believe that the small amount of good I am able to accomplish makes up for my errors. How petty to complain about competition and brutality, when it goes without saying that, as we all strive to realize our convictions and beliefs, we maintain the tact and standards of civilized people. I assure you: you mistake the purpose of our profession by raising the claim that nothing should be planned and no projects envisioned without prior consultation with others. I am sure that once you have thought this over you will not insist on such a premise.

The Insel Verlag, to name one example, decided to publish the recent poetry of Becher, Schaeffer, Gildemeister, and Pulver, who were associated with me through older contracts, without asking whether this suited me. (They could not know that it suited me very well.) And I have signed contracts with writers who had previously published elsewhere: Sternheim with Insel, Werfel and Brod with Juncker, Aage Madelung with S. Fischer, etc., etc. We all acted perfectly correctly in not asking each other's permission (provided, of course, that we were acting in agreement with the authors involved). If it were otherwise, it would be the authors who would suffer most, for they would then be confronted with a publishers' cartel. Please do not say now that the publishers named bear no comparison. Certainly authors know how to distinguish among us, but in the eyes of God and the reading public we are all equal (unfortunately). Thus we should each go our own way without looking anxiously over our shoulders, and the competition this independence brings with it is, I repeat, not the worst outcome of our work. Let me give you one example for many where one might see conflicts but shouldn't: I love *Göttinnen* [Goddesses] and *Die kleine Stadt* [The Little Town], works which had previously found fewer than 6,000 readers among 75 million Germans in fifteen and eight years after publication respectively, and it gives me immense pleasure that I was able to bring 100,000 copies to many hundreds of thousands of readers in a single year.[2] Should we really debate whether this result represents a lack of tact toward Langen, Cassirer, and Insel, upon whose shelves the books were piled up, gathering dust? If brutal behavior toward Mr. Kippenberg or Mr. Cassirer consists in helping a writer at the height of his powers finally to reach an audience, or in bringing a fine book already pronounced dead back to life, then I will gladly accept the charge of brutality . . .

I am afraid I have allowed myself to be carried away, and it now seems strange that this letter is addressed to Rainer Maria Rilke. —Perhaps letters are the wrong place to discuss such questions, especially for a man of action like me, whose writing ability is limited.

I did have the impression, however, that your last two letters took an approach toward my professional life which virtually demanded a clarification of my own position. It would pain me to lose your friendship, which I value highly, but if it has to be, it should not happen because of some idle gossip.

Yours very truly in sincere admiration,
Kurt Wolff

This exchange of letters, to which neither of us ever referred again either in conversation or writing, only strengthened our mutual trust and amity. I have referred to it today because it is another expression of my conviction that contracts should not impinge on an author's freedom.

This attitude, however, would get me into some highly problematic and ticklish situations.

I met Gerhart Hauptmann for the first time at a very small dinner party at the house of my friend Björn Björnson, who was then living in Munich. It was in the spring of 1921. For me as a young man,

2. Works by Heinrich Mann. [Translator's note]

Hauptmann was the venerable Nestor of the elder generation of writers and the greatest playwright of his time. The idea of becoming his publisher would never have crossed my mind. Apart from the fact that I would never have taken the first step in approaching any author associated with another firm, my admiration and respect for the Fischer Verlag were double cause for restraint. Only later did it dawn on me that the way the evening had been arranged was no accident; indeed Björnson later went so far as to let me know that Hauptmann had been rather taken aback by my reserve. Hauptmann did indicate on that evening that he had heard from his friend and publisher, Fischer, of preliminary talks on the subject of a possible merger, an idea of which Hauptmann heartily approved. He asked me to keep him informed.

When, somewhat later, these discussions with Fischer reached a dead end, I let Hauptmann know about it. To my amazement he replied immediately by telegram from Agnetendorf:

WOULD SINCERELY REGRET OUTCOME OF MATTER WERE IT DEFINITE
SINCE THE THOUGHT OF YOUR EXCELLENT ABILITIES AND VITALITY RE-
FRESHED AND INVIGORATED ME   I WILL NOT GIVE UP HOPE   REGRET I
LIVE TOO FAR AWAY TO TALK IN PERSON   WARMEST REGARDS

GERHART HAUPTMANN

At the same time Hauptmann sent me word through Björnson that he would welcome a visit from me. I let months go by. When I happened to be visiting a friend in Silesia in the fall of that year, I sent Hauptmann a line and at once received a "you-are-most-welcome" telegram in reply. On my visit to Agnetendorf, which was overshadowed for me by a case of food poisoning, Hauptmann, fortified by large quantities of "cold duck," spoke volubly until the small hours about ways for me to take over the literary side of the Fischer Verlag, above all with a more dynamic approach to publicity, something he thought was completely neglected. In vain did I point out that Fischer had the best adviser imaginable in Moritz Heimann, that the initiative in reopening negotiations did not lie with me, etc. Hauptmann stubbornly stuck to his guns.

He stuck to them both that night and for years to come. We saw one another frequently; he wrote to me now and again, and the topic of the merger of Kurt Wolff and the S. Fischer Verlag remained permanently in the foreground. In September of 1922 Gerhart Hauptmann wrote:

> Our last meeting inspired the wish in me once again that a merger might take place between you and Fischer. Personal considerations speak very strongly for this, apart from the confidence I would have in the business side of things . . .

In June, 1923 he wrote again:

> Where my friend Fischer is concerned, who would benefit so much from the kind of expansion you know about, it is the same old story. Always the same routine, competent but old-fashioned. I am convinced, along with many others, that in the case of my own work, for example, he has by no means exploited all the possibilities. I am the one to suffer from it, with daily bouts of depression, and at the moment there does not appear to be the least hope of remedy.
>
> Fischer is a dear personal friend, and I also have high regard for him as a businessman. But I have stayed younger. I miss a lively, youthful sense of initiative, and stimulating, forward-looking companionship. Now I have no choice but to press forward with energy for two, somehow to compensate for what is lacking . . .

And so forth. Who was pursuing whom here, and for what purpose? It was a game of cat and mouse. Hauptmann never came out and said that he wanted to be my author. I always had the feeling he was waiting for a proposal from me that never came.

No more will be said about my negotiations with Fischer in this context. They do not belong to the topic of author-publisher relations with which we are concerned here, and furthermore the reasons for their failure were so private that they cannot be revealed even today.

But many authors of other publishing houses approached the Kurt Wolff Verlag and offered us single books or their complete works, among them Romain Rolland, Ernst Bloch, René Schickele, Aage Madelung, Jakob Wassermann, Georg Simmel, and others. I had no objections to their coming, and why should I have? They were independent and free to do as they pleased with their work. Sometimes, however, there were psychological problems. The most serious and delicate case was Alfred Kerr, and here again the Fischer Verlag was involved.

Kerr, a Fischer author who for many years had been a friend of the publisher's family and whose books had always been published exclusively by Fischer, suddenly appeared in Leipzig on February 10, 1917. Declaring that he was under no contractual obligations whatsoever, he proposed to us a seven-volume edition of his complete works, gave us a detailed list of its contents—I have it before me—and asked for an immediate answer. When I said yes, he named his conditions, and I accepted them with slight modifications. Kerr asked for written confirmation and received it the same day. Four days later the contract was signed by both parties, and Kerr received five thousand marks toward a total advance of thirty thousand marks. Everything was settled.

Then a letter arrived from Kerr dated March 2:

> At meetings with Mr. Fischer it transpired that he not only takes offence at the publication of my main works by your firm, but that he regards it as a personal blow. He is truly shattered. I told Mr. Fischer how deeply I regret this, but of course also emphasized an author's right to take his work wherever he thinks it will be in the best hands. What Mr. Fischer wishes is an agreement with you concerning my main works *and* "Das neue Drama" [The New Theater]. To be more specific: He wishes to acquire them, with you to have a share, and is willing to take on complete financial responsibility. In reporting this proposal to you I do not mean to take sides. In principle, as goes without saying, I remain committed to the plan as arranged in our contract—with regrets about the offence caused to a man who is deeply upset. I told Mr. Fischer frankly why I preferred to sign with you rather than accept the offers from other publishers (of which there were several). I also said I was attracted by your open-minded, energetic, and decisive way of doing business. Quite apart from the legal obligations, I feel personally bound to you.
>
> So much for our case. What I have to say now goes above and beyond that. Please do not be too surprised. Mr. Fischer considers your firm hostile (because of certain allusions in trade publications about which I know nothing). He has now reached the conclusion that a merger might in certain circumstances be more fruitful than competition. Mr. Fischer is prepared to negotiate with you concerning possible joint

operations. He has informed me about the general outlines—and you may contact me to discuss the matter.

Let me sum up to avoid any possible misunderstanding: (1) I have been authorized by Mr. S. Fischer, Bülowstraße 90, Berlin, to open discussions with you about the merger of the entire S. Fischer Verlag and the entire Kurt Wolff Verlag. (2) Mr. Fischer considers such a step desirable, because a merger of two strong private publishing houses may be advantageous given the expansion of newspaper publishers such as Ullstein and Mosse into the book publishing business.

I offer this information as a go-between in good faith, but also on the assumption that publication of my own works will not be delayed in the least on this account . . .

This fanfare was followed by silence. I made no move of any kind. Then, on March 15, Sami Fischer paid an unannounced and unexpected call in Leipzig, distraught over the loss of his author. He requested that my contract with Kerr be transferred to him, and I gave my immediate assent, provided that Kerr agreed, and naturally without retaining any share for my firm. Kerr's complete works appeared with S. Fischer, where they belonged.

The author's freedom of choice had not been interfered with by either party, and there could be no question whatsoever of trying to "lure away" an author.

Kerr took leave of me in a friendly letter of March 18:

My feelings toward you remain as I described them in my last letter—and I hope very much that Mr. Fischer did not describe them in different terms.

Mr. Fischer's visit to Leipzig was reported to me afterwards by telephone, as a *fait accompli*. I am sorry that I could not take part in the conversation.

That you are doing Mr. Fischer a favor is obvious. Whether it is also a favor to me is not so obvious. I still very much wish to work with you.

All the same he agreed to the transfer without further discussion.

A telegram from April 1917 that has survived these many years reminds me of still another proposal from an author wanting to change his publisher (once again the Fischer Verlag):

ON "LURING AWAY" AUTHORS

In this case it was not moral scruples but an antipathy toward Emil
Ludwig's writings that kept me from following up on Mechtilde Lichnowsky's telegram; the matter was never pursued.

A number of other authors were quite willing to be recruited from
their current publisher, who was by no means always Fischer. In addition to those named above, Frank Wedekind also approached me
about his work in the winter of 1916–17.

At the time I naturally asked myself what all these highly flatter-
ing suggestions meant. What were the motives behind them; why did
all these authors want to join the Kurt Wolff Verlag? I was neither a
magician nor a publishing genius, and hardly a young millionaire.
Sami Fischer was a notable individual who had spent many years
building up a large firm with an outstanding reputation, aided by excellent advisers. There was also the Insel Verlag, and others of
undisputed standing. Why leave them for Kurt Wolff?

There were various reasons, no doubt: older authors may have
wanted to be seen in the company of the younger generation (although in addition to those born around 1890 we published authors
such as Heinrich Mann, born in 1871, and Meyrink, born in 1868,
etc.). However, another reason seemed more decisive to me both
then and now, banal as it may sound:

In 1914 Georg Heinrich Meyer had joined the firm; even the
generally acid-tongued Carl Sternheim once called him the best
book seller he knew. Meyer was no financial wizard (in fact two attempts to found his own publishing firm had ended in bankruptcy, in
spite of excellent starts). He was, however, an advertising genius and
beyond all doubt a past master at promoting sales. Furthermore he
was a fanatically dedicated worker who spent at least twelve hours a
day at the office, lived on cola lozenges, and was personally acquainted with every book seller in creation. And Georg Heinrich
Meyer was constantly after me with one message: advertise, advertise,
advertise—this is the only way to sell books. I took his advice. We

advertised in a fashion without precedent in the German publishing industry, without any concern for the budget. I gave Meyer a free hand, in part because I believed and trusted him, but even more importantly because I had observed the slow but steady climb of inflation setting in soon after the war and felt that it was preferable to spend what money we had rather than save it. Authors were delighted to see large advertisements for their books in the *Berliner Tageblatt* and elsewhere. The Kurt Wolff Verlag remained more or less alone with this advertising strategy. Fischer, at any rate, made no move to join us; whether it was for reasons of economy or because he thought it in poor taste, I cannot tell. I am certain, however, that many Fischer authors deplored it, since they could see that the Kurt Wolff Verlag's strategy often resulted in unusually high printings. It remains an open question whether the reasons named were behind some authors' tendencies to disloyalty. Authors' disloyalty, after all, has classical roots. I will resist the temptation to embark here upon a long historical digression, but I would like to note that Goethe was not loyal to his publishers either, and left Weidmann, Unger, and later Göschen before becoming a Cotta author.

But enough of "luring away" authors in an active or apparently active sense, and of authors who changed or wished to change from other publishers to the Kurt Wolff Verlag. Now, for the sake of symmetry, let me mention some writers of the Kurt Wolff Verlag who were "lured away" by other publishers and departed with my blessing and with no hard feelings on either side.

I will cite only two examples. In both cases the writers were close personal friends and continued to be so. Both expressed their wish to change publishers at a time when our personal relationship was most cordial, and our business relationships were also completely unclouded.

I am speaking of Walter Hasenclever and Franz Werfel. We had published Hasenclever's early poems and his play *Der Sohn*, which was celebrated as an overnight sensation by the entire German press after its premiere in Dresden. The Kurt Wolff Verlag had launched an all-out opening campaign that set the play on its way to fame.

Then Walter, one of my most intimate friends with whom I maintained close ties up to the Second World War and his death, wrote me out of the blue in November 1916 from Dresden, where he was cheerfully sitting out the remainder of the war with his friend Oskar Kokoschka, both feigning illness in the sanatorium of the appropriately named Dr. Teuscher:[3]

> Yesterday Paul Cassirer's agent Leo Kestenberg was here in Dresden from Berlin to negotiate with me. Cassirer made the following offer: an advance of six hundred marks payable monthly for five years, beginning immediately, against royalties earned from the sale of books published by him, including performance rights. Should there be an unearned balance he would absorb the difference. In conjunction with this he proposes a special agreement offering me the editorship of a magazine with a completely free hand and a separate honorarium. For the time being I answered that I could not agree to anything until I had clarified my position with you.
>
> Cassirer appears to take such an extraordinary interest in me that, as Kestenberg intimated, he wishes his publishing house to be centered exclusively on my future work, and he stressed that the art dealer Cassirer, having returned to Berlin from Dresden in a state of uncharacteristic enthusiasm, was quite prepared to permit himself this luxury. You know that for ages I have had plans for a magazine, and I am very eager to carry them out now. It appears that my plans and Cassirer's are similar in tendency, and I was very pleased to find us in harmony, since it guarantees my independence.

I received this letter on November 8, and sent my answer on the same day:

> I can't be anything but very happy about the offer Cassirer has made you, and it goes without saying that I release you unconditionally. In saying that I do not do this light-heartedly, I don't need to emphasize that it is no empty phrase. But do it I must, since in all friendship and with the best will in the world I cannot match what the Cassirer Verlag is offering, in either material or creative terms . . .
>
> I have not the slightest doubt, however, that our warm and friendly relations, of long standing but always retaining the freshness of youth, will continue unchanged over and beyond this professional parting of the ways.

3. The identically pronounced word *Täuscher* in German means "deceiver." [Translator's note]

Once again Walter Hasenclever wrote back within twenty-four hours after receiving my letter:

> . . . today I must tell you how very much I admire the spirit of your letter! You know that no one else identifies himself as closely with the stigma [sic] of the Kurt Wolff Verlag as I do—and you know how much links me to you, to Elisabeth. For one moment I was uneasy, for two moments cowardly, and for a whole morning I felt sad. But then I realized two things. I said to myself: how would KW act himself in my situation? And so I tried to act as you would. Then I realized that the business relationship that has been subordinated to friendship is now objectified (and I did not doubt for a moment *how* this happened): it is now inconceivable that the two could affect one another adversely. This is more decisive for every form of friendship than any attempt, however well-meant, to combine two areas that must be treated in such diametrically opposite ways. I am happy. I am your firm friend, wholly and entirely! Now there is no third factor between us, there is just— *us* . . . There used to be two dangerous obstacles between us: friendship on the one hand, and a business connection on the other— partnership here, conflicting interests there. I think we have passed this test. We have achieved a sphere of freedom. The friendship goes on . . .

This was exactly right, and so it remained. The fact that the connection with the Cassirer Verlag had come about largely because Tilla Durieux, Cassirer's wife, had taken a great fancy to young Hasenclever and wanted to play the lead in his next play was an aspect of the matter that Walter had passed over in gentlemanly silence. Since this fancy soon passed, however, the liaison Cassirer-Hasenclever was short lived, and he moved on to his old friend Ernst Rowohlt, who was in turn replaced by Propyläen Verlag. But no matter who happened to be publishing his works, we remained friends.

In the case of Franz Werfel the situation was similar. I had published a dozen of Werfel's works: poetry, plays, and prose. We were close friends; there had never been any difficulties, either of a financial or any other kind. I was most unhappily aware, however, that although Werfel's books were selling extremely well in Germany, Werfel was making no money on them. If he had been living in Germany and been paid in marks every week, he would have profited to a degree, devalued though the mark was, and would at least have been able to use the money for something, to pay the rent, buy food, or the like. But by the time our checks reached him in Vienna they were practically worthless. Werfel was living with Alma Mahler, whom he married soon afterwards. Alma's fortune had been eaten up by inflation in Austria; indubitably Werfel considered himself obligated to contribute some income himself. His books were selling in large quantities, and his play *The Trojan Women* was performed successfully in countless German theaters. But both economically and legally it was not feasible for me to transfer to him any amounts that would represent significant purchasing power in Austria. It was at this point that Werfel was approached by a young Austrian who knew the writer was working on a long novel. The young man in question was Paul Zsolnay, the son of a very rich man, chief supplier to the Austrian state tobacco monopoly. The son wanted to found a publishing house and was determined to begin it with a work by his idol Franz Werfel. He offered Werfel an advance of five thousand Swiss francs for his novel in progress. Not much? I wish I could give people today an inkling of what *five* Swiss francs meant in the Germany of 1923, when a street car ride or postage stamp cost 200 million marks, and when employees were paid their salary daily, so they could spend it the same day for purchases that would be unaffordable the day after. Those were the times in which the value of the dollar climbed from 550,000 marks to 600 million, then 1 billion and 1 trillion, an exchange rate that gave even Karl Valentin[4] pause, prompting him to observe: "But that's really about all the dollar is worth." The sum of five thousand Swiss francs was mind-boggling to a financial layman. It was during this legendary period that I received Werfel's letter informing me of Zsolnay's offer and pleading for advice on what his response should be. Even drawing on all my financial resources I could not have come up with one thousand francs for my friend and author, and so I obviously replied that he should accept. Which he did. His Verdi novel was published by Zsolnay in Vienna in 1924, and when

---

4. Celebrated German comedian of the era. [Translator's note]

Zsolnay later married the daughter of Alma and Gustav Mahler, such close personal ties were created that the author-publisher relationship benefitted in the most fortunate manner. Still Werfel, the author who had been "lured away," and his expublisher Kurt Wolff remained the best of friends.

Adventures in Publishing

SOME RATHER startling experiences came my way as part of my profession, though they had little to do with literature in the strict sense of the term. The first adventure dates back to 1913; its key word was Gauguin. Fortunately a small part of the relevant correspondence has survived, or I would be unable to tell the story, since memory alone might not suffice. By and large my memory is good and reliable, but as is perhaps true for most people, it was only when I knew someone face to face that a lasting impression was produced. Letters are not enough. I never met Gauguin or his son Pola, with whom I corresponded over a long period, but as I reread my correspondence with Pola a number of things came back to my mind.

Pola was the child of Gauguin's Danish wife, whom he had married in 1873 when he was still working in a Paris bank. Later in life Gauguin rather neglected his family, but his wife and Pola were his heirs. In addition, the son had inherited considerable artistic talent from his father. I published a portfolio of Pola's colored woodcuts some fifty years ago; they showed ability and unmistakable originality, but I do not own a copy myself and never saw them again.

The surviving correspondence with Pola Gauguin begins with a letter from Tønsberg, Norway, of September 3, 1913; it was sent to me in Leipzig in reply to a letter of mine that has been lost. From Pola's letter it emerges that a Mr. Neven du Mont, a mutual acquaintance whom I can no longer identify but to whom I must have referred at the time, had told me about an important unpublished manuscript of Gauguin's and given me the address of his widow. And so I wrote off to Madame Mette Gauguin, née Gad, in Denmark, without assuming for an instant that anything would ever come of it. That must have been in the early summer of 1913. For a long time there was no answer, until a letter from Pola reached me in September, written on his mother's behalf to say: the answer to my inquiry had been delayed so long because they did not want to risk mailing the original manuscript, and further, because the family had first wanted to make inquiries about me. The letter announced that they were sending a typewritten copy of the manuscript by the same post.

The typescript arrived; it was entitled "Avant et après" [Before and After] and was, I was delighted to see, a quite substantial, highly interesting, and extremely well-written book, in no way inferior to the already published *Noa-Noa*. Inserted were photographs of twenty-five Gauguin drawings, closely related to the text. I confirmed receipt of the material and inquired about publishing terms. Pola's answer, dated September 8, 1913, arrived at once. In essence it said: the family wanted either a lump sum of fifteen thousand francs for the world rights or a royalty contract for each separate edition.

I replied—although *my* letters are mostly missing and only the much more important ones from Pola Gauguin survived—that I wished to acquire world rights.

By mid-October the contract was signed, and Pola Gauguin sent us the original manuscript and all the drawings, on which a French edition and all translations were to be based. The manuscript as a whole was so exciting and beautiful in form, such an extraordinarily characteristic expression of Gauguin's personality as an artist, that I have to describe it briefly: 213 closely written folio sheets in Gauguin's very legible handwriting, a clean copy in which there are almost no corrections. The front cover of heavy cardboard is inscribed and richly ornamented in Gauguin's unmistakable style. Not until I read the date 1903 did it dawn on me that Gauguin had written this book in the year he died, and that the drawings must be among the very last he ever did.

On the back cover the artist had pasted a reproduction of Dürer's "Knight, Death, and Devil," and as endpaper he had used one of his own drawings: a man—probably a self-portrait—looking into a small mirror. There were also Japanese woodcuts at the front and back.

The manuscript contained twenty-nine drawings, some drawn on the same paper as the text in the same ink, and some pasted in, but all of them were related to the text, which I found both interesting in content and lively in style. It revealed Gauguin to have been a talented writer. The book begins, "Ceci n'est pas un livre . . . " and ends, ". . . Voilà Messieurs les inspecteurs, tout ce que j'ai à vous dire si toutefois cela vous intéresse, à moins que vous ne disiez comme Pangloss: Tout est pour le mieux, dans le meilleur des mondes." ["This is not a book . . . "; ". . . That, inspectors, is everything I have to tell you, if indeed it is of any interest to you, unless you were to say, like Pangloss: everything is for the best in the best of all worlds."]

I was tremendously excited and could not conceive how such a unique object had come to me, a young, only recently established publisher. I was determined to do all I could to acquire the publishing rights *and* the physical manuscript as well. I wrote to Pola Gauguin, and he agreed to my keeping the manuscript and the drawings made within the text itself: "Mais en ce qui concerne les autres dessins, je regrette vivement de ne pouvoir accéder à votre désir . . ." ["But with respect to the other drawings, I strongly regret that I cannot comply with your wish . . ."] In other words he wanted all other drawings back.

I felt, however, that drawings and text formed an inseparably integrated whole and wrote him again at the end of October 1913. This is one of the very few letters of mine to Gauguin fils that has survived, and I quote it here because it refers not only to the book *Avant et après* and the drawings that go with it, but also to *Noa-Noa*. I quote it somewhat reluctantly, since I wish today that I had written it differently:

> I am most grateful for your letter of October 25 and hasten to answer it without delay. I do not quite agree with your arguments, but I trust that we will be able to reach a satisfactory understanding with regard to the illustrations and earnestly hope you will be flexible on this point. I believe there can be no doubt that the illustrations drawn on the same paper as the text, that is, embedded in the text itself, are an integral part of the manuscript; the manuscript would be destroyed and therefore worthless if pages had to be torn out or cut. The situation is somewhat different for the few illustrations which your father pasted in the book and which are also on different paper.
>
> It is my wish, however, to preserve the manuscript's full charm by acquiring these drawings as well, but I can do this only provided you can quote me an extremely reasonable price. The sum you have re-

From Kurt Wolff, *Autoren, Bücher, Abenteuer*
(Berlin: Wagenbach, 1965), p. 44.

quested for the whole work is so exceptional that I would have to consider selling the manuscript eventually myself, otherwise I could not come close to breaking even. And this manuscript will be far more attractive, as I have mentioned, if it retains all its illustrations.

Without any intention to show disrespect for your father, for whom I have the greatest admiration, let me say that the drawings hastily sketched in this book are not on a par with the major drawings he did. Most likely they have only limited value as single pieces, and they would lose both their charm and their actual value if they were isolated from the manuscript. It is therefore not possible to pay the same prices for them that your father's other works can command.

I would much appreciate it if you would favor me with an immediate answer, and hope that you will see your way to grant my request, i.e., permitting me to keep the pasted in drawings as well for a modest additional payment.

In conjunction with this I would like to make another proposal: I know that the existing edition of *Noa-Noa* is imperfect and incomplete, and that the original manuscript, on which a satisfactory and complete text would have to be based, is owned by a friend of your father's in Paris (whose name escapes me for the moment). I am also aware that you and your mother would have every right to expect suitable remuneration if a new edition of this work were to appear. Since I have an avenue of approach to the owner of the manuscript, I might be able to undertake such an edition and would like to hear from you what terms you might have in mind. I would appreciate hearing from you in this matter, but most particularly regarding *Avant et après*.

In a letter dated November 6, Pola Gauguin replied from Bergen: he asked for an additional four thousand francs for all twenty-nine drawings, a sum he later reduced to twenty-five hundred francs. As far as *Noa-Noa* was concerned, he promised to do everything in his power to enable the Kurt Wolff Verlag to bring out a faithful and complete edition, but added: " . . . le manuscrit original qui d'après mon opinion appartient à moi, se trouve à présent entre les mains de Monsieur Georges-Daniel de Monfried." [" . . . the original manuscript, which in my opinion belongs to myself, is at present in the possession of Monsieur Georges-Daniel de Monfried."]

The correspondence on the subject of *Noa-Noa* dragged on for years. Pola made it absolutely clear that his father regarded the German edition published by Bruno Cassirer as a "forgery." Years went by until we finally reached a contractual agreement on an authentic edition of *Noa-Noa*, to be based on the original manuscript. Bruno Cassirer heard of this, and at his urgent request I transferred the publishing rights to him.

But getting back to *Avant et après:* the book came out in German, French, and English editions, but received little notice. Gauguin's time had not yet come. To my knowledge no French museum had yet acquired any of his paintings.

However, the story of the manuscript does not end here. I, Kurt Wolff, was a publisher, not a collector, and I could not afford the luxury of acquiring the manuscript and the drawings. And so in 1918 I had a faithful facsimile edition of *Avant et après* printed (now completely unavailable) and sold the manuscript and drawings to my friend Erik-Ernst Schwabach for twenty thousand paper marks. The Kurt Wolff Verlag retained the publishing rights. This appeared to be the final chapter in the strange story of Gauguin's manuscript. I had not given any further thought to it for forty years, in any case, when a headline in the *New York Times* of July 24, 1956 caught my eye: "Court Fight Is On for Gauguin's Manuscript." What had happened to the manuscript I had long since forgotten?

It turned out that Erik-Ernst Schwabach, although heir to part of the Bleichröder banking fortune, had been reduced to poverty, partly by inflation and completely by forced emigration, and had sold the manuscript. Perhaps it had changed hands several times over those many years. In any event in 1956 it belonged to a major New York dealer, who was offering it for sale. Then suddenly five people sued him, all claiming to be the rightful owner. The manuscript was sold nevertheless to an American collector, who paid eighty-five thousand dollars for it, a price the *New York Times* called "the most spectacular for modern manuscripts." Today, however, seven years later, this seems very low when you consider the number of drawings included.

This was my Gauguin adventure, with its beginning in 1913 and its epilogue in 1956, which stirred my memory and made me look up my files.

THERE WERE other adventures. I remember some, if by no means all of them. One, for instance, was a correspondence with Helmut von Gerlach, a prominent politician and journalist with democratic leanings. It begins with a letter I wrote to Gerlach, whom I didn't know at all, on October 8, 1919. Its content seems sensational enough for the letter to be included in full:

Luisenstraße 31
Munich
October 8, 1919

Mr. Helmut von Gerlach
Genthinerstraße 22
Berlin W. 10

Dear Sir:

If I take the liberty of writing you today as a complete stranger about a highly confidential matter, let me preface it by saying that this letter is prompted by the high regard in which I have held you, both as a politician and a journalist, over the years. I am assuming that the substance of my inquiry justifies the inquiry itself. If I were not involved in a highly complicated move from Leipzig to Munich, I would have come to Berlin to discuss the matter at hand with you in person. But since that is impossible for me at the moment, I have no alternative but to write.

You will receive by the same post, in two registered letters, a typescript of 155 pages containing a complete set of the letters of Kaiser Wilhelm II to the Czar, written between January 5, 1895 and February 26, 1914.

They have been entrusted to me by a special and absolutely authentic source, with permission to make such publishing use of them as I see fit. It is my wish to do so in book form and in such a way as to avoid all sensationalism. For this reason I am extremely concerned to avoid prepublication of any part of the manuscript in newspapers or magazines.

My question and plea to you now is whether you would be willing to edit the letters. I am thinking in terms of an introduction and brief bridge passages providing the necessary foreign policy context. Since you are so thoroughly familiar with the politics of the years involved, I assume that the amount of work required would not make excessive demands on your time. At the same time I believe that the task is a particularly attractive and interesting one. How you would want to proceed in detail I would of course leave completely up to you.

The matter is extremely urgent, since it is not within my power to prevent publication of a Russian, French, or English edition ahead of the German one. If this happens, then the book I have in mind would be virtually worthless, since German newspapers and magazines could print excerpts of the foreign edition in translation.

Nothing need be added concerning the contents of the letters themselves. A glance at the manuscript will suffice to show you that it is a political document of the greatest significance, quite apart from the psychological interest that the letters will certainly arouse.

Finally, for particular reasons I cannot go into here, I must ask you to keep this information absolutely confidential, to mention the existence of the letters to no one, regardless of whether you decide to edit them or not.

To make sure that the manuscript reaches you rapidly, I am sending it not as a package, but in two registered letters insured for two thousand marks each.

Yours very truly,
Kurt Wolff

Gerlach responded by agreeing to take on the editorship, "since the task appears to be both attractive and important. However, I would need more information from you regarding the letters' authenticity. If I assume responsibility for them, I must of course be absolutely certain on this point . . ."

I reassured him without becoming too specific about my sources, since I was not allowed to. The letters had come from Moscow, from the Soviet government itself:

Incidentally, I have been expressly promised by a member of this government, who is currently an inmate in Berlin-Moabit, that in case doubt should arise with regard to the genuineness of any passage in the letters, a photograph copy of the original could be made available at any time.

Gerlach would certainly have known that the member of the Soviet government who was in Moabit prison at that time was Karl Radek. Someone connected to the magazine *Die Weltbühne* had suggested that I pay Radek a visit—and this had led to my receiving the manuscript.

Gerlach prepared the correspondence for publication, and the book was supposed to be published in January of 1920. Was supposed to . . . But then on December 31 I had to inform him: "I have been away for several days; I returned to Munich today and read in the train last night that publication of the letters is scheduled to begin simultaneously in newspapers in London, Paris, and New York on January 1. This makes publication of the book . . . a complete illusion." And that was the end of it. It had made for a great deal of excitement and fun, however. With the Russians, who didn't believe in the idea of exclusive rights or copyrights, one had to be prepared for that sort of thing. I actually think that at the time I was relieved that matters took this course. The correspondence between Kaiser Wilhelm and Czar Nicholas would not have fitted in the list of the Kurt Wolff Verlag.

SOMETIMES things occur that seem completely insignificant at the time, and take on an adventurous character only in retrospect, often after many years have gone by. You might call them adventures with a time fuse. The following occurrence is perhaps a good example.

It is a complete accident that out of thousands of letters which were destroyed or lost, one small sheet of paper has survived that was utterly unimportant to me when it arrived. Here it is, complete with return address:

via Sanità, 2[III]
Trieste
Italy

Dear Sir:

Perhaps this novel written by me and of which I present to you several press reviews would be suitable in German translation for your series "Moderne Bücher." Some of my works have already been translated into German, Italian, and Swedish. If you so wish, I could acquire a copy for you.

Respectfully

May 1, 1920   prof. James Joyce

If I had any reaction at all on reading these lines in 1920, it was probably: Who is this idiotic "professor" who has written from Trieste in bad German about an English book he wants me to publish in German? It is possible that I went so far as to make inquiries and learned that Joyce was not only completely unknown on the continent of Europe, but also an obscure figure in England. Of course I can no longer recall what "this novel" was. In 1920 Joyce had published only two books, *Dubliners* and *A Portrait of the Artist as a Young Man*, and they were known only to a tiny circle. It was not until two years later that Sylvia Beach's Shakespeare & Co. in Paris brought out *Ulysses*.

The adventure in this case was finding the letter forty years later, and realizing that if the Kurt Wolff Verlag had published an early book by Joyce, it would certainly also have acquired *Ulysses*, the most important work to be written in English in our century.

THERE ARE quite a few other "if-only" stories I could add to this list:

If only the Kurt Wolff Verlag had published Axel Munthe's *Buch von San Michele* [*The Story of San Michele*], for instance, it would have acquired the rights to a best seller that sold over a million copies in the German edition alone, and for some mysterious reason has continued to sell until today.

I was the first German publisher to be offered *The Story of San Michele*. I read it in the German translation and found it so unbelievably trite, vain, and embarrassing that I did not hesitate for a moment

in rejecting it. I did find the rejection difficult for one particular reason, however: the German manuscript had been given to me by the
translator, a Baroness Uexkuell from Hamburg, and to this day I vividly recall her beauty and charm; she was a woman to whom it was
hard to refuse anything. But I am proud to say that the Kurt Wolff
Verlag did not publish Axel Munthe's book, and no sales figures have
ever changed my mind.

In another case the "if-only" is slightly different. Here I would
like to cite a letter in full, because although it is long, its content is
noteworthy, and it was written by a man who became world famous
far beyond his own lifetime precisely because of the book to which the
letter refers:

Munich
April 12, 1917

Dear Sir:

Enclosed you will find a large work dealing with the philosophy of
history, that I send to you with the question whether you might be interested in publishing it. It is entitled:

The Decline of the West
Outlines of a Morphology of World History

It represents the first volume (*Form and Actuality*) of a longer work and
contains a study of the fundamental problem of history that is entirely
new in both method and results. Chief emphasis is placed on formal
problems in the intellectual and social development of modern Europe,
as part of a *complete* analysis of human culture. It is approximately
thirty-two signatures of sixteen pages in length. The second and shorter
volume (*Perspectives of World History*), of which I have also enclosed a
table of contents, should appear after an interval of one year. It will contain a summary of specific historical, political, and economic questions
based on volume I and aims to present a psychology of the future of
Europe. In the meantime two *small* essays of five to six signatures each
will deal with several problems of world politics that are of the greatest
topical interest: the universal historical significance of Prussia ("Ro-
mans and Prussians: A Parallel in World History") and the phenomena
of nationalism and nations with a parliamentary form of government
with respect to their origins, interrelationships, and duration. These
will serve as preparation for the more general conclusions of volume 2.

In these books I will present to the public the results of many years of scholarly research. Volume 1 was written between 1911 and 1914; the first draft was finished when the war broke out. Now I have made some final additions and completed it.

I do not wish you to suppose that I have striven for any fleeting sensational effect—and as you will see, the book's content should banish any such suspicion. The title was decided upon in 1911 and refers strictly to a phase of world history comprising several centuries which has only just begun, and whose real significance is much more directly apparent in the structure of intellectual, artistic, and social developments than in the purely political sphere.

A look at the very detailed table of contents should convince you that the book will have an epoch-making effect on several fields of modern scholarship—as everyone who has seen the manuscript has agreed. It has been predicted that it will have a particularly far-reaching influence on the study of history, the history of art, and economics.

For this reason I believe I can truthfully say that the book's publication will be a success, also in the terms in which publishers naturally understand the word. In any case my conviction is shared by others that the book's argumentation is conducted on a level never attained before and certainly not during the war. The persuasive nature of the fundamental idea itself and the scope and plausibility of its implications—already confirmed in part by recent events—lift the work above the prevailing tendency toward short-lived relevance. My approach made polemics as such both unnecessary and impossible; on the contrary, in fact, it enabled me to use the results of modern specialized scholarship and to develop them further in the direction in which scholars were *unconsciously* heading. This is important for the effect the book will have in scholarly circles. I have given clear and definite expression to a vague feeling evident everywhere today but up to now expressed in unrelated theories applicable only to limited areas and therefore incomplete.

A good part of the book's success will depend on the publisher, however, since the fate of a work such as this will be determined, possibly for decades to come, by the way the public is made aware of its existence.

I have deemed it appropriate to suggest publication of the book to you, and I would be pleased if this led to a lasting association between us in the future. If you are inclined to accept my proposal, I would be most grateful to hear your terms.

Yours very truly
Agnesstr. 54, Munich   Dr. Oswald Spengler

There are no grounds for pride in the fact that I returned the manuscript of *The Decline of the West* to the author unread. It is hard to
explain this stupidity in retrospect. All the same I think I can recall a
few reasons:

First of all, I did not like the undistinguished handwriting of the
letter, and this may have created a foolish prejudice in me. More
important was the thought that certainly must have occurred to me:
if this Mr. Spengler was offering such a work to the Kurt Wolff Verlag,
then the manuscript must have already been rejected by all the
German publishers who ordinarily dealt with this kind of scholarly
work. These publishers, at least half a dozen highly respected firms,
employed well-trained academic readers; then as now, they usually
sent auspicious-looking manuscripts to experts in the particular field
for reports. One glance at this manuscript told me I was completely
unfit to judge its merits, and I had no reader available to me with the
necessary qualifications.

It was quite evident that virtually no German publishing house
could be less appropriate for such a work than the Kurt Wolff Verlag,
which dealt almost exclusively with literature. Even Spengler could
not be so out of touch with the real world as to be unaware of that. At
the time the Kurt Wolff Verlag was known as the publisher of Werfel's
poetry, Hasenclever's play *The Son*, Meyrink's *The Golem*, and the
little series *The Last Judgment*. Our representatives called on book
dealers to offer them these and similar books. Could I now expect
them to sell, alongside *The Golem*, this five-hundred-page volume 1
of *Outlines for a Morphology of World History?* Nonsense. And so
back went the manuscript to the author who—contrary to the usual
practice—had submitted it without any previous inquiry or referral
from a third party.

Now, looking back at my rejection of *The Decline of the West*, I
must say with regret: A pity, what if . . . or if only.

My answer to Spengler from 1917 has not survived. He certainly
bore me no ill will for the rejection, and immediately thereafter he

found in the Beck Verlag in Munich the ideal publisher for his book. Later, when the Kurt Wolff Verlag moved to Munich in the spring of 1919, I encountered the author several times in Frobenius-Dacqué's circle of friends.[1] I was impressed by the self-assurance and persuasiveness this strange genius displayed in conversations and discussions, but his personality was quite colorless and I could never warm up to him.

Strangely enough, and to my own amazement, evidence exists that Spengler and I had further dealings with each other of a professional kind. I cannot recall the details, but I still have a copy of a letter I wrote to Spengler on February 9, 1923, which begins: "After our conversation yesterday on the possibility of bringing out a limited edition of your work *The Decline of the West*, I discussed the matter with other members of the firm." The letter goes on to say that in my opinion luxury editions made sense only if they were limited, and the edition of five thousand copies he had proposed was too large. It thus appears that the Beck Verlag had given the author permission to have a special edition printed elsewhere. The fact that this project never materialized did not bother me—by 1923 the book was already famous and being discussed everywhere. Printing an expensive limited edition at that point had no appeal for me; it would not have demanded any creativity as a publisher.

LET ME CLOSE my recollections of adventures in publishing with these remarks about Spengler and the work of his I did not publish. I was not particularly happy with the choice of the word "adventures" for this account of my experiences, mainly because the stories I have told here do not in fact represent the true adventures of my professional life. The truth is that every past and present manuscript is an adventure when it arrives, one that makes my heart beat faster. And since the number of manuscripts was and is legion, almost every day is an adventure, even without all the other surprises that our profession may have in store for us.

1. The Frobenius-Dacqué circle was a Munich-based group of writers, explorers, and ethnologists interested in primitive peoples and cultures. KWV published Frobenius's *Hadschra Maktuba* in 1925. [Editor's note]

Essays
on
Individual
Authors

Franz Kafka

THE TEMPEST that once swirled around the person and works of Franz Kafka appears to be slowly subsiding. His writings have survived the catchwords to become classics. Kafka is discussed less these days, but he is read more. Numbers may be of some interest in this connection: Fifty years ago, in August of 1912, to be exact, Franz Kafka sent me eighteen small prose pieces which were printed the same year in an edition of eight hundred copies, under the title of *Betrachtung* [Meditation]. This was the very first book of Kafka's to be published. His later books were printed in editions of a thousand copies, and I cannot recall that any of his books required a second printing during Kafka's lifetime.[1]

In November 1917, he wrote to Max Brod: "[Received] a statement from Wolff today noting 102 copies of *Betrachtung* sold in 1916–17, an amazingly high number . . ." Five years after publication, however, this amazingly high number of 102 copies had by no means exhausted the original edition of eight hundred. Today, fifty years later, I have a Fischer paperback before me, *Das Urteil und andere Erzählungen* [The Judgment and Other Stories] by Franz Kafka; it notes that the 347,000th copy of this volume was printed in March 1961, and to this figure must be added the many other printings in separate editions, other collections, and complete editions of Kafka's works. Other works by Kafka published by the same firm also had total sales numbering in the hundreds of thousands.

Exceptions exist, but as a general rule one can predict that the

1. This applies only to the larger works; three volumes that appeared in the series *Der jüngste Tag* were reprinted: *Der Heizer* [The Stoker] twice and *Die Verwandlung* [The Metamorphosis] and *Das Urteil* [The Judgment] once. [Author's note]

success of a book which on first publication goes straight to the top of the best-seller lists will be short lived. If, on the other hand, such a success develops years or even decades after first publication, it promises to be long lasting. In the case of Kafka, who since the end of the Second World War has had an enormous international impact—including a complete edition in Japanese translation—he may certainly be counted among the classics of world literature; no writer in this century has exerted a greater influence on other writers than this young man from Prague, who led a retired life and died unknown. One cannot imagine the same for Camus, or Buzzati, or—but I mustn't go off on a historical tangent . . .

I do not recall how many meetings I had with Kafka, but our first encounter has impressed itself on my memory with almost uncanny clarity. It was on June 29, 1912. Kafka was on a vacation trip with Max Brod; the two of them had left Prague the day before and stopped in Leipzig on their way to Weimar.

That afternoon Max Brod, who was already associated with the firm, brought Kafka to the shabby little office we had rented from the venerable Drugulin Printing Company. Ernst Rowohlt and I received them together, since our partnership was not dissolved until a few months later. May Max Brod forgive me for what I am about to say, since I am the last person who would want to diminish the incalculable service he performed for his friend, both during his lifetime and afterwards—but in that very first moment I received an indelible impression: the impresario was presenting the star he had discovered. This was true, of course, and if the impression was embarrassing, it had to do with Kafka's personality; he was incapable of overcoming the awkwardness of the introduction with a casual gesture or a joke.

Oh, how he suffered. Taciturn, ill at ease, frail, vulnerable, intimidated like a schoolboy facing his examiners, he was sure he could never live up to the claims voiced so forcefully by his impresario. Why had he ever got himself into this spot; how could he have agreed to be presented to a potential buyer like a piece of merchandise! Did he really wish to have anyone print his worthless trifles—no, no, out of the question! I breathed a sigh of relief when the visit was over, and said good-bye to this man with the most beautiful eyes and the most touching expression, someone who seemed to exist outside the category of age. Kafka was not quite thirty, but his appearance, as he went from sick to sicker, always left an impression of agelessness on me: one could describe him as a youth who had never taken the step into manhood.

As he took his leave on that June day in 1912 Kafka said something that I have never heard from any author before or since, and that for this reason remained irrevocably linked in my mind with this unique figure: "I will always be much more grateful to you for returning my manuscripts than for publishing them."

Max Brod has described this meeting and what followed from it in his biography of his friend:

> The journey to Weimar was also important for the reason that it took us through Leipzig, where I brought Franz together with Ernst Rowohlt and Kurt Wolff, who were then running the publishing house of Rowohlt. For I had long cherished the burning desire to see a book of my friend's in print. Franz's attitude towards this wish of mine was very divided. He wanted to—and again he didn't want to. At times his disinclination won the day, particularly at the time when, having returned to Prague, he had to set to work and choose those short pieces of prose which he considered were ready to be printed out of the wealth of his manuscripts, that is to say, the diaries, and give them the final polishing up—which took place not without a lot of hesitation, looking-up of dictionaries, and despair at his uncertainty of the rules of spelling and punctuation. The publishers had already expressed their readiness— those were happy days!—after seeing the specimens I had taken with me to Leipzig. It was only up to Franz to submit a definite manuscript. And that was just the point at which he began to kick good and proper, and discovered that everything he had written was bad, and that piecing together these 'worthless' old fragments prevented him from getting on and producing better work. But I wouldn't let up any more. Kafka's diary is a witness to the resistance he put up against me, but it didn't help him in the least. The book had to be finished, and finished it was.[2]

One can see from this that the manuscript would never have been assembled or sent off had it not been for Max Brod's tireless insistence.

2. Max Brod, *Franz Kafka: A Biography*, 2d ed., translated by G. Humphreys Roberts (New York: Schocken Books, 1960), pp. 124–25.

A month later the short early pieces arrived that were published in the winter of 1912–13 under the title *Betrachtung*. Within a few days Kafka had regrets about submitting the manuscript, wanted to change his mind, and wrote in his diary of his hope the firm would return it, "so that I could be no more unhappy than before."

The conflict over whether to publish or not to publish remained with Kafka throughout his life. "The publication of any of my scribblings always makes me uneasy," Kafka once said to a young countryman, who replied, "Then why do you have them printed?" Kafka's answer:

> That's the trouble! Max Brod, Felix Weltsch, all my friends always manage to get their hands on something I've written and then confront me with a contract already drawn up. I don't want to cause them any difficulties, and so things end up being published that are actually only very private notes or trifles to amuse myself. Personal documents of my human failings are published and even sold, because my friends, with Max Brod in the forefront, insist on turning them into literature, and I don't have the strength to destroy these products of my solitude.
>
> What I say here is naturally just an exaggeration and a bit of spitefulness toward my friends. The truth is that I am so corrupted and shameless that I participate myself in getting these things published. Then to excuse my weakness I make the forces working on me out to be stronger than they are. This is fraud, of course. I am a lawyer, you see— that is why I can't keep away from wrongdoing.

I never had the slightest doubt that this ambivalence between fear of publishing and the wish to publish was utterly sincere and deeply rooted in Kafka's nature. His defensiveness seemed to me actually the stronger force, and I sensed that it was more than mere dislike of literary publicity. It was an attempt to hold the external world at bay altogether.

Although I tried to encourage productivity in other authors by prodding them both in conversation and letters, and actively sought their manuscripts, in Kafka's case I had inhibitions and was unwilling to intrude on his private world. Since our association had been brought about by Max Brod, contacts between this author and his publisher as a rule went via Brod instead of directly. My sense that I was complying with Kafka's wishes is confirmed by a letter of Kafka's to Brod from June 1918:

. . . thanks . . . too, for mentioning me to Wolff. It is so much more agreeable to have you remind him about me than to do it myself (assuming that you don't mind), since then if he doesn't like to do something he can say so openly, while otherwise—at least that is my impression—he doesn't speak openly, or not in letters at any rate; in person he is more forthcoming.

I did overcome my diffidence about sending to Kafka directly more than just short reports on current business matters at least once, in a letter of November 1921. I suspect that it is the only "appeal" I ever addressed to him, and since it also happens to be the only letter of which I still have a copy, I am able to quote the essential parts of it here:

> Our correspondence is infrequent and meager. None of the authors with whom we are associated approaches us so seldom with requests or questions as you do, and none gives us the same impression that the fate of the books we publish is such a matter of indifference. In such a case it seems appropriate for the publisher to reaffirm, from time to time, that the apparent lack of concern on the author's part about how his books are faring does not shake the publisher's belief and confidence in their outstanding quality. Among the writers we represent, there are two or three at most—and I say this in all sincerity—whose work affects me so intensely and personally as yours.
>
> Please do not take the visible success we have with your books as any indication of the effort that goes into selling them. You know as well as we do that it is usually the best and most estimable works which find little or no echo immediately and must wait for one; still, we are confident that the German reading public will one day be capable of giving these books the reception they deserve.
>
> You would do me a great favor by allowing us to demonstrate this confidence to the public: let us publish more of your books. Every manuscript you can bring yourself to send us will be welcomed and published in book form with loving care. If over the course of time you could give us, in addition to collections of short prose pieces, a longer, connected story or a novel—since I know from you and from Max Brod how many manuscripts of this kind are nearly finished or even completed—we would be especially grateful. It lies in the nature of things that the public's receptivity for a single extended prose work is greater than it is for collections of shorter pieces. This is a tiresome and senseless attitude on the part of readers, but it is a fact of life. The interest aroused by a larger prose work would allow vastly wider distribution

than has been possible up to now, and at the same time such success would help us to publicize your earlier works more energetically.

Do me this favor, dear Mr. Kafka, and let me know if we may expect something in the near future, and what it will be.

I hope this finds you in tolerably good health and send assurances of my unchanging regard and best wishes,

Sincerely yours,
Kurt Wolff

This letter is anticipating events, however—so let us go back to the publication of Kafka's earliest works.

In May 1913 the Kurt Wolff Verlag started publication of a new series, entitled *Der Jüngste Tag*. It was important to me to have Franz Kafka among the very first authors represented in it. When I suggested this to him, Kafka proposed that the first chapter of a novel he did not intend to publish appear as an independent short story. This was *Der Heizer* [The Stoker], the first chapter of his novel *Amerika*. I sent a request—apparently a very urgent one—for the manuscript and Kafka replied:

> Your very kind letter has just reached me late this evening. Under the circumstances I cannot get the manuscripts to you by Sunday even with the best will in the world, and even though I would find it more bearable to send off a still-unfinished piece of work rather than to let it seem that I was being even the least disobliging. To be sure, I cannot see in what way or what sense these manuscripts could be a favor to you, but for that reason I ought to send them all the more readily. I will indeed send you the first chapter of the novel, since most of it has already been copied; by Monday or Tuesday the manuscript should be in Leipzig. Whether it can be published by itself I do not know. To be sure, this first chapter does not expose the total failure of the next five hundred pages, but on the other hand it probably lacks sufficient coherence. It is a fragment and will stay that way; this prospect gives the chapter what coherence it has. [3]

These remarks, along with many others, make it clear that while he was alive Kafka would never have permitted "the total failure of the

3. Franz Kafka, *Letters to Friends, Family, and Editors*, translated by Richard and Clara Winston (New York: Schocken Books, 1958, 1977), p. 96.

following five hundred pages," in other words, the novel *Amerika*, to be published. —I have no intention of entering the controversy concerning the rights and wrongs of Max Brod's decision to publish Kafka's posthumous novels contrary to his instructions. I myself published his *Amerika* and *Das Schloß* [*The Castle*] reluctantly and with grave reservations after Kafka's death, although I was aware that only with these novels did Kafka's full significance as a mystical and philosophical thinker become evident.

Now almost forty years later, it seems inconceivable to me that the novels which add a new dimension to his oeuvre might have been burned as he desired. But then as now, I find the greatest appeal and the greatest formal perfection in the superb prose miniatures of the two small volumes *Betrachtung* and *Ein Landarzt* [A Country Doctor]. (I realize this is the relish of an aesthete, not the reaction of an Existentialist.) It always saddens me that most of the Kafka readers I encounter in life or in books are familiar with the novels but not the short prose pieces. (One can read in Simone de Beauvoir's autobiography, for example, how she and Sartre discovered Kafka.)

Is there any prose in all of German literature of the twentieth century, or far back into the nineteenth, that possesses a flawless purity comparable to these creations of Kafka's? I am thinking of such pieces from *A Country Doctor* as "Elf Söhne" [Eleven Sons] or "Auf der Galerie" [Up in the Gallery], a prose jewel 2 (two!) sentences long!

But it was a ceaseless struggle to be able to work, to write. Reading his diaries, one begins to understand what torments and resistance Kafka's creativity suffered. Apart from the fact that during his best years—fourteen long years of his short life—he had to meet the demands of full-time employment at the Workers' Accident Insurance Institute in Prague, his life was a heroic, desperate struggle against illness, a weak constitution, insomnia. And lastly, the circumstances of his home life, where he had no privacy or peace and quiet, were extremely unfavorable.

It was only thanks to the efforts of Max Brod that additional literary works of Kafka's achieved publication in the year 1913: "The Stoker" as the third volume in the series *Der Jüngste Tag* and the short story "The Judgment" in *Arkadia*, a collection edited by Max Brod. "The Judgment" is probably the only story about which the author himself had a good word to say, a work whose publication he approved. In a letter to the firm dated August 1913, he wrote: "The story is more lyric than epic; for this reason it needs a great deal of space around it, if it is to be effective. It is also my favorite work and thus it was always my wish that, if possible, it should be presented independently." "The Judgment" first appeared in *Arkadia*, but was later reprinted separately in *Der Jüngste Tag. Meditation*, "The Stoker," the collection *Arkadia*, all failed to arouse attention—one can say without exaggeration that everything published by Kafka during his lifetime failed to attract public notice.

As far as I can recall, none of the critics at that time responded to what Kafka had to say and how he was able to say it. Even a writer such as Musil, now ranked close to Kafka by literary historians, wrote quite an unsympathetic review of *Meditation* in 1914 for the Fischer literary journal *Die Neue Rundschau*, saying that "fifty years ago an author would have called the book *Soap Bubbles*" and commenting on how empty and flimsy Kafka's stories were.

Later Thomas Mann and Hermann Hesse were the first to recognize the extraordinary and unique quality of Kafka's genius.[4] Hesse coined the lovely phrase about the "secret king of the German language," and in 1922 Rilke wrote me from Muzot, "I have never read a line by this author that did not affect or amaze me in the strangest manner." This was a year and a half before Kafka's death. The poet W. H. Auden stated his conviction: "The author who comes nearest to bearing the same kind of relation to our age as Dante, Shakespeare, and Goethe bore to theirs, Kafka is the first one I would think of . . . Kafka is important to us because his predicament is the predicament of modern man."[5]

4. Both did so after Kafka's death, when the novels were published. One of the few writers to see Kafka's work in the proper perspective and appreciate its greatness during Kafka's lifetime was Kurt Tucholsky. [Author's note]

5. This quotation is from Mrs. Wolff's memorabilia.

FRANZ KAFKA

LETTERS

Franz Kafka to Ernst Rowohlt

Prague
August 14, 1912

Dear Herr Rowohlt:

I am herewith transmitting to you the short prose pieces you wished to see. They might well make a small book. While I was assembling them for this purpose I sometimes had the choice between appeasing my sense of responsibility and my eagerness to have a book of my own among your fine books. Certainly my decisions have not been perfectly pure. But now, of course, I would be happy if you liked the things only to the extent of your publishing them. Ultimately, even with the greatest experience and the greatest keenness, the flaws in these pieces do not reveal themselves at first glance. And the personal mark of each writer consists in his having his own special way of concealing his flaws.

Yours sincerely, Dr. Franz Kafka

Manuscript follows separately by parcel post.[6]

Kurt Wolff to Franz Kafka, Niklasstraße 36, Prague

September 4, 1912

Dear Dr. Kafka:

My partner and I have read your work and will be very happy to publish it. Technically, printing such a quite short book will present certain difficulties, but I think we will be able to find an attractive solution. Now I hope you will be so kind as to let us know the terms under which you would let us have the book and also whether you

6. This letter of August 14, 1912, and those of September 7, 1912, March 8, March 25, and April 4, 1913, are reprinted by permission from *Letters to Friends, Family, and Editors*, translated by Richard and Clara Winston (Copyright © 1958, 1977, by Schocken Books, Inc., published by Pantheon Books, a division of Random House, Inc., and by John Calder, Ltd.), pp. 85, 94–96.

have particular wishes about how it should be printed (e.g., Roman or Gothic type, and so forth.)

I look forward with interest to your reply and send my best regards.

Yours very truly,
[Kurt Wolff]

Franz Kafka to Ernst Rowohlt

Workers' Accident Insurance Institute
Prague
September 7, 1912

Dear Sir:

Many thanks for your friendly letter of the 4th. Since I can easily imagine the commercial prospects of publishing such a small first book, I gladly agree to any conditions you wish to propose. Conditions that limit your risk as far as possible will also be those I prefer.

I have too much respect for the books you have published to interfere with any proposals in regard to this book. I would only ask for the largest possible typeface consistent with your plans for the book. If it were possible to give the book a dark cardboard binding with tinted paper somewhat like the Kleist *Anecdotes*, I would like that very much—always assuming, however, that this would not disturb your plans.

Looking forward to further word from you, I am,

Sincerely yours, Dr. Franz Kafka

Franz Kafka to the Ernst Rowohlt Verlag

Workers' Accident Insurance Institute
Prague
September 25, 1912

Dear Sirs:

Enclosed please find a signed copy of the contract you sent, which I am returning to you with my thanks. I have delayed sending it for a day or two because I hoped to send an improved version of the little piece "Der plötzliche Spaziergang" [The Sudden Walk] along with it; in the present conclusion of the first paragraph there is a passage that revolts me. Unfortunately I haven't quite got this better version yet, but I will definitely be sending it in the next few days.

A further request: since the publication date is not mentioned in the contract (although I attach no importance whatsoever to this being done) and since I would naturally very much like to know when you intend it to appear, I would appreciate it if you could send me word about this at your convenience.

Yours very truly,
Dr. Franz Kafka

1 enclosure

Franz Kafka to the Ernst Rowohlt Verlag

Workers' Accident Insurance Institute
Prague
October 6, 1912

Dear Sirs:

I am enclosing the better version of the little piece "Der plötzliche Spaziergang" and ask that you be so good as to include it in place of the earlier version in the manuscript.

At the same time I would like to ask again for the information I requested some time ago about the publication date you contemplate for *Betrachtung*. I would be grateful if you would kindly send this information soon.

Yours very truly,
Dr. F. Kafka

1 enclosure

Kurt Wolff to Franz Kafka

October 7, 1912

Dear Dr. Kafka:

This is to confirm, with thanks, receipt of your letter of yesterday with the new version of the one sketch; I will replace the original version in the manuscript with it. Your book will certainly be out during November, i.e., in good time for Christmas. I am still having difficulties in finding a suitable typeface and appropriate format so that we can give the not very extensive manuscript a larger size.

Yours very truly,
[Kurt Wolff]

Kurt Wolff to Franz Kafka

October 16, 1912

Dear Dr. Kafka:

You have had to wait a long time for news from me; I hope you will be all the more pleased by the sample pages I am sending today, which seem to me to have come out quite beautifully.

Would you be happy to see your book printed like this?

I look forward with interest to your reply and remain

Yours very truly,
[Kurt Wolff]

1 sample proof

Franz Kafka to Kurt Wolff

Prague
October 18, 1912

Dear Sir:

The sample pages you were kind enough to send me are very beautiful indeed. I cannot agree quickly enough and with sufficient enthusiasm to this format and send my heartfelt thanks for the interest you have shown in this little book.

I do hope the page numbers in the sample are not the final ones, since "Kinder auf der Landstraße" [Children on a Country Road] should be the first piece. It was my mistake not to have included a table of contents, and the worst of it is that I cannot rectify this mistake, since apart from the piece at the beginning and the final piece "Unglücklich sein" [Unhappiness] I don't really know what order the stories in the manuscript were in.

"Der plötzliche Spaziergang" in the improved form did arrive safely, I trust?

> Yours very truly,
> Dr. F. Kafka

Kurt Wolff to Franz Kafka

October 19, 1912

Dear Dr. Kafka:

Thank you for your letter of yesterday; today I will give instructions to the printers to begin work immediately. The page numbers were inserted in the sample completely at random and have nothing to do with the order in which you placed the stories; naturally they will be printed according to the order in your manuscript.

> Yours very truly,
> [Kurt Wolff]

Franz Kafka to Kurt Wolff

March 8, 1913

Dear Herr Wolff:

I am sending the proofs for *Arkadia* by return mail. I am grateful to you for having sent me the page proofs since there was a ghastly printer's error on page 61— "bride" instead of "breast."

> With thanks, yours sincerely, Dr. F. Kafka

Kurt Wolff to Franz Kafka

March 20, 1913

Dear Dr. Kafka:

Mr. Franz Werfel has told me so much about your novella—is it called "The Bug"?—that I would like to see it, too. Are you willing to send it to me?

Yours truly,
Kurt Wolff

Franz Kafka and other of the firm's authors to Kurt Wolff

[Postcard. Charlottenburg; postmark: March 25, 1913]

BEST GREETINGS FROM A PLENARY SESSION OF AUTHORS OF YOUR HOUSE.

OTTO PICK   ALBERT EHRENSTEIN   CARL EHRENSTEIN

Dear Herr Wolff:

Pay no attention to what Werfel tells you. He does not know a word of the story. As soon as I have had a clean copy made, I will of course be glad to send it to you.

Sincerely, F. Kafka

CORDIAL GREETINGS FROM PAUL ZECH; [a drawing by Else Lasker-Schüler, signed:] *ABIGAIL BASILEUS III*

Kurt Wolff to Franz Kafka

April 2, 1913

Dear Dr. Kafka:

May I ask you most earnestly and urgently to be so kind as to send me the first chapter of your novel, if possible *at once*, since, as you and Dr. Brod both believe, it is well suited for separate publication, and please also send me a copy or the manuscript of the bug story. I am leaving the country for several weeks on Sunday and would like to read both before I go.

I would consider it a special favor on your part if you would accede to my request.

I hope we will meet again soon and in a more relaxed atmosphere than recently in Leipzig.

> Yours very truly,
> [Kurt Wolff]

Franz Kafka to Kurt Wolff

April 4, 1913

Dear Herr Wolff,

[The beginning of this letter is quoted verbatim on p. 58.] My other story, *The Metamorphosis*, is not yet transcribed, since lately everything has combined to keep me away from writing and from my pleasure in it. But I will have this story, too, transcribed and sent to you as soon as possible. Perhaps later on these two pieces and the "Judgment" from *Arkadia* will make up quite a decent book whose title might be *The Sons*.

With cordial thanks for your friendly words and best wishes for your journey,

> sincerely yours, Franz Kafka

Franz Werfel

IN MY TRAVELS in Europe and later to America, I lugged with me for fifteen years a crate I never opened, a bulky impediment for which there was never enough space. This crate contained mainly correspondence with authors of my earlier publishing house, or that part of it which was more personal in character. I had no very precise notion of what was in it. One day I got fed up with the whole business, and so in 1947 or thereabouts, acting on the suggestion of a friend who was a professor of German at Yale University, I sent the crate off to the library there, where there was already a major archive of manuscripts related to modern literature.

Beginning in 1948, the *Yale University Library Gazette* occasionally published reports on the crate's contents, and it emerged that it had contained many, many letters from Kafka and Rilke, from Romain Rolland, Maxim Gorky, James Joyce, Oswald Spengler, Paul Klee, Käthe Kollwitz, and others. Nothing amazed me more, however, than the announcement that nearly one thousand letters from Franz Werfel had been found. The archive is open to the public, but I never happened to be in New Haven, and it remains quite a mystery to me what these letters might contain apart from corrected versions of poems and the like. The only letters I recall are the ones Werfel wrote from the front during the First World War, when he was assigned to the 10th Austrian Field Artillery Regiment. He sent poems to me in Leipzig on several occasions, most of which were later included in the large volume of poetry entitled *Der Gerichtstag* [Day of Judgment]. Beyond that I do know that we did not maintain a regular correspondence; our lively friendship was sustained by frequent meetings, whenever we happened to be in Vienna, Munich, Paris, or

New York at the same time, or whenever we were living in the same city. This was the case in Leipzig before the First World War.

Franz Werfel was the only son of Rudolf Werfel, a manufacturer and owner of Werfel, Boehm and Co., makers of leather gloves with factories in Prague and Tuschkau. It was assumed that in accord with his father's wishes he would enter the family business and later take it over. At the age of twenty the son was sent to Hamburg, where he was supposed to acquire some commercial training in a shipping company, but his father, who was neither a tyrant nor a fanatic, must soon have realized that Franz was hardly likely to become a desirable partner of Werfel, Boehm and Co. Young Werfel appeared in my office in Leipzig immediately after finishing his unhappy one-year stint in Hamburg. *Der Weltfreund* [Lover of All the World], his first book of poems, had already been published by a Berlin book dealer and publisher, and its completely new tone, in which only few people in those days were able to recognize the strong influence of Walt Whitman, was making the young literati in the cafés of Prague, Vienna, and Berlin prick up their ears.

The astute critic Kurt Hiller, as a rule extremely hard to impress, surrendered immediately to the Werfel phenomenon and reported himself "swimming in a sea of pleasure"; "For the first time a grand wave has swept up again from the depths: the music of the feelings."

The aim of Werfel's visit to Leipzig was to explain to me the predicament in which he found himself and to find a way out with my help. In essence it was the old story: Werfel Senior had given up all hope of making Franz into a businessman, but he was not willing to regard writing verses as a legitimate career for a young man. He insisted that Franz enter a respectable profession. And so the son had come up with the idea of going to work for the Kurt Wolff Verlag, which was still in the very early days of its existence, hoping I would create a position with a real contract for a manuscript reader, which he could then fill. Franz Werfel, a few years younger than I, was a good sort, and I agreed to the suggestion without further ado. We signed a contract covering several years (which never ran its full course, however, due to the outbreak of war in August 1914), and Werfel Senior was given the illusion that his son Franz had become an upstanding young office worker. A letter from the father written in the fall of 1912 still exists, in which he says:

> As I assume you know, my son wishes to seek his future in a profession other than his father's, and after a long struggle I have resigned myself to it, on the condition that he choose an occupation which is compatible with his literary interests, but on the other hand will enable him to keep regular hours and do a certain amount of work on a daily basis. I would therefore be extremely grateful to you if you could offer him a position in your publishing firm, as he has told me is possible, that will require him to perform certain regular tasks in the firm for a specified number of hours each day.

A letter reflecting touching parental concern, which we ought not to make fun of, even if, as was naturally the case, the reality bore little resemblance to the father's desires: we hardly ever saw Werfel at the office. Mornings he was incommunicado in any case; if I wanted to talk to him, he could be found at noon at Wilhelm's Wine Bar, and afternoons and evenings at the Café Merkur. These were the places where four young men gathered at that time, all of whom were connected more or less loosely with the Kurt Wolff Verlag as readers or authors. In addition to Franz Werfel there were Walter Hasenclever, Willy Haas, and Kurt Pinthus, all names now closely associated with the Expressionist era. The last two produced criticism and essays, while Werfel and Hasenclever wrote poems and plays. Indeed, the young Franz Werfel was in my eyes the quintessential poet of those prewar days; it was inconceivable that he would ever write anything but poetry.

He was a poet, a visionary, a child: blind to reality, ungainly, clumsy, gauche, totally absorbed by verses and music. When I recall the young Werfel, I automatically think of Baudelaire's poem in which he compares the poet to an albatross. Franz Werfel was such an albatross, out of touch with the real world. He perpetually lost things, forgot appointments, didn't know whether it was Monday or Friday. His pockets were overflowing with old envelopes, empty cigarette packs, and bills from cafés and restaurants, all scribbled full of verses, stanzas, rhymes. You had the feeling that it was not he who created poetry, but rather that he was inhabited by a force creating poetry inside him, just as it created music inside him. He would drift down the street, singing or humming Verdi arias, and never notice that people were turning around to stare and tapping their foreheads.

The importance of music for Werfel's nature and personality cannot be overestimated. It was a passion, although an extremely one-sided one. He was a fanatic admirer of Verdi throughout his entire life, and this love expressed itself not only in singing and humming and his book *Verdi: A Novel of the Opera*; he also edited and translated Verdi's letters, and prepared three translated versions of Verdi libretti which led to resurrection of the virtually forgotten operas *La Forza del Destino, Simon Boccanegra*, and *Don Carlos*. These labors in the service of Verdi belong to his later years. During his time in Leipzig only the singer was active—and I do not mean this ironically. Franz had a beautiful voice and loved to sing the arias *à l'italienne*.

Otherwise these Leipzig years produced the abundance of poems published in the collections *Wir sind* [We Are] and *Einander* [Together] in 1913 and 1915. He also wrote *Die Troerinnen* [The Trojan Women] during this period, a work too far removed from Euripides to be called a translation. *Die Troerinnen* had a great impact when it appeared in book form in 1915, an impact which increased when it was produced successfully in theaters throughout Germany, beginning with the Berlin premiere in April 1916. In her book on Werfel, Annemarie von Puttkamer called it "a premonition and a portent of the future." This must have been the cause of the extraordinary response it evoked during the war, which marked the real beginning of Franz Werfel's fame. The three volumes of poetry from the years 1911, 1913, and 1915 had been immediate successes, of course, but were known to only a small circle of readers compared to theater audiences in the numerous cities where *Die Troerinnen* was produced. All of this took place in the absence of the author, who was in uniform and doing his duty somewhere in a war against which he had protested in his poetry.

The war naturally separated publisher and author; years passed, during which we corresponded but never saw each other. When I saw Werfel again, he had just met a woman, or perhaps one should say the first woman who was to play an important role in his life.

It is impossible to speak of Werfel's existence as a creative genius or as a man among men without mentioning Alma, the woman who exercised a decisive influence on his life and work: Alma Schindler the painter's daughter, Alma Mahler, Alma the companion of Kokoschka, Alma Gropius, Alma Werfel. The debate over Alma's effect on Werfel, and whether it was ultimately to his benefit or not, continued among his friends throughout his life and even after his death, and it should be noted right away that both those who saw their relationship as a blessing and those who regarded it more skeptically were united in their respect and admiration for the unique personality of this woman.

It is indisputable, however, that when Alma and Franz met, the writer's position was precarious: war, revolution, external and internal circumstances had all combined to create a state of disequilibrium such as Werfel had never known before or after. In an overwrought state he wasted his days in cafés, exhausting himself in fruitless political, pseudophilosophical, pseudotheological, and literary debates, until he was incapable of creative work. Years later Werfel included a superb ironical portrait of this period in his novel *Barbara oder die Frömmigkeit* [Barbara or Religious Devotion]. But it was truly a time in his life when the influence of an outstanding person whom he recognized as such, admired, and loved could point him in a new direction and provide support of a kind that cannot be valued too highly. Alma came and personally led him away from the café table, in a manner of speaking, into her own world, a world that was anything but a staid suburban household, however. Alma inhabited an artistic, bohemian sphere, but in comparison to the smoke-filled chaos from which she rescued Werfel, it was nonetheless one where order prevailed, where days were devoted to work and nights to sleep, and meals were served at normal times. They divided their time between Alma's apartment in the Elisabethgasse in Vienna, where they lived a life filled with music and musicians, poetry and poets, and a lovely country house in the mountains.

I remember many visits to their home in Vienna, filled with lively discussions and many guests, but I recall even more fondly a long stay at the house in the Semmering district, where I enjoyed the intimate atmosphere with just the two of them. Alma's country house in Breitenstein, far from cafés and the distractions of the city, was an

ideal place for Franz to work: the majority of the novels and short stories written while he was still in Europe were put to paper there. One
visit that has remained clearly fixed in my memory took place in June
of 1922; on that occasion we had a dinner table conversation highly
typical of both Alma and Werfel. My wife and I had just returned to
Vienna from Venice, and so it was only natural that the talk turned to
the subject of Venice. Suddenly Alma said, "Franz, we both have
such a passion for Venice. Why don't we have a house there, where it
is warmer than on this cold mountain. I would be content with a little
palazzo near the Grand Canal." Werfel: "But Alma, haven't we
enough on our hands with an apartment in town and this big house
out here? And we don't have any money at the moment, with inflation what it is in Germany and Austria. Why don't we go to Venice
and stay in a hotel?" Alma: "I never feel at home in a city if I know it
only from hotels. As for money, that's nonsense. I don't need this
ring, and maybe I will sell my Munch." And to us, the guests, she
said, "Next Easter you are all invited to Venice." One could see from
the expression on Franz's face that he knew her mind was made up.
Alma was a woman of action. Before the year was out they had pur-
chased a pretty house with a garden—a garden in Venice!—and we
know from Alma's memoirs what it meant to her and to Franz, who
loved Italy so dearly.

Werfel's own nature was such that he was not easily dislodged
from wherever he happened to be. I remember from the Leipzig days
that it was impossible even to lure him out for a walk. He preferred
travels in his imagination to train rides, and it was Alma who showed
him a large part of the world. His novel *Musa Dagh* [*The Forty Days
of Musa Dagh*] would never have been written if they had not first
gone to Asia Minor, nor *Paulus unter den Juden* [*Paul among the
Jews*] and *Jeremias: Höret die Stimme* [*Hearken unto the Voice*] without the visit to Israel. Werfel acquired his knowledge of the world, his
familiarity with the intellectual and artistic elite of Europe through
his wife.

Late in his life Werfel once remarked to a friend, "If I had not met
Alma, I would have written a hundred more good poems and then
gone to pieces." The significance of their relationship could not be
summed up better, and the remark reveals what his friends sensed: his

adoption of a disciplined work routine, a prerequisite for all his long prose works, was something he owed to her. A related circumstance, the fact that his preoccupation with prose fiction relegated poetry to the sidelines for years at a time, was the price Werfel had to pay, and he paid it gladly out of a sense of undiminished love and gratitude to this marvelous woman. He had, however, a group of friends to whom these hundred unwritten poems would have meant more than all the novels.

LETTERS

Franz Werfel to Kurt Wolff

April 24, 1913

Dear Mr. Wolff,

You are not annoyed that I haven't written, are you?—It is doubly disgraceful of me, since I must thank you with all my heart for the love and care you devoted to the appearance of my book.—It really looks marvelous and everyone likes it. So my very warmest thanks!

Der jüngste Tag has become terribly popular. This is inconvenient—manuscripts are now arriving for the firm and for me personally every day in the mail. I have made a selection from *Trakl*, but I am very much in favor of your publishing the whole book at some point. The *Hennings Poems* (there are only eight or nine of them) ought to be shored up by having the lady write a short autobiography or something similar and adding it to that issue.

I would recommend [Carl] Einstein as an author for the firm; whether there is something for *Der jüngste Tag* would depend on the writings.

The first series would seem to conclude with Trakl and should be ready for publication. We can then take our time with the next one. Wedekind (a terribly polite, nice, and clever old man) has said some very appreciative and friendly things about the firm, without a trace of hostility.—How are you getting along in Paris? Please give my warmest regards to your wife and all the best to you, too,

Werfel

Franz Werfel to Kurt Wolff

Leipzig
July 12, 1915
Haydnstr. 4/II

My dear Kurt Wolff,

This is my very first chance to answer your letter, which is now almost four weeks old. During all this time I have been traveling, and not to keep you in suspense, I have been given two months' leave after a small odyssey. In the meantime I have thought of you very often, my dear Kurt Wolff, and with an easier mind than before, since I hope you are out of danger now. —I have left Austria for the duration of my leave, and at the moment I am in Leipzig for two weeks. At the office I heard that all the news you send is good, and that you are writing frequently . . . I was glad to hear it, too, since initially I sensed the terrible things you had to endure were still weighing on you, an impression that came through in your letter as well. But I think these experiences will fade more quickly than other dreams, and because there is no truth in them, they will have to become untrue soon. I do hope all that has become a dream to you already.

About myself I can report only that I have been feeling all this time as if I were under water, half out of my mind and confused. All the same politically inclined very much toward one side. I long to hear what you think; I believe there have never been so many necessary tasks for us in the world as now.

You won't be annoyed if I speak of a book now?—Namely my *Einander* [Together], which is nearly done. By the end of my leave (March) I hope it will be completely finished.

Mr. Meyer thinks it would definitely be good for the book to be published at Easter. I am a little doubtful whether this is a good idea?

But this is almost a minor point. Now I have the firm and deep feeling that a book of mine is something that comes about only through the love and interest you invest in it.

I am touched when I remember *Wir sind* [We Are], for which you took more responsibility than I did, and for heaven's sake don't think I mean outward, practical responsibility by that. I mean the joy and affection I sensed in your attitude toward the book.

How I wish it could be like that again! At any rate I would be happy if you would send me a line, since I have grave doubts and misgivings about my work, as always. Forgive me for bothering you again with my concerns . . . but I am beginning to emerge from my abstracted state.

Do you still have your old assignment, and is what they are saying here true, that you are on duty at midnight? Is there no possibility for you to get some leave? You should copy me! They gave me leave in part on mental grounds. The feeling you wrote about (that you are homesick)—a version of it is familiar to me. At the beginning I suffered greatly from moral scruples, but now things have fallen into a different order in my mind. As I said, I am longing to have a talk with you.

How long will this waiting for one another last? Keep the same feelings for me as I have for you

Yours, Franz Werfel

Franz Werfel to the Kurt Wolff Verlag (G. H. Meyer)

[1915]

My dear Mr. Meyer,

Once again it has taken quite a long time for me to reply to your kind letter.

But recently I have been feeling so tired and terribly apathetic that I have had to interrupt all my work.

I have read Hasenclever's manuscript. [1] It is not easy to know what to say about it. The view of life he takes, the protests, many lyrical passages all appeal to me, but there is too much disparity in it as a whole. Despite its great verve, startling turns of phrase, etc., I have the feeling that a terribly difficult question is being *discussed*, in too off-hand a manner. Unfortunately it seems to me to be nothing more than a poetically heightened discussion, interrupted by dramatic gestures which are not really necessary. It is neither dialogue nor drama,

---

1. The manuscript referred to is Walter Hasenclever's play *Der Retter* [The Savior], which was published in 1915 by KWV. Hasenclever received the Kleist Prize in 1917.

but a kind of helpless form that is not really convincing, despite all the agitation the author has put into it. It seems to me to lack scruples in both respects, in terms of both literary form and intellectual argument. One is constantly falling back on the other as an excuse. (Incidentally I say this knowing full well that my own dialogues *Versuchung* [Temptation] and *Über den Krieg* [On the War] have similar flaws.)

If I were to give Hasenclever any advice, I would tell him not to publish the play for the time being. He should let some time pass, since everything that has been written during the war about the war probably just contributes to the lack of clarity. I am very annoyed myself that two poems in *Einander* refer to the war. In spite of all this I must say again and again that there is so much that is beautiful in this book, so much that is Hasenclever at his best!

What do you and Wolff think of it?

The novella *Montezuma* is unfortunately still not finished, but on the other hand *Die Hölle* [Hell] is coming along nicely. Do you really think prepublication in *Der jüngste Tag* would be harmful? If I think it over carefully, you may be right.

Are you now completely restored to health? The increased work load will certainly be a drain on you again.

I am very glad that thanks to your effectiveness the firm has grown so much during the war.

The Kurt Wolff Verlag is mentioned everywhere in what one hears and reads. Your advertising (particularly in the press) was as intensive as can be imagined.

The success of *The Golem* is due more to the publisher than the author. I am firmly convinced of your skill and only hope that you also have faith in me, although I have always liked the way you openly admitted your reservations about my writings.

As far as the anthology is concerned, I would like (speaking with complete frankness) to delay it.

First of all, the work I have done does not seem comprehensive enough to warrant publication of excerpts.

Secondly, I am no longer very attached to it and would prefer to replace it by something more memorable.

Thirdly, I feel too young to publish a piece of retrospective impertinence.

In any case I would like to wait until my book of odes and ballads is finished, which I intend to make a deserving and not an accidental success.

I worked very hard until December, but since then, as I said, I have been paralyzed by a number of things. It may be a few months before I am finished, but then I want my true self to be there for the first time.

I would like to copy and send a little volume of reminiscences (fifty pages) called *Bozener Erinnerungen* [Recollections of Bozen] (title will be changed) for *Der jüngste Tag*, if you have any use for it. It is quite interesting. In addition, quite a bit from a *dramatic legend* (with theatrical possibilities).

I want to send you *New Poems* for the *Weiße Blätter* in the next few days.

At the moment my outward situation is not exactly pleasant either. I toss and turn here in the hospital day and night, where it is both dirty and boring. Perhaps my father will call you from Berlin and tell you a little about it. Please don't be annoyed that I don't feel up to the anthology yet, but I think there will be time enough if it appears simultaneously with a large-size volume.

Sincere and repeated regards,

Yours,
[Werfel]

Kurt Wolff to Franz Werfel

May 2, 1916

Dear Franz Werfel,

For the first time in almost two years a short leave has brought me back to Leipzig and allowed me to work in person again for the publishing house. I have grown even fonder of my profession than before and will be participating more actively than has been possible when I was serving far away with a mobile army unit—you know that for the past six months I have been in Macedonia.

You know it is no empty phrase when I tell you that of all the many useful and useless, lovely and unlovely things that go to make up the name of the Kurt Wolff Verlag after the first seven years (they must have been the seven lean years, since they will now be followed by seven fat ones), none are so dear and important to me as Franz Werfel and his work.

Let me congratulate you on the great effect the premiere of *Die Troerinnen* has had on discriminating people. I am optimistic that the firm will soon be able to report to you the acquisition of the performance rights by several large German theaters as a *fait accompli*. It will probably also be performed on tour by the Barnowsky ensemble at several other theaters. Allow me to pass over in silence the horrible complications that have arisen over *Die Troerinnen* in connection with the names Barnowsky and Reinhardt and only lament the nerves that have had to suffer from it, without going into the question of who is guilty. I don't know if you happened to see what an exceptionally large advertising campaign the firm has mounted for you and your work in the major newspapers following the production of *Die Troerinnen*, a campaign whose immediate effect can only be slight and in fact, to be frank, has remained slight. Nevertheless it remains Georg Heinrich Meyer's and my most earnest desire to continue advertising the four books *Weltfreund, Wir sind, Einander,* and *Troerinnen* with the greatest intensity and energy. However, after reconsidering all the possible ways to do this with some prospects for a genuine internal and external success, we have once again reached the conclusion that we must create a bridge between the relatively expensive and intellectually demanding books of poetry and the large circle of readers we wish to win. This bridge can only be a small volume of selected poems by Franz Werfel, which we would sell at an extremely low price and provide to book sellers at an enormous discount, so that in essence it will be merely a less blatant and more sophisticated form of advertising than a reprint of more or less meaningless articles and reviews represents. You know that I have always wanted such a small-sized book, and I have been told that you are against it and why. Forgive me if I say frankly that I cannot completely accept your arguments and that I see them as a considerable stumbling block for my work as a publisher. You say: I don't want to think retrospectively and would rather look ahead and work only toward the future. I find that both right and completely understandable—and a completely inaccurate description of what I want to do. If it were a matter of bringing out a collected edition of your work published so far, with a grand gesture of voilà!, then you would be right to oppose it, and I would oppose it with you. But all we want is to say to the thousands of potential readers for the books you have already written but who barely know the name Franz Werfel: here is a poet by the name of Franz Werfel; if these few poems communicate something to you, then buy his books. I am very optimistic with regard to such a small-sized book and convinced that the people we would win by these means for the Franz Werfel of the past and present would be irrevocably won over for the Franz Werfel of the future . . .

Dear Franz Werfel, why do I have to write at such length? I wish I could talk with you in person, so that there would be no misunderstanding me: I am really not concerned here with the values of the literary marketplace, but my feelings are very, very much involved. I have no legitimate right to ask you for a great favor, but I am doing it all the same: please send me the booklet I have described and allow me to take care of everything connected with it as the pleasantest possible task I could have during this leave.

The specifics of my ideas concerning this book are in a separate enclosure. Will you send me a telegram or at least an immediate letter?

My wife Elisabeth and I send our regards in old friendship and in memory of unforgettable past evenings and nights in this Saxon city of Leipzig, where the sun sometimes used to shine as it does today,

Very truly yours,
[Kurt Wolff]

Kurt Wolff to Franz Werfel, c/o Rudolf Werfel Co., Mariengasse 24, Prague

May 5, 1916

Dear Franz Werfel,

I hope that my letter of May 3 reached you without delay. Today I am able to report to you that *Die Troerinnen* will be performed in:

Vienna, Budapest, Breslau, Hanover, Munich, and Leipzig by the ensemble of the Lessing Theater; in Hamburg at the Deutsches Schauspielhaus; in Dresden and Frankfurt am Main either by the ensembles of the Hoftheater and Schauspielhaus or by the Barnowsky ensemble. In the places where the Barnowsky ensemble appears on tour, your play will become available again as early as October 1 of this year, so that in cities which have an appropriate hall to perform it and where Barnowsky's production was successful the local theater companies can include it in their own repertory of the season.

Another pressing matter to which I urge you to reply as soon as possible: you know that for two years now the firm has been asking you for materials regarding a new edition of *Weltfreund*. We still have not received them, and it is impossible to delay the printing any longer. You will have noticed that it is under way from the first proofs we sent you on May 1. I would deeply regret it if the edition did not correspond to your wishes, but you must realize that the firm cannot possibly advertise your work as extensively as it is doing at present and then not have copies in stock when the orders start coming in. We still have a few copies left, but if we really want your poetry to have a wider circulation we must be able to send considerable quantities on commission, and there are not enough for that.

Please, dear Franz Werfel, assist us in our efforts and take care of this immediately.

Yours very truly,
[Kurt Wolff]

Karl Kraus

THE MOST INTENSE period of Karl Kraus's creativity fell in the years during and immediately after the First World War. In these years his work was familiar and important only to a small coterie confined almost exclusively to Austria. As the Wagnerian clamor of the Nazi twilight increased and Hitler seized power, his voice grew subdued. "Hitler doesn't inspire me," he said. This is a comment you could translate in a number of ways. I would suggest something like: "You can't say things are going to hell if you're already there."

The only book by Kraus to appear after 1930 was *Die Sprache* [Language], and this was not published until 1937, after his death. When Kraus died in 1936, a generation had grown up in the German-speaking countries without any opportunity to get to know his work. It was not until 1952, when the Kösel Verlag in Munich began publishing his collected works in Heinrich Fischer's superlative edition, that Kraus's writings became available again, writings which for the most part dated from half a century earlier.

Was this delayed first edition of his complete works a success? My own guess would be that many more copies were sold of each volume of the Kösel edition than of all the fourteen volumes I had the privilege of publishing between 1916 and 1920. And there can be no doubt that Kraus's collected writings in the form in which they exist today will remain a significant and integral part of twentieth-century literature in German. Many years had to pass after his death before a few distinguished writers produced the studies that clearly established the place he had earned in German letters as a satirist and dramatist. I am thinking of the publications by Walter Benjamin, Erich Heller, and Werner Kraft among others.

The modest recollections I propose to offer have nothing in common with these studies. If I venture to speak *on*—or more aptly, *about*—the most controversial figure in German literature of his time (and for decades this time was also mine), then it is only because accounts of this literary phenomenon that combine knowledge with some degree of objectivity are so scarce, and accounts of Kraus the man are even scarcer.

In the years in which I knew, saw, and published Kraus—roughly the decade from 1912 to 1922—it was startling to learn that the people who stood in any kind of relationship to him at all were divided into two opposing camps: fanatic admirers and fanatic enemies. From among the members of the admiring group Kraus had accepted a very small number who were granted access to his table at the Café Pucher; the vast majority had to be content with worshipping him from afar and approaching their idol through letters overflowing with pledges of their devotion and esteem. I found the two extremes quite similar to one another, inasmuch as they were all obsessed with Kraus.

Most of the fanatic enemies had started out as fanatic admirers. Once in the camp of opponents, a return to the camp of idolizers was out of the question, but admirers were constantly being converted into enemies. (I will mention a few examples of this later on.)

There were a few exceptions, to be sure, but they were very rare—at least in the period before the First World War. The architect Adolf Loos, Oskar Kokoschka, and Peter Altenberg, were all acquaintances I owed to Kraus. They were his friends, genuine friends, and as such able to maintain their personal independence. Others, for instance Berthold Viertel, Ludwig von Ficker, Sigismund von Radecki, and Theodor Haecker should also be mentioned. But the climate surrounding Kraus was determined by the "obsessed."

It was immediately apparent that Kraus suffered more from the admirers than from the opponents, a feeling he also expressed often in his writings. I do not intend to go into what caused this permanent state of tension here, however; I am trained neither in psychology nor "psychoanality" (as Kraus used to call it). But the fact that these tensions existed is something no one who ever came in contact with Kraus's world would dispute.

As he struggled to hold these negative and positive forces at bay,

Kraus struck me when I met him in 1912 as tragically lonely. The few friends just mentioned, the architect, the painter, and the poet, had their own sources of creative stimulation, but these were unrelated to the events which stirred Kraus's emotions. Often it was the tiniest of sparks that set off his apocalyptic creations. Loos or Kokoschka probably never even registered the journalistic inanities written by the likes of Hermann Bahr or Felix Salten. But in Kraus the hypocrisy, baseness, and sheer idiocy that leapt out at him from the pages of newspapers, magazines, books, and even from billboards inspired ghastly visions. In his prophetic imagination they foreshadowed the last days of mankind, the black magic that would bring about the end of the world. In the midst of this appalling vision, which constantly preyed on his mind, he was alone. I did sense later that there were women who loved him and whom he loved, but this was on another plane, and the topic was naturally taboo. Only once, in connection with the poem "Wiese im Park" [Meadow in the Park], did he mention the Czech Baroness Sidonie Nadherny, to whom "Worte in Versen I" [Words in Verse I] is dedicated.

The substantial body of literature on Kraus—not counting the studies of his work by critics and literary historians—was created almost exclusively by the fanatics; true orgies of worship, addressed to an idol, are thus to be found alongside the venomous babble with which opponents hoped to annihilate their apelike devil.

As far as I know, there is no account of the *human being* who had a genuine and intense interest in people and animals, in flowers, trees, and mountains. My own contacts with Kraus were too short lived for me to be able to fill this gap. But after waiting for decades for others to do so, I want to record what little I know and witnessed. Perhaps this will bring forth more substantial testimony from better qualified sources.

But let us begin at the beginning. When Werfel arrived in Leipzig in 1912 to become a reader for the Kurt Wolff Verlag, I had never seen an issue of *Die Fackel* [The Torch] or read a book by the author Karl Kraus—scandalous when you consider that many of his important works had already appeared: the volume of essays *Die chinesische Mauer* [The Great Wall of China], the brilliant work *Heine und die Folgen* [Heine and the Consequences], and the two volumes of aphorisms *Pro domo et mundo* and *Sprüche und Widersprüche* [Dicta and Contra-Dicta]. Werfel showed me issues of *Die Fackel*. His admiration for Kraus knew no bounds. At twenty-two, Werfel was one of the "fanatics," and I—twenty-five years old at the time myself—found his youthful exuberance and enthusiasm appealing.

Werfel claimed that Kraus was not comfortable with his publisher, Albert Langen, that it bothered him to be published under the same imprint as the magazine *Simplizissimus*, which he loathed, as well as a score of other writers repugnant to him. In my own view, Kraus had found an excellent home in the company of authors such as Hamsun, Björnson, Strindberg, and Wedekind and under the eye of Korfiz Holm, the distinguished and tactful editor-in-chief of the firm's literary department. But Werfel insisted: I should go to Vienna, see Kraus, and try to win him over to us.

And so off to Vienna I went—unfamiliar with his work, unprepared, and with an openness and naiveté that I certainly would not have had a few years later. Kraus had made an appointment with me at his usual café for the evening of my arrival. I don't remember who else was at our table that night, but I remember very well that I was ill at ease and uncertain about how to make contact with this man. After perhaps an hour or so, Kraus suddenly suggested that we leave and go to his place, saying, "We could have a cup of coffee and talk." Delighted and relieved, I agreed. (I learned only much later that this invitation was out of the ordinary, almost a special honor; Kraus was usually fiercely protective of his privacy and reserved the evening hours at home for work.) We arrived at the Lothringer Straße, and almost the moment I entered the room my uncertainty and discomfort vanished. We talked into the early hours of the morning on that night, the following nights, and on many others over the course of the next few years. I recall how surprised I was at my own lack of shyness and inhibitions, considering that this was Werfel's idol and that there was a thirteen-year difference in our ages. At thirty-eight, Kraus seemed to me like an older man.

Back at the hotel and thinking about the hours I had experienced, I suddenly realized that I had seldom if ever met someone so acutely sensitive to others. Kraus must have sensed my malaise at the café and for that reason left so brusquely; apparently he also sensed how full of gaps my knowledge of his work was—so he avoided bringing it up as we talked. On this first evening it never crossed my mind to broach the question of publishing him, even though this was the reason I had come to Vienna in the first place.

Of course I can no longer recall every detail of that first conversation, but I do remember very clearly the general topics of that evening and the others that followed. We did not spend much time discussing literature, but at one particular moment we did make contact—quite unintentionally, I think—a contact that survived some foolish blunders I was later guilty of committing.

It was in the early hours of the morning; I was dead tired and feeling drained by Kraus's intensity, which never flagged for a second. Suddenly he said, "Before you go, I have a nice present for you," and he went over to his bookshelves, which seemed to me to contain a rather meager library. Taking down an old book he had probably picked up somewhere or other not long before, he began to read aloud from it. I thought he read very well and could see how moved he was by the poems he was reciting. He read "Der Tod und das Mädchen," "'s ist leider Krieg," and "Mondlied" [Death and the Maiden, Alas, There's War, and Moon Song]. The poetry itself barely penetrated the fog of my fatigue; I was spellbound not by the familiar verses but by the singular man who was reading them. Mechanically I began to recite the last few lines of the "Mondlied" along with him, but soon found myself speaking alone as Kraus fell silent:

> Verschon uns, Gott, mit Strafen
> Und laß uns ruhig schlafen,
> Und unsern kranken Nachbar auch!
> [Spare thy wrath, Lord, we entreat;
> Let our sleep and dreams be sweet,
> And those of our sick neighbor, too.]

He stared at me in astonishment and asked in a tone of voice that betrayed dismay as well as surprise, "But how do you know that? Matthias Claudius is completely unknown!" "Perhaps in Austria," I replied, "but not where I'm from. When I must have been between five and eight and tired of the usual bedtime prayers for children, my mother used to recite the "Mondlied" with me every night. I adored it . . . 'Der Wald steht schwarz und schweiget' ['The woods stand dark and silent'] . . . I loved it then just as I do today." His joy at finding someone to share his enthusiasm was greater than the disappointment over not being the first to introduce me to these poems.

I had enjoyed those hours in the middle of the night, and I took a great liking to Kraus, who struck me as very different from what I had expected after Werfel's extravagant praise—entirely natural and without affectations or pretensions. His readiness to invite me home and to spend long hours talking, his proposals to accompany me to my hotel and to meet again the next day, as if all this were the most natural thing in the world, made me feel I was in Vienna as his guest. I was looking forward to our next encounter and decided to skip the visit to the Brcughel paintings I had planned for the next morning and to get some sleep in preparation for the night to come.

Werfel had warned me about the pace. "Kurt Wolff, I know you," he had said, "you won't be up to it. If Kraus accepts you at all, then be prepared: he won't leave you alone for a minute. He is as jealous as a woman. Only more so. If he wants to walk you back to your hotel, you mustn't take it for a polite gesture and refuse. Kraus walks people home. He can't bear the thought that they could meet someone else after being with him. If you want to disentangle yourself, there's only one excuse that Kraus will accept, though with bad grace. Somewhere between midnight and one o'clock, you may hint at a rendezvous with a woman. It's your only chance . . . " I remembered Werfel's advice, but at the time I didn't know any woman in Vienna I could have or would have visited at that hour, and so despite the toll it took I preferred to linger on into the small hours with Kraus.

If memory serves me right, our meeting the next day was for our first meal together. Since almost every meal with Kraus followed the same pattern, it makes for a good story: then and later, we met at the Hotel Imperial on the Ring, where everyone from the concierge down to the last waiter knew Herr von Kraus and greeted him enthusiastically. He studied the menu at length and finally ordered cold roast beef with *sauce rémoulade* and toast. It took a long time for me to appreciate the comedy of this ritual: every single time I had a meal with Kraus in Vienna—and this happened frequently in the years following that first visit—Kraus invariably ordered cold roast beef . . . There was one exception; once, in 1914, he took me on an excursion to the Kobenzl and invited me to a superb meal there; on that occasion he went so far as to depart from the self-imposed monotony of his diet. But with these observations on roast beef we are getting ahead of the story. At the moment it is still the year 1912, and it is time to describe my second evening with Kraus, and the second night: I put the question to him, naïvely and directly, whether he didn't have a new book I could publish. The answer was a partial and surprising yes: there wasn't a *new* book exactly, but I could take over an older but still unpublished book if I liked. It was called *Kultur und Presse* [Culture and the Press]; the type for it had been set some seven years earlier. He, the author, would be perfectly happy to let me publish this; the reason it had not been printed and published during these seven years had to do with his reservations about the Langen Verlag.

Of course I agreed, although I hasten to add that the Kurt Wolff Verlag never published *Kultur und Presse*. When it was almost ready for press, Kraus could not accept the thought that something of his would appear alongside works and authors he found objectionable. In his own words, "In April 1914 I sent Mr. Kurt Wolff a letter setting forth the dilemma but also acknowledging our friendship, for whose sake I would sacrifice my right to offer it to another publisher. I asked him to release me from our agreement, since it was apparent I had consented not to a favorable contract but a terrible contrast." The contract was revoked without hard feelings on either side or any ill effect on the personal relationship between Karl Kraus and Kurt Wolff. How I did actually come to publish some of his works will be related at the appropriate point in our story.

Kultur und Presse was *one* topic of that second night. I also recall the second main topic of conversation clearly, because its importance to Kraus was very evident. Lichtenberg's name had cropped up, and I happened to mention that I had learned about Lichtenberg from Gundolf. Kraus pricked up his ears and began pumping me for information. He wanted to hear everything I knew about the circle around [Stefan] George. How long had I known Gundolf, Wolfskehl, George himself, and how intimately? I had to describe George's apartment in his parents' house in Bingen, and give a report of our conversations;

Kraus wanted to know how dependent or independent Gundolf and Wolfskehl were from the master, and so on . . . Obviously he had never met anyone who had any contact with the George circle and was extremely interested, indeed fascinated by this world, so very remote from his own world in Austria.

Gundolf and I had been friends for some time, and I owed a great deal to his enthusiasm and talent as a teacher; I knew Wolfskehl well, too, and was familiar with his life and background in Darmstadt. As a young man of twenty I had spent an unforgettable day with George at his house in Bingen. These contacts sufficed to give me an inkling of something I later saw clearly and convincingly demonstrated: even though in many ways there could be no greater contrast than that between the priestly bard of the Rhineland, who had been influenced by Mallarmé and the French Symbolists, and Karl Kraus, the polemicist, philosopher and aphorist in the tradition of Lessing, Kierkegaard, and Lichtenberg, nonetheless they shared some decisive common ground—both were solitary figures who intentionally kept aloof from the literary and intellectual society of their day. It was impossible to imagine either Kraus or George as members of a literary academy, a PEN club, or similar group. Both were perfectionists who demanded the utmost of themselves. Both would have insisted on scrapping an entire printing if a book contained a single major typographical error. Both were totally impervious to financial enticements and considered a connection between the life of the mind and money to be unworthy of them, and vile. Both demanded the utmost integrity from anyone who wished to associate with them. Within their own very different circles they were such evidently towering figures that the dominant role they played seemed utterly natural. And finally, both were always right, in their intellectual as well as their human judgments, although this should not be understood to mean they insisted on always knowing best; I seriously mean they had an unerring instinct for the proper attitude, action, or opinion in a particular situation.

These qualities which George and Kraus had in common distinguished them from their contemporaries and were significant at that time, extremely significant. Their attitude isolated them, set them apart from other writers and poets of their day. It is legitimate, indeed appropriate to recall: if the *Berliner Tageblatt* wired to ask for a quick text to commemorate a celebrity who had just died or on some other topical matter, Gerhart Hauptmann would not refuse; Thomas Mann would not turn down a writer's request for a commendatory comment on a mediocre manuscript, to enhance the prospects of its publication or sales, and what Rilke sometimes recommended or praised, because he was too weak or good-natured to say no, would make your hair stand on end. If I mention this here it is to emphasize how different the two solitary and uncompromising figures of Kraus and George were; I do not mean to disparage the others in the slightest.

Kraus's great curiosity about the George circle was rather touching, and I was sorry not to be able to tell him more. Kraus and George never met in person, nor do I think that Kraus would actually have wanted to meet him or his disciples, even though I know that Wolfskehl and Gundolf, at least, regarded Kraus's work in a very positive light.

As the years went by, Vienna came to be identified in my mind with Kraus's apartment in the Lothringer Straße. Whenever I was in Vienna I saw Kraus; of the city itself I saw nothing. Through Kraus I encountered Altenberg occasionally, Kokoschka rarely, and I saw the amiable and nearly deaf Adolf Loos and his charming young wife quite often. I did not get to know the Hofmuseum, the Albertina, or the National Library until many years later.

During the war, from the spring of 1915 to the summer of 1917 to be exact, I served as a lieutenant, later first lieutenant, with an army unit stationed in the Balkans. I frequently had occasion to travel on the Orient Express between Nish and Frankfurt, a journey which gave me an opportunity to stop over in Vienna on the way to or from Germany. I never saw as much of Kraus as during the war. I had no choice but to travel in uniform—Kraus must have hated it, but he never said a word; I assume he accepted it as a kind of necessary disguise.

In these war years I had only one close friend in the army, who belonged to the same unit in Macedonia. How I ever hit on the rash idea of telling Jesko von Puttkamer, who was going on leave, to stop in Vienna and convey my regards to Karl Kraus is now a complete mystery. Kraus was not the sort of person to whom one casually sent friends and acquaintances. Not until Jesko had left did I realize that my very tall friend would doubtless make Kraus, who was quite short, feel particularly dwarf-like and irritable, a not uncommon phenomenon; in any event I awaited the outcome of my rather daring initiative with some trepidation.

My fears were groundless. As I soon learned, Kraus gave my friend Puttkamer a warm welcome and apparently took an immediate liking to this young man whose purity of vision and intellectual gifts were accompanied by equally extraordinary good looks. On his return from Vienna Puttkamer reported that he had been fascinated and swept away by Kraus's personality, artful conversation, and the depth and richness of his mind, which could shift from deadly satire to the most affable good humor and from there to a display of aphoristic verbal fireworks with the speed of lightning.

Soon I was beginning to worry whether Jesko Puttkamer had joined the "fanatics." I fear this was so. A flow of letters from Macedonia to Vienna followed, and there was no trip on which Puttkamer had to pass through Vienna that did not result in his getting together with Kraus, indeed Kraus himself insisted on it. When my friend suffered a severe nervous breakdown near the end of the war and had to be taken away, he left behind two long letters that formed a kind of last will and testament, and one was addressed to Karl Kraus.

I have recounted this episode not only because it affected me very deeply, but especially because in this case—in contrast to others I will mention later—Puttkamer's admiring "fanaticism" never underwent a transformation into its opposite. I should mention, however, that Puttkamer was not a writer.

I cannot recollect the various wartime stopovers I made in Vienna as separate occasions; all I can only say is that, by and large, the impressions I have retained are of happy and lively encounters. By this time I had become an attentive, regular reader of *Die Fackel*, but our conversations rarely touched on the magazine and Kraus's work. When now and then I might mention how much an essay or brief satirical piece had impressed me, Kraus would change the subject and talk about whatever happened to be more on his mind at the moment. He would ask me, "Have you read Jean Paul's *Rede des toten Christ* [Speech by the dead Christ]?" or "Did you know the passage I quoted from Kierkegaard?" (Jean Paul came up again and again; he admired him greatly.) But even though Kraus might refuse to talk about his polemical prose, his poetry was a different matter. *Die Fackel* began to publish more and more of Kraus's poetry, single poems at first, but later the *Worte in Versen* [Words in Verse], which took up more and more space. It was obvious that the poems meant very much to him. Whenever he would mention them or read one aloud to me, it was done with a mixture of embarrassment and pride. Later, when he gave public readings, this attitude was not evident. The first suggestion to publish a volume of poems came from me, and he agreed to it more enthusiastically than to any other project on which we worked together.

This brings us to the subject of our relationship as author and publisher. The story of how it began is quickly told—and not without its amusing side. Let me preface it by saying that in 1914 the Kurt Wolff Verlag published an enormous book—although in a tiny edition—containing Kraus's marvelous essay "Die chinesische Mauer," taken from his first volume of essays of the same name that had appeared in 1910. Kokoschka did eight lithographs in over-size format to go with the piece. To my mind it was primarily a Kokoschka book; it certainly did not seem to make me in any way Kraus's publisher. On the other hand, the intention of becoming Kraus's publisher was what had led me to seek his acquaintance. Once my first attempt in this direction had failed, as I described, our personal conversations and friendship continued almost as if we had forgotten it—almost, but not quite. It became a standing joke between us that, whenever we parted, I left with the same question: "When will I finally have the honor and pleasure of publishing Karl Kraus?" At this Kraus would laugh and give the standard reply: "My dear fellow, you know I can't possibly become the author of a firm that would advertise my books in the same catalogue with those hacks X and Y . . ." The joke was carried on for a time with no serious discussion. But one night, probably in the summer of 1915 on one of my first stopovers between the Balkans and Germany, an idea occurred to me, and as I was about to go, I varied the routine and said to Kraus: "I am delighted to be your publisher at long last—all I need now is some manuscripts. I can't forgive myself for not seeing how to surmount the one obstacle long ago . . ."

"What in the world do you mean?"—"I mean that tomorrow, as soon as I am back in Leipzig, I am going to have a new publishing house registered. It will be called the 'Verlag der Schriften von Karl Kraus' (Kurt Wolff). The firm will have no other authors. Agreed?"

Kraus hesitated for a moment and said: "Agreed." "Fine," I said, "I will take over all the books you did with Albert Langen and reprint them, those out of print and those in print. Please instruct Langen that you have agreed to this and send me the manuscript for a volume of poetry as soon as possible." Such was our conversation, more or less, and the plan was actually carried out with even fewer formalities. The author-publisher relationship in this case was based on a gentlemen's agreement we never needed to discuss again. Creating this *chambre séparée*, our private nook, gave me great pleasure, and I think my interest in the poems, my wish to begin the association with their publication, gave Kraus pleasure, too.

In the postwar years, as I recall, I was rarely in Vienna, but seeing Kraus in Munich, my own city, was an enjoyable experience in itself. One evening in the spring of 1919, without any warning, he suddenly turned up in the large hall of the Hirth Building into which we were moving from Leipzig. He could not have chosen a worse time and place. I had just started to unpack eighty crates of books, my personal library that I intended to house at the office. Coming straight from the railroad station, Kraus walked into this chaos, good-humoredly sized up the situation and told me I shouldn't let him disturb me. Picking up a few books, he clambered onto a pile of crates where he perched mischievously and began to read, looking for all the world like a little bespectacled monkey, with every intention of not getting in the way. Before long, however, some violent swearing demanded my attention. Kraus had been reading Goethe's "Pandora" in one of the volumes of the *Inselbücherei* and found the line:

Auf, rasch! Vergnügte . . . ["Away, quickly! Revelers . . ."]

He had sensed immediately that the line could not be correct, that a punctuation error had distorted the meaning of Goethe's text: "in a delightful abbreviation," as Kraus later wrote, it should have read:

Auf! rasch Vergnügte . . . ["Away! you who are quickly amused . . ."]

Kraus thundered his displeasure and outrage from the top of the crates, and there was no peace until, after enormous exertion and much searching, it was finally established that the Insel text was erroneous and Kraus's intuition, confirmed by consulting a facsimile of Goethe's manuscript, was correct . . . His description of this event is entitled "The Violation of Pandora" and was included by Heinrich Fischer in the collection *Die Sprache* [Language].

Kraus appeared even more cheerful and relaxed in Munich than he was as a rule in Vienna: here he did not have to check proofs at the printer's and could enjoy a few days' rest far from all his obligations, reading and going for walks. He spent many hours in the Wolff Verlag's large library, ignoring the incunabula and other bibliophilic treasures that were the pride and joy of my collection, and completely absorbed in German and French poetry, in first editions or reliable(!) later ones. Since he enjoyed reading aloud, it was easy to persuade him to give a reading in this same room, to which about 150 guests were invited. Kraus's only condition was that the press not be admitted. The evening made a deep impression on the audience. The April 1920 issue of *Die Fackel* contained the program of the reading, which took place on January 29, two days after Kraus had given a public reading in Munich. Kraus described it as follows:

> The second evening was more of a social occasion, to which I had agreed, once all *literati* were removed from the guest list, not so much for the sake of the Kurt Wolff Verlag as for its amiable owner, who also publishes my own writings. It was combined with a charity appeal for needy children in Vienna, to which the guests responded with somewhat less reserve than to the reading itself. The latter proved once again that an intimate setting destroys intimacy. This is essential to the reader, however, a need arising not from a desire for applause but from the awkwardness of being the only person in a group of individuals to speak. A speaker must be able to sense how his listeners are reacting—the liveliness of the reading depends upon it—and he must be able to sense it immediately and not through the medium of a later report. Certainly not by means of a printed review (in the Social Democratic paper the *Münchner Post*, of January 31), which is not really appropriate for a private occasion, but it is reproduced here to prevent my own frustration from creating a one-sided picture:
>
> "A Reading by Karl Kraus. On Thursday evening Munich pub-

lisher Kurt Wolff invited a number of guests to a reading by Karl Kraus in the firm's library. Kraus, a familiar figure to only a small group in this city, appeared not in his role as the fearsome and acid-tongued essayist, but as a poet and dramatic interpreter. He read a number of his own poems, which projected a wealth of musical sonority, poetic imagery, and rhythmic power. (Or rather, the poems flowed melodically from the fountain of his inspiration.) As in the essays, his work is permeated by a profoundly serious and reverent sensibility, further heightened by hymnic melody and solemnity: the poet Kraus distilled from the Kraus of *Die Fackel*. I would give all the rest of modern Austrian poetry for certain poems of his.—In addition Kraus gave a masterful reading from Hauptmann's *Die Weber* [The Weavers], a play resounding with the desperate cries of the starving. Here one could sense that true art, even if for the time being it goes by the name of "Naturalism," demonstrates its claim to immortality when the heart and voice of the true artist come alive. Karl Kraus was able to make this happen. He deserves special thanks for using this dramatic cry for help to raise money for the hungry children of Vienna."

Occasionally, when Kraus visited Munich in the summer or fall, he would take short trips into the Bavarian countryside. One telegram has survived (apparently from September 1919); it reached me from the Schiffmeister Inn on the dark and beautiful waters of the Königssee near Berchtesgaden and read, "Don't you want to come in quest of this magnificence?" All my memories of this period are of contented harmony—despite the fact that we had already entered into the precarious union of author and publisher.

I had begun publishing Kraus's books with energy and enthusiasm, and in rapid succession there appeared four volumes of poetry, the first of them in 1916; the volume of aphorisms entitled *Nachts* [At Night] in 1918; *Weltgericht* [Last Judgment], almost six hundred pages long, in two volumes in 1919; *Ausgewählte Gedichte* [Selected Poems] in 1920, a small book that gave me particular pleasure, because I was permitted to make the selection myself; and also in 1920, a fifth volume, *Worte in Versen*.

In addition to these new books the firm had taken over the following, some of which appeared in new editions: *Die chinesische Mauer, Sprüche und Widersprüche, Pro domo et mundo, Sittlichkeit und Kriminalität* [Morality and Criminality], *Heine und die Folgen, Nestroy*

und die Nachwelt [Nestroy and Posterity]. These fourteen titles represent a major part of Kraus's total output. But—the time came, and it
wasn't very long in coming, when the happy days of the "Verlag der
Schriften von Karl Kraus (Kurt Wolff)" ended; the *chambre séparée*
had to be closed. The reasons for it, which had nothing to do with me
as a person, were symptomatic, and a development I should have
foreseen . . .

In speaking earlier about the Kraus fanatics, I remarked that as a
rule Kraus haters had first been Kraus idolators, and I promised to
offer some evidence for this claim. Let me give here two examples,
both excerpts from a "Rundfrage über Karl Kraus" [Questionnaire on
Karl Kraus] that appeared in the magazine *Der Brenner* in 1913 and
was later brought out in book form by the Brenner Verlag of Innsbruck in 1917. There Willy Haas (who was associated with the Kurt
Wolff Verlag as an adviser) wrote:

> Karl Kraus is for me the incarnation of unskeptical moral philosophy.
> This is what gives him the authority and quality as judge over the ac-
> tions of other men . . . He is not one to seek the heart of a matter
> analytically, since his powerful intuitive sense tells him that from the
> very beginning . . . His eroticism is the eroticism of a virtually unalien-
> ated and undivided spirit and has not the slightest similarity with
> Weininger or Strindberg . . . But here the point is to show one's col-
> ors . . . So I would like to add that I venerate Kraus to the highest
> degree of which I am capable, for I believe in his purity and integrity. It
> goes without saying that journalists have no right to pass judgment on
> such a man as he, either favorably or unfavorably.

This was the tenor of Willy Haas's tribute to the living Karl Kraus. In
his autobiography of 1957, *Die literarische Welt*, Haas wrote after
Kraus's death:

> Today, looking back decades later, I am firmly convinced that Karl
> Kraus was a born sadist, with the sadist's fine instincts for inflicting a
> wound where it will hurt most. He applied his skills in seduction—and
> his poison—with full intent. The human, intellectual, and moral
> worth of his victims—often innocent young people on the threshold of
> an outstanding career—was a matter of complete indifference to him. I
> am certain that his sadism had a hidden and unfulfilled homosexual
> component at its root . . . But there was something else in him, too, a
> way he had of ingratiating himself with people, of fastening on and

clinging like a leech and, as soon as he sensed a response to his over-
tures, plunging in a poisoned dagger. His triumph was boundless when
he sensed he had made someone else suffer . . . He . . . sympathized
with Weininger's anti-Semitism . . . Weininger committed suicide . . . Kraus found another way out, less tragic, but more diabolical:
he dulled his own pain, his own self-hatred from time to time through
his addiction to others' suffering, by sucking their blood—just as Cesare
Borgia had himself wrapped in the bloody raw flesh of animals to allevi-
ate the terrible pain of his illness.

I myself never knew any "innocent young people on the thresh-
old of an outstanding career" who became the victims of an
intentional seducer. Trakl, Janowitz, Viertel, Kokoschka can hardly
be called "victims," and even Werfel would have laughed if you had
called him that; Werfel was indeed far more than a promising young
man destroyed by Karl Kraus.

Kraus must have been a thorn deep in Haas's side to call forth
such a reaction twenty years after his death. It is not the about-face as
such that seems so pathetic or ridiculous, as when the "moral philosopher" becomes the "born sadist" or the second reference to
Weininger claims the exact opposite of the first; what is sad and pathetic is the insinuations, the defamation of the dead. So great was
the hatred of a journalist who had denied himself the right to "pass
judgment on such a man as he [Kraus]" that he went on to do something far worse. Whoever would like to learn the reason for this attack
on a man who could no longer answer his accuser should read the
section "Briefwechsel mit der Literarischen Welt" [Correspondence
with the Literary World] in Kraus's book *Literatur und Lüge*
[Literature and Lies] or in *Die Fackel* of February 1930.

Let me emphasize that what is objectionable and deplorable here
is not the conclusion, but the position from which it is reached. Of
course anyone has a perfect right to contradict the views expressed by
Wedekind, Thomas Mann, Lichnowsky, Haecker, Kokoschka,
Trakl, and others, outstanding personalities who expressed their admiration for the moralist Kraus without ever joining the fanatics. But
in this case Haas describes an author as a diabolical sadist out of personal resentment, accusing him of despicable actions instead of seriously discussing his work. One cannot indulge in vituperation of
this kind for pages and note in passing that *Die letzten Tage der*

Menschheit [The Last Days of Mankind] is a remarkable work. Haas presents this "remarkable" man to his readers as a deliberate poisoner.

The second example is Franz Werfel, and is of a very different nature. When love turned to hate in his case, he attacked the still living Kraus like a reckless Don Quixote, although he had been declaring his passionate devotion only a moment before. Werfel's expression of idolatrous veneration went beyond anything of the kind I had ever seen, as a brief quotation should demonstrate:

> . . . I had mystically experienced the nameless personality of the word . . . The next morning I was awakened by a letter from Karl Kraus in which he informed me he had accepted for publication in *Die Fackel* some of my poems that a friend had submitted, unbeknownst to me.
>
> A year later I saw Kraus face to face and, shaken by the tremor of life's mystery, I recognized in him the apparition of my dream . . .
>
> Yesterday I wrote a few pages of philosophy on Kraus.
>
> I will not send them to you—they are inadequate!
>
> Inadequate to describe the experience through which this man inexplicably entered my life.
>
> For behind any essay I could write on Kraus there would always stand, sovereign and immovable, the hour that attaches my planet to his.

This was also written in 1913 and republished in the "Questionnaire" book in 1917. In the meantime, however, the mystical attachment of the planets had come unglued. Within a short time an extremity of admiration and love had been transformed into an extremity of hate. In November 1916 Werfel wrote Kraus from the front; the elaborate commentary with which Kraus responded in *Die Fackel* is understandable only in conjunction with a poem published there shortly before, entitled "Elysisches, Melancholie an Kurt Wolff" [Matters Elysian, A Dirge for Kurt Wolff]. Aside from the manifest content, there is also the parodistic intent of its intonation and rhythm; in those days Werfel was apt to go overboard in imitation of Schiller's rhapsodic mode. Kraus's poem is a satirical imitation of Werfel's "Vater und Sohn" [Father and Son], which begins:

> Wie wir einst im grenzenlosen Lieben
> Späße der Unendlichkeit getrieben . . .
> [As we once in boundless love
> Played tricks of infinity . . .]

KARL KRAUS

This is Kraus's satire with its touch of Yiddish, which goes far beyond
a parody of Werfel's rhapsodic Schillerisms:

ELYSISCHES
Melancholie an Kurt Wolff

Dort in Prag, wo neukatholsche Christen
heimisch sind, teils aber Pantheisten,
hingeschwellt am Tag,
dort ertönt manch morgendlicher Triller
aus der Jugendbrust des andern Schiller;
ausgerechnet das geschieht in Prag.

Aus dem Orkus in das Grenzenlose
wird gewendet eine alte Hose,
was Ergetzung schafft.
Der dort schaukelt auf der Morgenröte,
der hier hat den Ton des alten Goethe;
denn Gewure heißt auf deutsch die Kraft.

Aber besser noch sind zwo Gewuren,
denn das zeucht dann hin wie Dioskuren,
was nur mich nicht freut,
unterscheid' ich unbeirrter Mahner
junge Prager, alte Weimaraner;
doch Talent hat schließlich jeder heut.

Wer im Himmel oder unberufen
gar an des Olympus heiligen Stufen
wie das Kind im Haus,
morgen hat er wieder andre Sorgen,
etwa zwischen Hölty und Laforgen
kennt er sich mit jeder Note aus.

Wer entzückt im Flügelkleide wandelt
oder andrer Art mit Büchern handelt,
Gott gefallen mag.
Die hier gehn nur—merkt auf das Exempel—
nebst der Kirche in den Sonnentempel
und erscheinen auch im Jüngsten Tag.

Reingebadet in entlieh'nen Lenzen,
läßt der Seele Überschwang nicht Grenzen
fremdem Element.

Heute ist sie à la Rimbaud tropisch,
morgen schlicht kopiert sie schon den Kopisch,
hat ein ausgesprochenes Formtalent.

Solchem Wesenswandel wehrt kein Veto,
hin zu Goethen geht es aus dem Ghetto
in der Zeilen Lauf,
aus dem Orkus in das Café Arco,
dorten, Freunde, liegt der Nachruhm, stark o
liegt er dort am jüngsten Tage auf.

Wer in altem oder Neugetöne,
jedenfalls in ausgeborgter Schöne
sich dahin ergeußt,
pochend mit der Jugend Nervenmarke
letzt sich noch mit seinem letzten Quarke
an der Quelle, die da für ihn fleußt.

Denn vom schönen Einfluß der Kamönen
können sie sich nun mal nicht entwöhnen,
und kein Hindernis
ist es für der Phantasei Erfindung
und die literarische Verbindung.
Diesen Faden keine Parze riß!

Und geklagt sei es dem ewigen Gotte,
daß der Literaten heutige Rotte
ihr Elysium
findet, denn wer nur am Worte reibt sich,
wird gedruckt bei Drugulin in Leipzich.
Edler Jüngling Wolff, ich klage drum.

MATTERS ELYSIAN
A Dirge to Kurt Wolff

There, at Prague, where new Catholic Christians
Are at home (though still half Pantheistians),
Lolling at voluptuous ease,
From the larynx of a pseudo-Schiller
Tweets his verses many a morning triller—
And all this in Prague, if you please . . .

Out of Orcus to unbounded views
They reverse a worn-out pair of trews;

What a savoury tonic!
This one seesaws on the edge of dawn,
That one finds Geheimrat Goethe's tone,
For *Gewure* (Yid.) means *Kraft* (Teutonic).

Even better: harness *two* Gewuroy,
They would forge on like the Dioscuroi,
I alone demur;
I can tell apart, unerring judge,
Vintage Weimar and Bohemian fudge
(Though we *all* have genius now, yes *Sir*).

He who too familiarly passes
Now through pearly gates, now up Parnassus,
(May he not, one hopes!)
Can tomorrow nonchalantly barge
Anywhere 'twixt Hölty and Laforge,
Knowing all the subtleties and ropes.

He who wends in ecstasy and wings,
Or cuts deals with books like other things,
He may walk God's path;
These types just attend—mark the example—
Both Our Lady's and the *Sonnentempel*
And still make it into "Day of Wrath."

Scrubbed and purified in borrowed springs,
Soul's exuberance will tie no strings
On exotic "lifts":
Now it deals, à la Rimbaud, in *tropisch*,
Other times it plainly copies Kopisch,
Showing most pronounced mimetic gifts.

No injunction bars such sweeping change,
From the Ghetto, nimble verses range
Right to Goethe's path,
And from Orcus to the Café Arco;
There renown, o friends, comes hot and stark-o
As it is embalmed in "Day of Wrath."

Who for classical or neo grace
(Decked in borrowed plumes in either case)
Thither thrusts his vim,
Throbbing to his youthful pith (or such),

Still is drawing for his meanest *Quatsch*
On the freshet bubbling there for him.

For from the Camoenas lovely sway
They just can't break free, let come what may,
And it is no let
To the volatile imagination
Or the literate association:
No—no Atropos can cut *this* thread!

Ah—had but eternal Zeus not suffered
That today's low breed of scribes be offered
Its Pierian bourne!
Sophomoric drivel, froth unstinted—
Leipzig's Drugulin will gladly print it.
Wolff, o noble youth, know that I mourn.
[Tr. Walter W. Arndt]

This was the satirical poem to which Werfel responded by writing
a letter to Kraus; in it Werfel reproached him for using a variant form
of the word "dort" [there], calling it a regrettable betrayal of the German language. This letter in turn prompted Kraus's satirical comment entitled "Dorten."

In Werfel's high school in Prague pupils must surely have been
taught Schiller's classical poem in which the wanderer going to Spar-
ta is asked to take some news "there," in the variant form "dorten"; but
hatred made Werfel forget these (and many other beautiful) verses. In
any case Werfel's letter is so blinded by hate that a Karl Kraus could
not resist the opportunity to respond; this was the background of one
of the most brilliant polemics Kraus ever wrote.

The rather foolish letter of 1916 was probably Werfel's first attack
on Kraus. But the embarrassing "Dorten" sequel and the satire in *Die
Fackel* must have given him no peace. He followed it up with a ram-
bling open letter to Kraus in *Die Aktion* for April 1917 entitled "Die
Metaphysik des Drehs" [The Metaphysics of the Twist], to which
Kraus in turn replied in a twenty-two-page article in the October 1918
issue of *Die Fackel*. Needless to go into further details of this wran-
gling.

In 1919 the Kurt Wolff Verlag brought out a large collection of
Werfel's poems under the title *Der Gerichtstag* [Day of Judgment],

which included a poem called "Einem Denker" [To a Thinker]. As I was reading the manuscript it did not occur to me to connect it with Kraus; I thought it an appealing poem and was later surprised to learn that it was indeed Kraus who was targeted; it showed him in a completely false light . . .

EINEM DENKER

Dein Blick, mein Bruder, hat mich erschreckt.
Ich habe um deinen Mund und über deinen Brauen einen
    fremden Mangel entdeckt.

Meine Sphäre war traurig,
Ihr mißfiel deine Art,
An der Spitze des Tisches zu sitzen, zierlich geduckt,
Mit gekreuzten Armen, freundlich, listig, kätzchenhaft.

Tu' dieses Ducken aus deinen Augen, mein Freund!
Laß ab von der Bereitschaft des Anklägers und Angreifers!
Wie deute ich mir,
Wie verstünd' ich's,
Daß du den feurigen Talar des Richters unverbrannt durch die
    gleichgültigen Räume trägst,
Daß dein Wort dir gelingt, dein Schlaf dir gelingt, du
    Schläfer, an dir vorbei, du nicht Erwachter!

Wie soll ich dein Gebrechen nennen, Schläfer?
Ich will dein Gebrechen Selbstgerechtigkeit nennen, Schläfer!
Denn wer zu Gericht sitzt
Über die Sünder,
Sitzt hinterm Kreuz, ist im Recht, braucht seiner Schuld
    nicht zu gedenken, darf seine Sünde vergessen,
Und der Henker erspart die Pflicht, sich selbst den Kopf
    abzuhaun.

TO A THINKER

Your threatening gaze, my brother, gives me pause;
About your lips and brows I discovered alien flaws.

My sphere was saddened,
It disliked your way
Of sitting at the table's head, daintily crouched,
With arms crossed, affable, crafty, kittenish.

Take this crouch out of your eyes, my friend!
Desist from the accuser's and attacker's readiness!
How am I to take it,
How could I fathom
Your wearing, all unsinged, a judge's flaming robe through the indifferent
     rooms,
Your managing your word, your sleep, you sleeper, past your self, you
     unawakened one!

What shall I call your frailty, sleeper?
Let me call your frailty selfrighteousness, sleeper!
For he who sits in judgment
Over sinners
Is safe behind the cross, is in the right, need not assess his guilt, may forget
     his sin:
The headsman is exempt from the duty to chop his own head off.
                                                  [Tr. Walter W. Arndt]

   Kraus was not the *judge* Werfel saw; he was the *conscience* of the
times, and he was a righteous man. Whatever the psalmist may have
meant by the reference to the righteous man who must suffer much,
one can't help thinking of it here. One is fated—you might even say
cursed—to be a righteous man. Someone who is born righteous has
no choice: he *must* speak the truth as he sees it; he *must* castigate what
seems to him wrong and unjust. He will inevitably wound others in
the process, but it will cause him as much pain as it does them. The
"others," the unrighteous men who encounter him and recognize
him for what he is, will tend toward enthusiastic admiration and devotion at first—but there are very few who can endure the continuing
awareness of their own all-too-human failings called forth by the
other's personality and works.
   Is there any defense against the righteous man's superiority? Tilt-
ing at windmills like Don Quixote is quite senseless; withdrawing in
resignation is possible but sad. There is only one way to defend
oneself. Goethe realized this and recommended it with the words: "If
another person's good qualities far outshine our own, there is no recourse but love."
   It is painful to talk about Werfel's next attack. Its vulgarity can
neither be glossed over nor excused. I did my best to suppress this sad

lapse, but without success. In the summer of 1919 the Kurt Wolff Verlag received a manuscript from Werfel, probably his weakest work in dramatic form: *Der Spiegelmensch: Eine magische Trilogie* [The Mirror Man: A Magic Trilogy]. Through letters, telegrams, and the intervention of friends I tried to persuade Werfel to delete an offensive and obscene passage directed at Kraus. He refused. The book edition of the play appeared in early 1920. It prompted Kraus to publish a *Magische Operette*, entitled *Literatur oder man wird doch da sehn* [Literature, or Let's See About That], also one of Kraus's weaker works, in my opinion. As preamble, Kraus juxtaposed excerpts from Werfel's tribute of 1913 and from *Der Spiegelmensch*; the last, alas, may not be skipped here:

> I have nothing planned for the next few days—what project could I begin? Wait! I will become a prophet, a major one, of course!—The first thing is to found . . . a magazine. I will call it: The Beacon? No! The Candle Stub? No! The Torch [Die Fackel]? Yes!—I will turn local gossip into a cosmic event—I will juggle puns and pathos so excellently that everyone who thinks after one line that I am a comic stool pigeon and fart-catcher will have to admit after two lines that I am Isaiah in person . . . My character, with its unfortunately all too dependent side, does include a great talent for acoustic mimicry.
>
> In brief, since I cannot look at people *eye to eye*, I can look into their backsides, to see whether they have the proper ethics there.

So swiftly was the man he loved, adored, idolized, to whom his planet was attached, transformed into a fart-catcher. I know no more drastic example of the devastating effect Kraus's personality could have on infatuated young writers, an effect which by no means convinces me that Kraus was a sadist. He was no more a sadist than Lessing in attacking Pastor Goeze or Heine in attacking Platen.

In my view, it was not the fact that they were inferior to Kraus in dialectics—as they undoubtedly were—that made Werfel, or Haas, or others unable to rise to Kraus's polemical level. The problem was that there was no answer, because Kraus invariably held the position of the uncompromising moralist, leaving them no line of defense.

Many others whom Kraus "attacked," if you will, recognized that he was not concerned with them as individuals, and that he was only using them to point out certain symptoms. The Prague group (including Max Brod, who was also a detractor of Kraus after his death), and Haas in particular, believed Kraus meant to satirize them personally—you might say they felt he had singled them out for the honor of being his targets. This was a naïve error, pardonable in the young, but less comprehensible in an older man. For today's readers most of the figures who inspired Kraus's acid commentaries are completely unknown; it would make no difference if the names of Hans Müller, Stefan Grossmann, Paul Zifferer, and others were replaced by the letters x, y, and z.

Haas never outgrew his experience with Kraus, but this was not true of Werfel. Kraus was never mentioned between us in later years, because I sensed he had remained painfully aware that, after initiating my relationship with Kraus, he had also been the one to destroy it. But shortly before he died Werfel once remarked to a mutual friend, "If Kraus had been forced to emigrate as I was, then I would have gone to see him and made up."

It was clear that the *Spiegelmensch* episode meant the end of my publishing relationship with Kraus. The divorce occurred without fuss. In October 1923 the following notice appeared in *Die Fackel*: "The 'Verlag der Schriften von Karl Kraus (Kurt Wolff)' of Munich and Leipzig was dissolved in August and its rights transferred to the 'Verlag *Die Fackel*' of Vienna and Leipzig. New editions of out-of-print titles are in preparation." That was all.

When the *Spiegelmensch* bomb went off, I waited for a lightning bolt from Jupiter to strike me. It seemed to me I had earned it, for I had not protested strongly enough against Werfel's publication of an unworthy and base piece of polemics. I should have prevented its ever being printed and published under my name, and if I had done so, I would not only have shown more loyalty toward Kraus; more importantly, I would have done a service to Franz Werfel who was, after all, still a young man of not yet thirty. I deserved the bolt of lightning . . . but it didn't strike, never struck . . . a miracle. It was inevitable that the incident and the ensuing cessation of our business relationship also put an end to my personal relationship with Kraus. Yet my attitude toward him and his work never changed. At the same time my close friendship with Franz Werfel remained unaffected by all this. Does that seem strange?

During this feud I had never been interested in taking sides. But the affair brought another element to the fore, a question that has occupied me all my life: it was a quarrel in which one person was in the right, had right on his side, clearly and beyond all doubt, and the other had done something asinine and was in the wrong. Surely one ought to take sides, one ought to support the party who had been insulted and who was in the right. But although I have always admired and respected those with right on their side, I have never really been able to *love* them. I have always preferred *d'être du côté des vaincus*, to be on the losing side.

I remain grateful to my friend Franz Werfel for putting me in touch with Karl Kraus fifty years ago, and I remain grateful to Kraus for showing me his warm human side—I regard it as a privilege, a gift, a source of happiness. Reading the great polemical essay "Dorten," which sparkles with wit, satire, and irony at the same time that it carries a weight of deeper meaning, I still feel humbled, forty-five years later, by the courtesy, affection, and warmth I experienced in my acquaintance with Karl Kraus. It is better for me to say this before others say my recollections are colored by prejudice. They are, and I admit to this prejudice openly.

I knew three sides of Karl Kraus, although I had only superficial glimpses of two of them. He rarely spoke of his feelings for nature, of his travels, the grandeur of an Alpine valley or lake, the beauty of a park in Bohemia. Only once did I stand with him on top of the Kahlenberg and observe his pleasure as he surveyed the mountain ridges and the enchanting view of the Vienna Woods.—It was also only on rare occasions that I witnessed the side of Kraus that flourished in café conversations, an activity to which he sacrificed thousands of hours—although "sacrifice" is probably the wrong word, since he clearly thrived in this atmosphere. Surrounded by an attentive audience, he improvised a great deal that was later carefully shaped and polished in long nights of labor. And the café was where he picked up a great deal of information not to be found in the newspapers, which sooner or later he could put to good use.

The side of Karl Kraus I came to know well, however, was the private one, at home in the Lothringer Straße, where he could be relaxed, humorous or serious, cool-headed or heated in debate, but always completely natural, unaffected, and open. His words were always on target, though not deliberately weighed. Naturally it was more of a monologue than a dialogue; his visitors needed merely to interject a word now and then. But in these conversations Kraus displayed the immense scope of his mind: in the course of a single evening, a single night he would range from the inspired to the scurrilous and every shade in between. These talks also revealed a characteristic side of his thinking that is reflected in his commentaries, the unbelievable discrepancy that could exist between a stimulus and its outcome, between a tiny incident and what he would make of it.

I would never claim that Karl Kraus was a friend of mine, but I can truthfully say that the Kraus I knew was an extraordinarily appealing person, who always treated me with warmth and kindness and who taught me much. As a young man in my twenties, hardly precocious for my age, I experienced the hours spent with him in Munich or the peaceful oasis of his home in Vienna, far from the feuds and commercial bustle of the literary world, as a great enrichment.

LETTERS

Kurt Wolff to Karl Kraus

July 2, 1913

Dear Sir:

By the same post I am sending you the proofs of the luxury edition of *Die chinesische Mauer*; when you have looked them over please return them and let me know whether you would like us to send you a copy of the revised version in proof.

I would like to take this opportunity to ask once more whether, as I hope, you would be interested in continuing the association with our publishing house that this project started. May I assure you how much I desire to see your work obtain the recognition in Germany and Austria that it deserves. I personally believe that as a practical matter this can only be accomplished by the publisher, and to do this is my greatest professional ambition, one that has nothing to do with financial and commercial considerations.

I have heard talk that you have completed a new work. Perhaps by entrusting this new work to me you will give me an opportunity to do for you what has been left undone before now. It goes without saying that in your case the physical presentation and advertising would be handled according to your wishes and instructions.

I would appreciate hearing from you and remain

Yours very truly,
Kurt Wolff

Karl Kraus to Kurt Wolff

Vienna
December 9, 1913

Dear Mr. Wolff:

Last spring, when I happened to see the introduction to an anthology published by your firm in which, without direct mention of my name and in the most inappropriate context, I was maligned by one of the most unfortunate hysterics among the scribblers who devote themselves to loving and hating me, namely by the well-known character *Brod*, your assurance that you had no knowledge of the target at which this attack was directed was sufficient to make me disposed to accept your kind and repeatedly proffered offer of publication. As you know, I am not seeking and have not sought a publisher; I am thoroughly content if I succeed in bringing my books safely into the world through the agency of my nearby printer, without any prospects of large-scale publicity on the part of a publisher. You may take my agreement to your proposal as an indication that your unusual enthusiasm and desire to be of assistance made an impression on me strong enough to overcome my profound reservations, reservations which were inevitable after a mere glance at the neighbors I would acquire by joining your firm. I would be surrounded by precisely the worst of those bad apples in the garden of literature who have preyed on my nerves for years with their hysterical interest in me and disruptive concern with my existence, the more so the better I get to know them. I made no secret of my hesitancy and told you straight out that as a mercantile setting I prefer my current publishers, colorless and lethargic as they may be, to the latest Berlin-style fuss, for my own good as well as for the good of literature; I consider the best interests of both less threatened by the most bumbling mechanics than by the most talented jellyfish. I expressed a desire to do without company rather than to have to endure the deformed creatures most recently spawned by German literature, and as an example I cited my opinion that a thousand Reznizeks are less of a hindrance to a man like Kokoschka than one Oppenheimer. Your undisguised antipathy in the Brod case seemed to offer some assurance that along with my work you would also welcome my opinions on how to go about creating a publishing firm for genuine art over time. As far as that particular case is concerned, I explained at the time that in my view I would have every right to withhold my books from a firm that was simultaneously publishing attacks on me, but that I would never exercise this right as long as it was a matter of honest and manly differences of opinion. It is only natural, after all, that I would find a manly expression of a hostile attitude, if such a thing exists, vastly preferable to adolescent crushes, which sometimes turn into their opposite. Thus I explicitly and from the start renounced my right to draw the consequences should my opponents attack me within the same firm, and I am prepared to show the same generosity even in the case of this perfidious attack, since I have been assured that it took place behind the publisher's back and behind the backs of the authors of the anthology.

Now, however, your firm has brought out a book containing an attack on me that while not hidden is offensive enough to render absurd the notion that the same firm could be longing to acquire me as an author. On p. 221 of a book entitled *Die Weisheit der Langenweile* [The Wisdom of Tedium] the author claims that my criticism of Mr. Kerr's style was either "uninformed or *insincere*," and that no one could "be angry with Mr. Kerr for reacting with far more unjustified claims." Mr. Kerr's reaction consisted in fact of muttered curses and threats of physical violence, and rather than reacting with anger, any housebroken German reader would have felt like puking. Yet even here I assure you that I have no objection to attacks on me published by the publisher of my own books, from whatever quarter they may come, and that I am completely indifferent to seeing my opinions branded as "uninformed" in the very place where these opinions will later appear. I will gladly leave it to my publishers to explain their impartiality to the purchasers of their books. What I cannot accept, however, is approval of base invective against me, above all the charge of insincerity. Under no circumstances can I allow my opinions to appear in the same place where their sincerity is being called into doubt. I have nothing against being called an incompetent writer by my publisher's other authors, but if I am invited to join a circle then I must insist that its members acknowledge my honest intentions. I do not doubt for a moment that you, my dear sir, are indeed the gentleman I have come to know and that you make every effort to observe the rules of gentlemanly behavior even among the literary tribe with which your profession requires you to deal, nor do I doubt that you will find my discomfiture understandable as I find myself in a situation where on the one hand my arrival is welcomed and on the other I am received not with mere disparagement but with suspicion. The particular kindness, even self-sacrifice of the head of the firm has helped me to overcome the serious reservations I had about taking this step, and although I did not quite understand why he would not rather do without such dubious guests, I could at least hope that out of regard for my presence he would keep this crowd under control and prevent them from throwing dirt at me the moment I arrived. I have just received new confirmation of how untrustworthy they are as neighbors, even though I will not deny that, while they hold their noses and accuse me of insincerity, the stink they produce is genuine. I have received such confirmation from the author of the book in question himself, who sent it to me with an adoring letter. I am not so hard-hearted as not to regard all the emotional outbursts in which I figure in one way or another as completely sincere, but I do not wish to experience these fluctuations at close hand. Since this letter was brought to me unsealed by an intermediary, I think I have a right to enclose a copy, and you will see from it how much valuable criticism can be produced by an hysteric who has got hold of some printers' ink. The author of this book, which is only just out, now comes forward unbidden to ask my forgiveness for the opinion expressed on p. 221, never suspecting that the state of my nerves would derive greater benefit if he would only be consistent and stand by his negative judgment. Crushed by his guilt, he freely admits that the words about me published by your firm were a "lapse," a "sin," a "poisonous affront." I would not use such strong language. I forgive the author, who has asked for forgiveness. I would rather have to forgive suspicion being cast on my work than the adulation of a newspaper critic, and I will go on forgiving even if I am declared a non-god and banished from the much bemoaned "battle of the Titans," because I know I truly do not deserve the honor of being assigned a place near heaven and the adulation of such worshippers: let the author be forgiven this time, once and for all. But then I would like to make the publisher all the more responsible for printing the remarks of juveniles or hysterics. The public knows nothing of the author's regrets, which have surfaced simultaneously with the book, and people can only be puzzled that the publisher of Karl Kraus's books permits another of the firm's authors to accuse him of insincerity, or they will come to believe in the end that the many expressions of esteem also contained in the book make up for this trifling reproach. Not only is this not the case, but what wounds him even more than the accusation of intellectual dishonesty is the feeling of being condemned to the society of the most vacillating of the unstable characters the literary world seems to bring forth these days. I do not believe, my dear sir, that you can clear up either the anomaly of the one contradiction for your readers or the underlying situation for me. If it were possible, it would give me great pleasure, for I have pleasant memories of the proofs of your regard for me. But I by no means believe that the sincere debt of thanks owing to you for your personal kindness could be large enough to cancel out the charge of insincerity which has now been leveled against me in one of your firm's publications, or that the present situation of your firm could encourage me to hurry with the book *Untergang der Welt durch schwarze Magie* [Decline of the World through Black Magic], since here I criticize everything which seems to have found a home there and make an issue of precisely the kind of case which is causing me such annoyance now. I believe I would then be guilty of insincerity and lend support to the very charge against which I am trying to defend myself. For this reason I ask you to release me from my guest appearance as an author of your house. I will not conceal from you the intention I had of making the fulfillment of our agreements dependent on a resolution of the current unpleasantness and the assessment I would have made after a year or so of the situation I was about to enter, for which period of time I would have refrained from having the work brought out by another publisher. By merely postponing a hope and not requiring you to give up the idea of its ever being fulfilled, I wanted to express my gratitude for the kindness you have often shown me. But now, I sincerely regret to say, I must give up this plan, because it might appear as if I were asking you to choose between us, and as seriously as I take my obligation to combat the bad apples, I do not claim the right to interfere with the interests of a literary undertaking that—whether I like it or not—already exists. It is legitimate for me, as a writer, to describe the circumstances that enable worthless characters to become writers, but not to use the power I possess within the same professional group, although it is accidental and certainly undeserved, to damage those who have already achieved such status. Since I must avoid even the appearance of using my all too real possibilities for influence and censorship in publishing, I have no choice but to withdraw. I could not do so without real provocation. If you, my dear sir, will examine the matter without prejudice, you will be forced to agree that this is the case. You will realize that the attempt to make my voice heard amidst the kind of cackling that is its own echo would be doomed, impossible, or at best a literary joke. You will realize that I am right to refuse the publicity efforts of the most eager publisher if their side effect will be to involve me, again and again, in misunderstandings and annoying quarrels, and that in the Germany of today I must be my own publisher and choose the isolation that entails, even if it amounts to my own funeral, over any form of resurrection. Just as I have never doubted your good intentions in the cause of literature, so you will now not doubt the sincerity of my decision to avoid a path on which I see only obstacles.

With repeated thanks and sincere esteem I remain

Yours very truly,
Karl Kraus

Enclosure

Kurt Wolff to Karl Kraus

December 14, 1913
Sunday

Dear Mr. Kraus:

On October 22 of this year you agreed to two contracts with me for two books. —Naturally I will not hold you to them in any way if you wish to be released, because a book *Weisheit der Langenweile* has been published by my firm. I am also willing to withdraw *Die chinesische Mauer* with Kokoschka's lithographs from publication if that is your wish. I wanted to preface my reply to your letter of December 10 with this explanation, for two reasons: first, because a response of this kind was my first impulse, and at my age I am still inclined to act on them, but then because, as I thought over the present situation, I would have found it awkward to carry on a frank discussion of the matter on the basis of a contract which one partner regards as a pleasure but the other as compulsion and duress. But let me add at once that nothing would be sadder and more painful for me than your insistence that we dissolve our publishing relationship completely. No one can desire to invest his labor and energy for you more passionately than I do, but this passion does not prevent me from realizing clearly that I have lost all right to be or become your publisher.

Yesterday I was ready to go to Vienna to discuss the matter in person, but then I decided against it. Since I know how extraordinarily kind you can be, I would not feel right if I made it harder for you to settle the matter entirely according to your own wishes and desires by paying you an unscheduled visit. But I am prepared to come if you call. And now I will reply to the actual content of your letter as well as I can. You seem to understand the publisher's profession as similar to an editor's, rather like the managing editor of a magazine that appears at irregular intervals in the form of books; he is responsible for its contents, should ideally allow every contributor to have his say, but must maintain a coherent editorial point of view. —I for my part consider a publisher to be—how shall I put it?—a kind of seismographer, whose task is to keep an accurate record of earthquakes. I try to take note of what the times bring forth in the way of expression and, if it seems worthwhile in any way, to make it available to the public. (This is being a seismographer, not a seismologist.) I could imagine that one person could simultaneously be the publisher of Wagner and Nietzsche, but not that one magazine could print writings or texts by Wagner and Nietzsche's *Der Fall Wagner* [The Case of Wagner] at the same time. But these general views have nothing to do with the painful case for me of K. H. [Kurt Hiller].

I lack the necessary skill of a writer to justify these views in detail. Perhaps there will be an opportunity to discuss them with you in person.—I know that I will be able to learn much from your views, just as I have learned a great deal from the case of K. H.

What I have told you was a rather personal matter that may not have interested you at all. But I wanted to mention it because you, Mr. Kraus, have always been very kind and interested in my welfare. I have been punished for a very foolish blunder and unpardonable negligence. I well understand that I must take the consequences for my actions, which must seem more than mere carelessness to you. Up to now I have been able to pay for my mistakes with financial losses and a bit of annoyance. In this matter I am richer by one piece of experience, but I have had to pay for it with the most painful loss I could possibly incur.

Please preserve your good will and esteem for me. I remain with the very highest regard for you,

Yours truly,
Kurt Wolff

Rabindranath Tagore

IT IS THE YEAR 1913, and the best seller lists in Germany are headed by books such as *Alraune, Die Heilige und ihr Narr, Der Tunnel,* and *Die Biene Maja* [Alraune, The Saint and Her Fool, The Tunnel, and Maja the Bee]. For the more discriminating reader, there are Kafka's first stories, Annette Kolb's *Exemplar* [Specimen], Thomas Mann's *Tod in Venedig* [Death in Venice], and Eduard von Keyserling's *Abendliche Häuser* [Houses at Twilight]. At that time contemporary Asian writing lay completely beyond most people's ken.

I am no longer certain who mentioned to me that a book of poems by an Indian writer by the name of Rabindranath Tagore had just been published in London, poems with a unique flavor which nonetheless appeared to be eminently translatable. I think it possibly, or even probably, was Franz Blei, since he was always sniffing out new talent and had an excellent nose for it. He and I met occasionally in those days in connection with *Die Weißen Blätter*, a new magazine to whose editorial board Blei belonged.

I learned that Tagore's poems, translated into English by the author, had caused quite a stir in England. They had been published by Macmillan, the large and well regarded firm that would go on to supply the country not only with many good books but also, rather unexpectedly, with a prime minister. It wouldn't do any harm to inquire about the book and the German translation rights, I thought. The title of the book was *Gitanjali*. A copy arrived, and with it the information that no other German publishing house had made an inquiry. And then, sad to say, it fell victim to an all-too-common vice in publishing houses: the book lay around for weeks before anyone took a look at it. I, the publisher, was unfortunately unable to do so, since at the age of twenty-six I could neither speak nor read English;

my schooling, with its emphasis on the classical languages, had neglected this skill. *Gitanjali* was sent out to readers and, as so often happens, what they had to say was so contradictory that the reports cancelled each other out.

"Our German Rückert wrote more inspiring poetry on India," said one. "These are beautiful verses of great delicacy and originality, with a monotonous strain characteristic of Eastern lyric poetry," said another. The third reader reported, "These are not poems but elevated prose, and setting them typographically in verse form does not make them poetry. Poetry without rhyme has always been considered an unacceptable hybrid form in Germany. I strongly advise rejecting it."

After brief vacillation I decided in favor of publishing—not least because everyone agreed that there would be no translation problems, since the poems involved neither rhymes nor complicated meters. This decision then received support from a most unexpected quarter: Rabindranath Tagore was awarded the Nobel Prize for Literature in 1913, even before the German edition appeared. No one had reckoned with this possibility in their wildest dreams, neither the author, the English publishers, nor the German one. Gerhart Hauptmann had won the prize in 1912, and Maeterlinck the year before that; the inclusion of Eastern literature in the Nobel committee's deliberations represented a sensational departure. It had never happened before, and has not happened since. In India itself the award met with a mixed reaction, for reasons I will go into later.

The German edition of *Gitanjali* appeared and was a solid, but not overwhelming success—the usual fate of a Nobel Prize book. Additional Tagore books followed—volumes of poetry, plays, novels, short stories, autobiographical works and philosophical reflections. The most successful of these were the novel *The Home and the World* (which appeared in German as *Das Heim und die Welt*), the book of poems *The Gardener* (*Der Gärtner* in German], and the philosophical work *Sadhana: The Realization of Life* [*Sadhana*].

The huge volume of titles that appeared within a period of about ten years were not all written during this period, of course. Born in 1861, Tagore began publishing in English in 1913, but the original editions of his works in the Bengali language had been appearing in his homeland since 1874, when he was only thirteen. *Gitanjali*, the first collection of his poems which the author himself had translated into English, was taken by him to England in 1912, and it appeared first that same year in a privately printed edition of the India Society before it was published by Macmillan in 1913.

Tagore was an extraordinarily prolific writer. I would estimate that the eight-volume edition of his collected works published by the Kurt Wolff Verlag in 1921 contains only one-fifth or one-fourth at most of his literary output, to which have to be added his numerous essays and articles on politics and other topics, works for the most part unknown in the West. Only three of Tagore's twelve novels, for ex-ample, have been translated into European languages to my knowledge. And one begins to grasp the full extent of his creativity only when one considers that in addition to his writings he com-posed, painted, and drew. He began painting in earnest in 1928. Recently, in 1962, an exhibition of Tagore's paintings and drawings was held in France.

In the years I am speaking of here, however, from 1913 to the twenties, public interest in Tagore in Europe was limited to his liter-ary works. The period of Tagore's success, fantastic for the time, was the years during and after the First World War. By the end of 1913 the works of his published by the Kurt Wolff Verlag had sold more than a million copies. And these were normal, hardcover books; the era of paperbacks still lay decades ahead. It should be noted in passing that neither author nor publisher made any money from these editions, enormous though they were. The profits were eaten up by inflation, and the income from one book was never enough to finance the next.

What were these books like, whose phenomenal popularity with German readers lasted for ten years? Why were they read, and who had written them? Let me begin with a few words about the author. I first met Tagore in 1921, although we had corresponded before the war. Then in the course of an extended trip through Europe he came to Munich, accompanied by one of his sons and some friends. On the very first or second day of his stay he accepted an invitation to lunch at our house.

It is difficult to describe my first impressions of him without sounding gushing or overdramatic. I had had my doubts about the success of this meeting; as Tagore's German publisher I had been bombarded with letters, telegrams, and telephone calls long before his arrival. There were requests for interviews, for speaking engagements, readings from his work, and what not. It was a three-ring circus, and while Tagore could of course in no way be blamed for it, it was still not particularly pleasant. When word got out that Tagore was staying at the Hotel Continental during his visit to Munich, there were always a few curiosity-seekers gathered at the entrance, hoping to catch a glimpse of "the Indian."

The Indian celebrity arrived in the Königinstraße for lunch, alone, as I had requested. He was dressed in the Indian style; as far as I know he never wore Western clothes. With his long grayish-white beard and great dignity he presented a most impressive figure, so that it seemed a completely natural error when my three-year-old daughter assumed God was paying us a visit, and settled contentedly in the lap of the Lord. But there was nothing theatrical in Tagore's appearance or manner. His way of moving and speaking was simple and direct. We sat down to lunch, and he ate the foods he ate everywhere—only bread, vegetables, and fruit, I believe, without any wine. From the first moment the conversation was natural, relaxed, but not trivial. Even when he was inquiring about such things as family matters, one had a sense of genuine interest and human warmth, never of mere empty phrases. But what interested him most was Germany, and he posed simple, precise, intelligent questions, saying, "Tell me about the men who came back from the war, the youngest generation, and your interests, your hopes; tell me about your profession and about contemporary literature in Germany." Continental Europe was then still unexplored territory for Tagore; he had lived and studied in England for prolonged periods of time, but he sensed that continental Europeans were a different breed and that at that particular moment, in the year 1921, significant differences existed between the countries of the victors and the vanquished.

The conversation continued for hours until suddenly, sometime during the afternoon, Tagore asked if he could take a rest. He refused the offer of a bedroom or a chaise longue; he would prefer to stay where he was if he were not disturbing us. We withdrew and left him alone. I can still see him sitting on a Regency sofa, his right arm resting on its arm, in a very large, very low room, which had been designed by the architect Josef Hoffmann of the Wiener Werkstätten with windows overlooking the English Garden.

And then something happened which I have never forgotten: a few minutes after leaving the room I realized that I had left behind a notebook I needed urgently. Overcoming my disinclination to disturb Tagore, I very quietly pushed the sliding glass door a bit to one side and thought I saw him asleep. I tiptoed over to a bookcase in another corner of the room and turned around. I saw—although I could not believe what I was seeing—that Tagore had remained in the same position in which he had conversed for hours, with his large, beautiful eyes wide open. I saw *him*, but *he* did not see me, even though I was less than ten yards away. I gazed at him for a long time and grasped the fact that his open eyes were seeing nothing, not the room, nor me, nor the trees; I realized that he was resting by withdrawing, in some way that seemed quite natural to him, from his outer existence into an inner one. I could not grasp what I was seeing and made no attempt to find a rational explanation for it; I knew only that I was experiencing a marvel and that this sublime man from the East had an existence on two different levels which, for him, constituted a natural and indivisible unity. Here was a man such as you or I, a member of the species *homo sapiens* and not a ghost or a magician, who could draw energy from mysterious sources inaccessible to Westerners. Where was the Rabindranath Tagore of the preceding hours, where had he withdrawn to? Had he descended to the mothers of Goethe's *Faust*, or was he absorbed in the pure contemplation of God? He was in some infinitely remote place, where no one could or should try to follow him.

What I experienced during this first encounter with Tagore had nothing to do with the question of whether his literary work made him a writer of world stature. This was a question to which I gave hardly any thought at all, either on this day or on those that followed. I was overcome instead by the unforgettable and profound impression which left me convinced that this man was completely and utterly uncorrupted and genuine, a man from a distant world, whose being included a dimension which we Westerners lacked. The experience of that hour gave a new meaning to later conversations with the poet;

my knowledge of the other, mute side of his nature provided a kind of counterpoint, as it were, to the spoken word. For my part, I had no urgent desire for *conversation*; in fact, I preferred listening to what he wished to communicate or express. He loved to talk about Santiniketan, for example, the school and university he had founded twenty years previously, which was constantly changing and developing. It was in Santiniketan, more than any of his other achievements, that he saw his lasting contribution to his country. He regarded it as an important undertaking in truly liberal education and hoped that it would serve as an example to other universities not merely to teach facts, but to serve the development of human potential in his countrymen. At my last meeting with Tagore in 1926, in Zurich, I asked him which form of poetic expression was most important for him. With a motion of his hand he brushed the question aside. "None," was the answer, and seizing on the word "important," he became more emotional, more passionate than I had ever seen him in previous conversations. Only Santiniketan was important, he said, nothing else, now and always.

His educational efforts took precedence over everything else. He proceeded to talk at great length about the school he had founded twenty-five years earlier with five pupils, one of them his son. He spoke feelingly about the hopes entertained by him and his colleagues that the seeds planted in the hearts of students in his country and many other countries would bear fruit, ushering in an age of higher human development and peace.

But let us return to Munich and to the year 1921, in which the topic of Santiniketan was already so prominent in Tagore's thinking.

Tagore gave a talk in the Kurt Wolff Verlag library, and I attended other lectures and readings from his works. I had many opportunities to hear him converse with Germans interested in the inexhaustible subject of East and West. One such encounter which I recall clearly is the meeting between Rabindranath Tagore and Hermann Keyserling. Much of what has been said and written about their relationship strikes me as so inaccurate that I would like to digress for a moment and say a few words on the subject.

Keyserling's "Schule der Weisheit" [School of Wisdom] in Darmstadt has often been described as a counterpart to the school founded in Santiniketan by Tagore (or vice versa), but this is absolute nonsense. Tagore's institution, situated on an old family estate far from the noise of the city and developed from a school for boys into a full-fledged university, offered instruction to pupils of all ages in a variety of subjects including music, painting, sculpture, and crafts. Tagore himself established the pedagogical principles on which it is run and served as its headmaster. Education was his primary interest; he had never forgotten the disappointments of his own school years in Calcutta, and his later experiences in England had left him dissatisfied from a pedagogical point of view as well. Founded in 1901, the school continues to exist to this day; after Tagore's death the Indian government assumed responsibility for it, and all indications are that it will continue as a genuine institution of learning.

Keyserling's "School of Wisdom," by contrast, was never a school in the real sense of the word. It had no classrooms, no pupils, and no teachers. In an essay on his father's relationship to Tagore, Keyserling's son suggested in 1961 that the Nazis destroyed the school after they seized power in Germany; this is somewhat misleading, however. What Keyserling sponsored under the name of the "School of Wisdom" in Darmstadt was actually a series of lectures attended by some people with a genuine interest in the topics presented and a great many others who came because it was fashionable. I recall with gratitude some truly valuable lectures by men such as Max Scheler, Richard Wilhelm, and C. G. Jung.

In 1921 these Darmstadt lectures were decisively influenced by Tagore's presence, even though it needs to be mentioned that he strictly refused to appear in the guise of a philosopher. Largely because of Tagore, that year more than any other saw not only lectures, but also exchanges and discussions.

A greater contrast in personality than that between Tagore and Keyserling would be hard to imagine. Tagore's stature lay in the complete identity between his teachings and his own self, in the harmonious purity of his personality. Keyserling's importance was based on his high intelligence and rare ability to absorb the ideas of others with immense speed and to explain them to others, frequently in clearer, more precise, and more comprehensible language than that used by their originators. Tagore, although disclaiming to be a philosopher, epitomized in his attitude our ideas of what a philosopher is or should be. Keyserling, the self-declared philosopher, gave precisely the opposite impression to those who knew him and were familiar with his intensely emotional attitudes and alcoholic instability. What most impressed one in contacts with Tagore was his ability to remain silent and to listen, whereas a dialogue with Keyserling was a virtual impossibility; he overwhelmed his partners, who could not get in a word, with a ceaseless cascade of talk. Thus for me, as doubtless for many others present, encounters between the two served as a distressing example of the differences between East and West and were painful to witness. This impression persisted, even when one took into account that Keyserling had known Tagore for a long time, had met him twenty years before the Darmstadt discussion in England and ten years earlier in Calcutta, and that Tagore took a lively interest in this man who was exerting a growing influence on the intellectual life of Germany in those days. It was a comfort to know that Tagore had met and made friends with other Europeans, including William Butler Yeats, the great Irish poet, who admired Tagore and gave readings of his poetry in England. Romain Rolland, the revered French writer and friend of Gandhi, was another, who at his home in Villeneuve, in the 1920s, once spoke to me warmly, discerningly, and at great length of Tagore's qualities as a poet, thinker, and human being. Tagore, for his part, had a sure instinct for nobility of character and was deeply devoted to Rolland, once writing of him in a letter: "De tous les hommes avec qui j'ai été confronté en Occident, c'est Romain Rolland qui m'a le plus ému, comme le plus proche de mon coeur et le plus étroitement apparenté à mon esprit." ["Of all the people whom I have met face to face in the West, it is Romain Rolland who has touched me most deeply, as the closest to my heart and most closely related to me in spirit."]

I have mentioned here the names of some European, but not German, admirers of Tagore and his work, men of high intellectual and artistic abilities, with a particular purpose in mind, and I would like to add a few more to the list, for a German audience in particular. There is a long-standing tendency among German intellectuals to look down on authors who are very successful. Of course it is ridiculous to regard a writer as suspect because his books sell well, just as it is to praise a book because it does poorly and attracts few readers. Tagore and his works are a typical example: as their popularity grew (and he was more popular in Germany than in any other country in Europe), so did the number of those who denigrated his work as "kitsch" and referred to him by disparaging nicknames such as "Gangeshofer."[1] Under such circumstances it seems appropriate to recall how some of the leading figures in Western literary and intellectual life responded to the appearance of Tagore's work.

The very first to comprehend the Indian's great poetic genius was Ezra Pound, whose sure instincts enabled him to recognize the talent of Yeats, T. S. Eliot, and many others. In September 1912 he wrote to Harriet Monroe, the editor of *Poetry* magazine in Chicago: "I'll try to get some of the poems of the very great Bengali poet Rabindranath Tagore. They are going to be the sensation of the winter . . . W. B. Y. is doing the introduction to them. They are translated by the author into very beautiful English prose, with mastery of cadence." Some of Tagore's poems did in fact appear in the magazine in 1912, their very first publication anywhere in the West.

Yeats, the great Irish poet, has already been mentioned. He wrote to the Indian poet about the strong influence Asian thinking, transmitted by Tagore, had exercised on his mode of life: "What an excitement it was, the first reading of your poems, which seemed to come out of the fields and the rivers and have their changelessness."

Men so different in spirit as Bernard Shaw, the Americans Robert Frost and Hart Crane, and the Alsatian Albert Schweitzer admired and revered Tagore. Schweitzer sent a copy of his own book on Indian philosophy to Tagore with a letter in which he told him how much he revered him and his ideas and that he had referred to Tagore in his book as the Goethe of India because he appeared to have the same significance for India that Goethe has for Europe.

It is also a reflection of the universality of both Tagore and Einstein that each of them appreciated the other's extraordinary qualities. Einstein wrote to him, "Thou sawest the fierce strife of creatures, a strife that wells forth from need and dark desire. Thou

---

1. A pun on the Indian river Ganges and the popular and prolific Bavarian writer Ludwig Ganghofer (1855–1920). [Translator's note]

sawest the escape in calm meditation and in creations of beauty. Cherishing these thou hast served mankind all through a long and fruitful life, spreading everywhere a gentle and a free thought in a manner such as the Seers of thy people have proclaimed as the ideal."[2]

In the West many people felt Tagore's work to be of international significance. Robert Frost expressed his sense of happiness that Tagore's poetry had broken down international frontiers when it reached the West in the poet's own English, and as his friend he was proud to participate in the celebration of his greatness.

Close ties of friendship existed between Tagore and two other great figures of contemporary India, Gandhi and Nehru, ties which remained unaffected by the fact that although all three pursued similar goals, their paths often diverged considerably.

These few names and quotations should suffice to show how Western intellectuals in Europe and America responded in the first half of this century to the fifty-two-year-old Indian poet when he suddenly appeared on our horizon in 1912. It was only natural that in a first encounter with him a Westerner's first impression would be predominantly of a man from India, with an Eastern calm, serene wisdom, and reserve. I found myself responding in this way on our first meeting in 1921 and on later occasions. As a conversation continued, however, one would forget that the speaker had grown up in Bengal and actually received a very small part of his education in England, so thorough was this Easterner's familiarity with the cultural and intellectual traditions of the West. In such talks, which revealed the universal breadth of Tagore's learning, one was forced to conclude that without doubt he knew far more of the West than most of the Europeans he encountered knew of the East. I am thinking here not only of Dante, Shakespeare, and Goethe, whose works he knew and admired, but also of his interest in modern literature and his astonishing ability to follow the most recent developments. This is proved by his essay on "Modern Poetry,"[3] among other things, in

2. Krishna Kripalani, *Rabindranath Tagore: A Biography* (New York: Oxford University Press, 1962).

3. *A Tagore Reader*, ed. Amiya Chakravarty (New York: Macmillan, 1961).

which he remarks that Robert Bridges, the British poet laureate, should not really be considered "modern" and then goes on to discuss T. S. Eliot. It is quite remarkable that someone born in India in 1861 should display such an interest in and grasp of an Anglo-American poet thirty years his junior.

I remarked earlier that my personal impressions and experiences on the day of our first meeting had nothing to do with the question of Tagore's stature as a creative artist, a remark I must now modify to some extent by adding that once I became convinced that the *creator* was utterly pure and genuine, I could not possibly doubt that his creations were the same. Naturally my recollections here are those of a publisher; I would not presume to express an opinion as a critic or literary historian. All the same, my subjective impression remains: all of Tagore's works—poetry, fiction, plays, essays, and autobiographical writings—express the same unflagging love for the natural world of mankind, animals, and plants, and a love and reverence for the divine principle, a respect for human dignity, and an untiring effort to understand, to see, to feel, and to give poetically pure expression to what has been felt, seen, and understood—sometimes in a lighter spirit, sometimes with more seriousness, but never in a loud, ponderous, vehement, or accusing tenor.

How was this quiet, gentle voice able to make the whole world listen? And how is it to be explained that its effect was greater in Germany than anywhere else in the world and that literally millions of Germans became intimately familiar with Tagore's works? His impact was considerable in England, less so in Italy, Spain, and France, but in Germany so enormous that it sometimes took embarrassing forms. Tagore's publisher was not pleased, I can assure you, to see the camera zoom in on a copy of his book *Der Gärtner* in the sentimental film "Die Lieblingsfrau des Maharadscha" [The Maharajah's Favorite].

It seems to me that one—although certainly not the only—possible explanation of Tagore's phenomenal popularity in Germany can be found in the historical context: Eastern themes are something of a tradition in German literature, and there have been several surprisingly sudden spurts of interest in the East, from some of Goethe's later works and the poet Rückert to Hermann Hesse in our day. One could also mention Schopenhauer, the numerous nineteenth-century translations by Daumer and others, Count Hammer-Purgstall, etc. Later, a perception of the West as a civilization in decline and an increasing rejection of their orthodox creeds by both Catholics and Protestants, accompanied by a search for new and unorthodox forms of faith, had set in among the more intellectual circles of the German bourgeoisie even before the First World War, particularly among the younger generation. The military defeat and its consequences, perceived by many Germans as a breakdown of the ideas and ideals of Western civilization, contributed immensely to the spread of this mood. I can still see the university students of those days in parks and cafés and shop clerks on the tramway immersed in their copies of Buddha's sermons, published by Piper Verlag in three small volumes that were on sale everywhere. Half a dozen translations of Lao-tsu were available, and they were all read. "Ex oriente lux" was Germany's hope for the future, which also helps to explain the seductive appeal of young Communist Russia to the intelligentsia. Poets such as Becher and Brecht, who were intellectual offspring of the bourgeoisie, fragile personalities such as Heinrich Vogeler-Worpswede, and many, many others were seduced—permanently so.

The reading material available to still this hunger for Eastern philosophy and poetry was all from the distant past until, in the years just after the war, a contemporary figure suddenly emerged: a poet, a cosmopolitan, a religious man who nonetheless sought no converts, a moral authority who did not moralize. He came bringing poems and verses which offered themselves freely, demanding nothing in return; possessed of a new innocence, they remained outside the sphere of ideology, vessels of human wisdom that introduced a fresh breath of Eastern beauty. As people read, they felt in the presence of something magical and beyond reason. Touched by waves of a secret, mysterious force, they could sense that the author of these poems was that oh so rare phenomenon, a case in which creator and creation are one, parts of a single whole. There is something miraculous about this, which gives the figure of the poet an almost messianic significance. Are we not experiencing a similar phenomenon today in the figure of Albert Schweitzer? Who of us knows, or would claim the ability to judge, whether Schweitzer is an important theologian, philosopher, musicologist, organist, or physician? But the whole world senses that for him ideology and action are inseparable, and reveres him for it. Figures such as Schweitzer and Tagore are rare, appearing perhaps once in the span of a generation.

Certainly one factor which contributed to Tagore's success in Germany was the relative ease with which his works could be translated by someone with a good knowledge of English and a sense for the subtleties of poetic German. All the translations into German were based, in accordance with the author's wishes, on Tagore's own English translations from the Bengali. It was this circumstance, that the poet wrote in his mother tongue of Bengali, a language not understood by his countrymen in other parts of India, which led to a mixed reaction there when it became known that Tagore had been awarded the Nobel Prize in 1913. The pride felt at having an Indian writer finally receive this most important literary award was dampened by the fact that so many Indians could not read his work in the original.

André Gide was Tagore's first translator in France, where *Gitanjali* appeared as *L'Offrande lyrique*. "L'incomparable pureté de ce petit livre rayonnait à mes yeux d'un tel éclat que je tiens à l'honneur d'en apporter un reflet à la France." ["The incomparable purity of this small book shone so brightly in my eyes that I consider it an honor to bring some of its reflection to France."] That Gide in France and Juan Ramón Jiménez in Spain, both themselves later Nobel laureates, were willing to serve as Tagore's translators indicates in what high regard he was held by the literary elite of Europe. The German versions, prepared by various conscientious translators who were enthusiastic admirers of Tagore, were, I believe, competently done, although I did not always find the translator I ideally wished for.

I knew Rilke well enough to turn to him in this matter. In late 1913 I wrote to him in Paris, asking whether he would consider taking on a translation. On December 6, 1913 he replied:

> I am looking forward eagerly to the German edition of Rabindranath Tagore. Here André Gide has just told us about his response to this poet and enthusiastically read us some samples of his translation of *Gitanjali*, which truly seems to be carried along by the flow of these poems. The book edition has just been brought out by the Nouvelle Revue Française.

A later letter, dated January 1914, goes into my proposal in more detail:

17 Rue Campagne-Première
Paris XIVe
January 7, 1914

Dear Mr. Kurt Wolff,

A bright sunny day—I took your proposal with me on a long walk, since such difficult matters are more easily dealt with while walking and seem to fall into place better out of doors, almost by themselves as it were, than if one is mulling them over hunched over one's desk. Then, on my way home, I wired you my answer: in the negative. Not an easy decision, since for one thing I don't like to refuse your requests and also, as you may have sensed, the thing itself is quite tempting.

But there is one objection, which renders all other reasons superfluous: I don't feel myself irresistibly called to the proposed task, as I would have to be to produce a definitive and responsible version. Though there is much in these verses to which I feel a close affinity, it is conveyed to me on a wave of foreignness, so to speak, whose movement I could not reproduce without imposing constraints on my own nature. This may be due in part to my lack of feeling for the English language; I lose my sense of it so quickly that again and again I have found myself floundering unless I have a great deal of help. Also, I have undertaken a few translations from other languages, small experiments really, that I turn to now and again while continuing with my own work, hardly worth mentioning, in fact, but too precious for me to give them up; such a large assignment, if I decided to take it on, would not only take priority over them for some time, but also over all my own inner life that presently absorbs me; this, to be frank, would be painful, since I had hopes of devoting myself to it here, in complete seclusion, rather than to reproducing what has already been expressed, no matter how beautiful it may be.

This, my dear Mr. Kurt Wolff, is about the extent of what I have to say. You see the course my deliberations have taken; my questions to myself lie open to your view, and so, I trust, it will not occur to you to think I fail to appreciate your fine proposal.

I have not read enough in the German edition to be able to judge the necessity on which your inquiry is based; is it really necessary to replace the quite significant amount of work that has already been done? When I think of certain familiar passages that I consulted, I could not say offhand whether they could be rendered better.

I am grateful, as I say, for your confidence in me and remain, in this spirit, most cordially yours,

R. M. Rilke

Since these are unknown Rilke letters, I have quoted them at length. They say as much about Rilke as about Tagore and prove, in any event, how seriously Tagore was taken in Paris, and by Rilke personally, immediately upon publication of his very first book.

MY CORRESPONDENCE with Rilke now lies some fifty years in the past, and the blaze of German enthusiasm for Tagore burned out more than thirty years ago. Whether the publication of a handsome volume for the centennial of Tagore's birth, containing an extensive selection from his works, has rekindled some of the sparks is something I do not know. But I do know that Tagore has left a legacy to the world, even if many of those who have felt the influence of his thinking and his work have never heard his name. In a time when ideologies are propagated with brute force, Rabindranath Tagore of India embodied the principles of a higher plane in his teachings, poetry, and life in an exemplary manner. This became a part of the awareness of many people and has been passed on, never to be lost.

Lou Andreas-Salomé

IN 1916, when Rilke asked me to pay a visit to his friend Lou Andreas-Salomé, her name elicited only vague associations in my mind. I thought I recalled that she had published several books, but I hadn't read them (either then or later). Rilke had once spoken about his journeys to Russia at the turn of the century, and told me that on both occasions he had been accompanied by Lou von Salomé. (Only a short time ago I came across a letter from Rilke of July 28, 1914—a somewhat unsettling date—in which he announced his visit for the following day, mentioning that he was coming to Leipzig after a stay with his friend in Göttingen; I know that the meeting took place but can no longer recall what we talked about. The outbreak of the war probably erased my memories of that day.)

Naturally I was willing to call on Frau Salomé, particularly when I learned that she was stopping over in Leipzig, where I also was at the time, on leave from the Balkan front. But I wasn't looking forward to it. Meeting a writer when you haven't read a single line of her work is an uncomfortable position to be in, all the more so if you are a publisher. And I assumed it was the publisher to whom she wished to speak.

I left the Hotel Hauffe in the early afternoon at the agreed-upon hour and had only to cross the street to the hotel where Lou Salomé was staying. She came to the point immediately: Rilke had advised her, she said, to make a final copy of a manuscript which she had finished some time before but withheld from publication, and to show it to me. He had also recommended that she talk with me about possible changes or additions. The book was to be called "Three Letters to a Boy" and consisted, as the title suggested, of letters, written between 1907 and 1913 to a boy in three different stages of development. The subject was a very young person's confrontation with the problem of sexuality. Lou Salomé spoke simply, quietly, and matter-of-factly about her approach to this task and to what degree it had been eased by her close connection with the recipient, a boy of whom she was very fond. Her aim had been to write plainly and undramatically but to stress unequivocally the importance of linking desire with love or at least some notion of feeling—a crucial point particularly during puberty, with its ever-present danger that the sexual drive might become autonomous and crave satisfaction without any connection to the young person's emotional life. She wanted my opinion on whether she had succeeded in this. I got the impression that she wanted to read some of the manuscript aloud to me, a suggestion I resisted, asking her permission to read it myself later. I did say, however, that I would be happy to hear any further comments she wanted to make about the book and asked whether she desired my reaction to any particular passages . . .

She would like to have my reaction, she said, to her allusions to homosexual love affairs in the third letter, where she had taken care to avoid any negative insinuation; she mentioned that here it was crucially important to keep the age of the recipient in mind. But even more important would be my opinion on a different matter: in the last letter she had originally intended to touch upon the mysterious connection between the desire and willingness to love and the urge to suffer pain, but she had then limited herself to one allusion concerning the fine line dividing passionate and sadistic behavior. She wasn't quite sure whether she could or should have gone further. Since the first time she had discussed this enigma of love, with Nietzsche . . .

Up to this point my attitude had been one of professional courtesy; I had been listening to Frau Salomé but without any sense of being personally stirred—I had not even looked at her closely. Now, however, I suddenly came awake with a jolt and a certain sense of confusion, and took a very good look at the woman sitting across from me:

A broad face; a strong, perhaps even stubborn chin; a beautifully curved mouth; intelligent, expressive eyes, which were always turned directly on the person to whom she was speaking or listening. A thoroughly feminine person, but conveying a sense of unusual strength.

Hadn't I heard Rilke say that his friend was Russian? That he had begun learning Russian with her, after their first trip and in preparation for the second, and for the pleasure of being able to read the great Russian classics in the original? Yes, she was certainly Russian, but she spoke German without any trace of a foreign accent. Her age? She looked to me as if she could hardly be older than fifty. But hadn't she only a moment or two before said something like, "When Nietzsche and I . . ."

I was bewildered. I knew Nietzsche's main works, but I had never read a biography or any of his letters. For my generation Nietzsche was already a figure of legend. I knew the major sites of his great and tragic life: the famous school at Pforta—Leipzig—Basel—the Engadin—Italy—Torino—darkness.

Lou Salomé continued speaking, but I was barely listening. I was hoping that she would soon be finished with what she had to say about her manuscript and that I might find a not too obvious way to bring the conversation around to other subjects. "As to the letter from Rilke I cite in the second piece," I heard her saying, "of course I have asked for and received Rainer's permission to publish it." She handed me the manuscript, which I promised to take with me and read soon. I had spent perhaps a quarter of an hour with her, certainly not much more. I sensed that it would be not only possible, but even polite to stay a little longer. Lou Salomé immediately began inquiring about my professional plans, my own literary interests. My answers, which were larded with more questions to her, seemed to stimulate her and to create an atmosphere of mutual understanding and trust.

What followed was not exactly a conversation. More accurately it was an account given by an older—although by no means old—woman of the most important intellectual and human encounters of her life to a younger visitor, in whom she must have found an attentive, interested, indeed eager listener, and whose interspersed comments and questions encouraged her to continue. The atmosphere was one of warmth and trust; though the distance that always exists when two people meet for the first time was preserved, it was nonetheless possible to refer to highly personal and even intimate experiences.

Lou Salomé talked about her life. She did so in a way which removed the distance of time from the events she recounted, and this, in turn, made her listener, who had been stunned into attention by his inability to grasp the temporal dimension in what he was hearing, forget the passage of time altogether. No matter whether she was talking about Richard Wagner or Pushkin, Malwida von Meysenburg, Rilke, whom she had just seen, or Nietzsche, with whom she described herself taking walks in Lucerne—it all became utterly real and vivid as she spoke, breaking down all barriers of time. This created the atmosphere of enchantment in which her visitor found himself that afternoon, for what is enchantment, after all, if not a loss of awareness of time and space around us . . .

There was no doubting, either then or later, that everything she said was true and real and had happened just that way. Everything seemed to have happened now or once upon a time and always and in no particular order.

But what in fact did I learn from her on that most extraordinary afternoon in 1916, in the midst of the war? The most profound impressions in Lou Andreas-Salomé's life stemmed from her childhood in St. Petersburg and a number of encounters during her adult life in Western Europe, encounters with towering personalities of whom at least three will no doubt be remembered beyond this century: Nietzsche, Freud, and Rilke. She had been Nietzsche's fiancée, Freud's pupil and friend, and Rilke's lover.

She hardly touched on her experiences with Freud and Rilke as she spoke, probably from a disinclination to talk about living persons, but also because my questions, both voiced and implied, were not particularly concerned with them. She spoke of Russia, her home, her early years in which a decisive human and religious experience occurred, but above all she spoke of her travels in the years before she settled in Göttingen as the wife of Friedrich Carl Andreas, a professor of oriental studies at the university there.

"Please tell me about Nietzsche as a young man; we—or I, at least—know virtually nothing about him . . ."

"But Nietzsche was not all that young when I knew him. I had just turned twenty-one, and for me he was an older man, almost forty, a professor who had published books. Malwida gave me *Human, All Too Human* to read, and his aphorisms. The marvelous part was that in conversation he was not like an older professor at all; he was younger, more passionate than any person I had ever known. We loved talking to one another, for hours and hours and hours. He never gave me the feeling I was a little girl and he was instructing me. I didn't learn from him; I experienced things with him. He took me seriously. He asked many questions. He even praised my early poems—something he really shouldn't have done. In fact he set one to music; you know that, as a student in Bonn, he was vacillating about whether or not to become a musician. Later he had the song arranged for chorus and orchestra. He mentions it in *Ecce Homo*. His praise didn't do me any harm. I knew that my poems were no good and never had them published.—Don't worry, I haven't changed my mind on that point! But Nietzsche gave me a beautiful poem as a present. And all the days we spent talking, just the two of us—they were indescribable . . ."

As Lou Salomé talked, one could sense how intoxicating this encounter was, how present the memory of it is, thirty-four years later. (One could also sense that her experiences with Nietzsche had by no means filled Lou's life in those years to the exclusion of everything else, but I thought it better not to ask too many questions . . .) Over and over again: those passionate, exhausting, consuming orgies of talk, occasionally painfully interrupted by one of Nietzsche's severe migraine attacks, which Lou recalled vividly. Religion seems to have played a major role in their conversations, but literature was also an important topic.

Nietzsche's letters to Lou Andreas-Salomé have been preserved in part; her letters to Nietzsche were destroyed. Naturally it was his jealous and interfering sister Elisabeth who poisoned his relationship with Lou . . .

It seems to me that many hours have passed since I entered this room. I make an attempt to leave, but she objects. "No, do stay, there is something more I have to say to you. You are a publisher. Tell me why more isn't being done in Germany for Russian literature, why do they go on bringing out the same old Dostoyevsky and Tolstoy novels? You should publish a good edition of Turgenev. Turgenev is a great writer. I knew him well. I've read all his works; I would be happy to advise you."

It no longer makes any impression on me that this woman has

personally known Turgenev, Strindberg, Wagner, and many others—
I still have not absorbed what I heard earlier. Afternoon has turned
into evening. I take the manuscript and depart. I believe I said, "Auf
Wiedersehen," but I did not mean it seriously. I was so caught up in
the uniqueness of this experience that the idea of actually meeting
her again never crossed my mind. This was in the year 1916. A year
later the small volume *Drei Briefe an einen Knaben* [Three Letters to
a Boy] was published by the Kurt Wolff Verlag, an event that seemed
of no great significance to me. Its author survived it by another twenty
years; Nietzsche's friend died in 1937.

WHAT I have attempted to recount here is my own experience in
the fragments I recall; I have written down what occurred as I remember it.

In the meantime two books have appeared which in a certain
sense confirm my recollections, but above all contain material to un-
derpin and round them out. In 1951 and 1958 Ernst Pfeiffer, who was
close to Lou in Göttingen during the last years of her life, published
two highly interesting books of memoirs assembled from her unpublished papers. In addition to the author's text they contain
copious editorial notes; both provide important information and
make the reader aware that the attraction Lou Andreas-Salomé's personality exerted on many important men spanned a period of fifty
years; her influence has become an inseparable element of this era
and the lives of those who were close to her.

In the first of Pfeiffer's two volumes, entitled *Lebensrückblick*
[Looking Back], he cites a letter from Nietzsche, written *before he met
Lou* in Rome. Paul Rée had sent a letter to Nietzsche in Genoa, mentioning that he was going to meet a young Russian woman at the
house of his friend Malwida. Thereupon Nietzsche wrote this—prophetic—reply to Rée from Messina on March 21, 1882:

> Please give this Russian my regards, if that makes any sense at all: I lust
> after this breed of soul. I plan to go out and abduct some soon—in view
> of what I want to accomplish in the next ten years, I need them.

The second volume, entitled *In der Schule bei Freud* [*The Freud
Journals*], contains a great deal that has little or nothing to do with the

title but is still of significance. It will be recalled that Lou asked me a question in regard to the third of her "Letters to a Boy," concerning the mysterious topic she had first touched upon with Nietzsche. In Lou's diary for the years 1912–23, which is reproduced in the second volume, I found the following note:

> Cruel people being always masochistic also, the whole thing is inseparable from bisexuality. And that has a deep meaning. The first time I ever discussed this theme was with Nietzsche (that sadomasochist unto himself). And I know that afterward we dared not look at each other. [1]

I ASSUME that if one were to take a survey of "educated" people between the ages of twenty and fifty today and ask if the name Lou Andreas-Salomé meant anything to them, the answers would probably be largely in the negative. A few would recall having seen letters addressed to her in the published correspondence of Rilke, Nietzsche, or Freud. That would be all. But who is interested in the recipients of letters? People read them because they are interested in the writer, not the recipient, and often, as in the case of Rilke, authors of letters are actually writing to themselves; the nominal recipient is relatively unimportant. In other words: it is understandable that Lou Andreas-Salomé has been largely forgotten. She was not a gifted writer, even if she did occasionally find excellent formulations, clear and convincing, for what she wanted to communicate. One example connected with our topic here is a letter she wrote to Paul Rée in the fateful year of 1882. The following excerpt is reproduced in the chapter "Freundeserleben" [Experiences with Friends] of her posthumously published memoirs:

> (August 18, 1882) At the very beginning of my friendship with Nietzsche, I wrote about him to Malwida, saying that his was a religious nature, and this aroused the strongest concern in her. Today I would emphasize this phrase doubly. —We shall experience his emergence as the prophet of a new religion, and it will be one which wins heroes as disciples. —We think and feel so much alike on the subject, we can virtually take the words and thoughts out of each others' mouths. We have

1. Lou Andreas-Salomé, *The Freud Journals*, translated by Stanley A. Leavy (New York: Basic Books, 1964), p. 143.

been talking ourselves to death for these past three weeks, and strange as it seems he is suddenly strong enough to spend about ten hours every day chattering away.—Odd that we unintentionally keep arriving at the brinks of precipices, those dizzying spots where one once climbed on one's own, to be able to gaze into the depths. We always took to such paths like mountain goats, and if anyone had been listening to us, he would have thought two devils were conversing.

"It was inevitable," Lou continues, commenting on this letter, "that I would be fascinated by precisely that aspect of Nietzsche's nature and conversations which found less expression in his talks with Paul Rée. In my case he evoked memories or feelings of which I was only half aware, stemming from my earliest but most personal, indestructible childhood. Only, it was just this that would never have allowed me to become his disciple, his successor: it would have made me suspicious every time to take a step in the very direction from which I had had to escape to find clarity. The fascination and an inner resistance to it were bound up together."

How illuminating this letter of 1882 and the later passage are for her relationship with Nietzsche! One tries to imagine the conversations between the thirty-eight-year-old philosopher and a twenty-two-year-old girl and is tempted to ask: has such a girl existed more than once? It seems clear, however, that she did not take herself particularly seriously as a writer. Characteristically, Lou's first book, a novel, was the result not of a creative urge but of a wish to demonstrate her abilities and autonomy to her mother and brothers, her right to live her own independent life. Her talents did not lie in the field of writing fiction.

Peter Gast, a friend of Nietzsche's, met Lou only once, when she was twenty-one, and wrote of his impressions immediately afterwards: "She is a real genius, and truly heroic in character . . . Her ideas reveal that in her thinking she has dared to approach the uttermost limits of the possible, both in the moral as well as the intellectual sphere—as I say, a genius in mind and spirit." Peter Gast's conclusions of 1882 are complemented by a passage of a letter Freud wrote to her in 1916: "You understand, you are a grasper of ideas par excellence, and what is more, you grasp more than what has been presented to you." It is possible to be a genius and a person who can grasp the ideas of others (we can imagine what this rarest of qualities meant to Rilke!) without producing important literary works of one's own.

If I have emphasized the names of Nietzsche, Freud, and Rilke here, it should not be misunderstood to mean that Lou Salomé's life is fully described by her relationships as fiancée, friend, and lover, respectively, of these men. They are only three of the best-known figures today who played a role in it, and perhaps for her they were not even the most important. In her youth she formed a deep attachment to her Dutch mentor and friend in Russia, an attachment that strongly influenced her over many years. Her close, sisterly friendship with Paul Rée may have meant more to her in the long term than her love affair with Nietzsche, an intellectual and emotional burst of fireworks destined to burn itself out. Her life brought her many other relationships, some of them close, which meant much to her and even more, as a number of accounts reveal, to her partners. All were men of outstanding intellectual caliber, among them Alois Biedermann, Georg Brandes, Hans Delbrück, Paul Deussen, Heinrich von Stein, Ferdinand Tönnies, and others in later years. But this is not the place to go into such relationships, and I would not be the appropriate person to do so.

The mysterious power of Lou Salomé's personality defies precise definition, and what the "Lou experience" (as it is referred to in the Nietzsche literature) meant in the last analysis to the philosopher, who descended into the darkness of insanity a few short years after they separated, will never be known. This uncertainty also remains in the case of the poet Rilke. The surviving letters do not reveal the secret, and neither left a Marienbad elegy for posterity to interpret.[2] We know only that for these two utterly different men an encounter with the same woman had a fateful dimension, and such encounters provide a lasting source of inspiration for creative artists. People capable of arousing such responses in others will not necessarily leave their

2. The reference is to Goethe's love poem "Elegie" of 1823, with the motto "Und wenn der Mensch in seiner Qual verstummt / Gab mir ein Gott, zu sagen was ich leide" ["While mortal men are silenced by such pain / A god gave me the gift to speak of my torment"]. [Editor's note]

own mark on the world, however. This seems to be true of Lou Sa-lomé. She radiated light while remaining in the dark herself. Pfeiffer speaks of her "total lack of a need to seek the limelight," a form of modesty which has its own greatness.

Letters

Rainer Maria Rilke

Rainer Maria Rilke to Kurt Wolff

17 Rue Campagne-Première
Paris XIVe
December 6, 1913

Dear Mr. Wolff,

It is only just at this moment, having reread your very kind letter before writing to express my thanks, that I realize you mention sending off the most welcome books by the same post. Now I am almost afraid that the package has gone astray: it still has not reached me by today.

Your thoughtful and considerate desire to give me pleasure by now and again sending one or the other of the books your excellent firm publishes almost puts me to shame, since, as you rightly assume, I have quite given up expressing public support for any books at all, even those I find most convincing. However this withdrawal has made my preoccupation with what does concern me that much more intense, and so it would cost me great effort to refuse your kind offers, even though I am the only one to benefit from them. Still, to salve my conscience, I do ask you to make me such presents only rarely and by way of exception, as it were, so that I may continue to feel the pleasure I take in your publications, and nothing more, is suitable recompense for your generosity . . .

With most grateful thanks I remain

Yours very truly
Rainer Maria Rilke[1]

1. This letter and that of February 10, 1917, are published with permission of Insel Verlag.

Kurt Wolff to Rainer Maria Rilke

Hotel Post and Riv-Alta
Silvaplana
January 10, 1914

Dear Sir,

Your kind gift reached me up here, where for a few days now I have found the fresh winter air and relaxation I came in search of: A. Gide's French translation of *Gitanjali*, for which I send you my sincere thanks. I began reading it at once and found the lovely French form of the Indian poems pleasing; at the same time I felt how much is still lacking in the German edition I am publishing. Then I thought of you, who were so kind to send the book, thought of your marvelous translation of the Browning sonnets—and sent you the telegram via Leipzig (as I don't have your address with me); I hope you will excuse its boldness.

In the meantime I have received the news that you have declined and that a letter from you is en route. Even without having read it, I appreciate and respect your reasons for declining. I can only ask you to forgive the request, sending assurances that I continue to hold you in the highest regard and remain

Yours very truly,
Kurt Wolff

You will receive from the Leipzig office a copy of the *Weiße Blätter* containing a poem by Princess Lichnowsky; from a conversation with the Princess I inferred that it would be of interest to you.

Rainer Maria Rilke to Kurt Wolff

Keferstraße 11
Munich
February 10, 1917

My dear and esteemed Mr. Kurt Wolff,

My apartment, constructed for summer living, has broken down under this winter's severity; the water and gas pipes froze, and as the first inconvenience led to a flood in my bedroom, I have been driven out of my quarters for more than a week; this is the reason for my tardiness.

I was reassured to hear that my answer is rendered somewhat less urgent by the fact that Insel has already accepted "Merlin." Dr. Pulver is very pleased; he told me about it obviously on the assumption that he owed this acceptance in some part to my influence. As a rule I am more than cautious in recommending manuscripts to a publisher with whom I am associated; I refrain completely in fact, and in Pulver's case I would have had considerable difficulty in writing a precise and clear report for Insel. When Dr. Pulver, after giving a reading of "Merlin," told me that he had also submitted it to Insel, I did decide to write to Frau Kippenberg to suggest that the manuscript be read immediately, and not in strict order of receipt; as I did so I realized all I could say in its favor was simply that on the basis of a certain integrity and sincerity it deserved very careful consideration. I tell you this in such detail, my dear Mr. Kurt Wolff, because I have then expressed everything I have to say concerning my approval or reservations about Max Pulver. The questions you addressed to me have been my questions, too, whenever I had dealings with him and have remained questions from occasion to occasion. That his somewhat aggressive stance as a man of letters works to his own disadvantage is something I have tried to explain to myself, as far as possible, as stemming from the worries and intolerable circumstances of his present state. When I first met him, for one evening, this ambitious contentiousness of his did not strike me; at that time he rather seemed to have the grave and ponderous temperament of his writings and was not particularly talkative; where he did attempt to describe a deeper impression (I am grateful to him for a first convincing recommendation of the marvelous Gilgamesh epic), he radiated a youthful warmth that won me over more than anything else of which he delivered himself. This was the high point of my impressions: for in his poetry (I am not familiar with his two plays yet, although I have copies of them) it is no doubt more a case of responding to its self-discipline and firmly outlined seriousness than of being overwhelmed by any inherent radiance. Certainly he has powers that deserve to be supported and tended, all young people are questionable, after all,—this particular young man strikes one as a poet who occasionally plays the literary pundit, whether in self-defense or because it is his ultimate calling, or out of a sort of desperation—indeed, that remains to be seen.

Your letter, dear Mr. Wolff, was not only a pleasure to receive, but also arrived at quite an opportune moment, since as it happens I have been giving some thought in the last few days to turning to you for some advice or even real assistance.

You know that my wife, Clara Rilke-Westhoff, is a sculptress and studied in her youth with Rodin, who has often spoken decidedly well of her. Three or four years ago we discussed the possibility of whether she should apply for a teaching post at a German art academy. Her technical abilities are great, in Rodin's opinion "complete," and when she has accepted private pupils in past years, they made good progress under her; she herself found enjoyment and confirmation in the activity of teaching. No real attempt has been made to acquire a post for her, however. Now circumstances, both external and internal, have combined to suggest that we really ought to take steps in this direction, and I think with fondness of Darmstadt as a first choice; the thought that my wife and our daughter (and I myself now and then) could find a more settled abode there is a pleasing one, and I would not hesitate to undertake the right steps to achieve such an aim, if only I knew exactly what they ought to be. I have in mind employment under the patronage of the Grand Duke, who received me once most graciously many years ago and may not yet have given up entirely his active interest in the arts; at the time it was so lively that our conversation about Rodin, which filled the short time of the audience, long remained engraved in my memory.

You are familiar with Darmstadt, my dear Mr. Kurt Wolff, and with the court in its present state, the situation of the arts, the people whose good will and assistance should be gained for a purpose such as mine; you yourself are thinking of settling your own life and work in this city. Presumably it will not be too far from your mind to give an occasional thought to my plan in the light of circumstances there, so that its practicability or impracticability will become evident before we do any more about it.

I am addressing myself here most particularly to your esteemed wife and would be most appreciative if I could rely on her advice as well. I would supply all the required information, and even come to Darmstadt myself if necessary, in order to call upon the relevant persons myself, and should there be any prospects of success, I would endeavor to obtain an audience with the Grand Duke, in order to secure the pending plan through the intermediary party. Presumably, however, many other efforts and attempts to gather information would be required first; in a word, if the matter is not burdensome or distasteful to you, we would like to entrust it to your kind consideration and discretion. Let me have your reaction at your convenience and please pardon the boldness with which I have presumed to approach you, and particularly your wife, in this connection.

Lastly I must ask you to forgive my handwriting, which even I find illegible. My apartment is still so cold and inhospitable that I have had to press forward with this letter with stiff fingers, in the most uncomfortable haste. May it assure you of my most sincere good wishes, with which I remain

Yours very truly,
R. M. Rilke

Kurt Wolff to Rainer Maria Rilke

Luisenstraße 31
Munich
January 30, 1922

Dear Mr. Rainer Maria Rilke:

Your continuing and active interest in the work of many young writers gives me such great pleasure that it is for me to thank you when we send you a parcel of books; there is no need to thank me. I was pleased that you asked about Unruh's new play *Stürme* [Storms]. The book will be sent to you as soon as a printed copy is available, presumably in March.

Please do not consider it excessively forward of me if I now and again select a work published by the Hyperion Verlag or the Kurt Wolff Verlag and send it to you unasked. If one or the other of these books captures your attention or is aesthetically or artistically pleasing to you, then these shipments have fulfilled their purpose. Nowadays there is little enough that fits this intention. With this in mind a small package is being dispatched to you today, containing the books noted on the reverse.

Yesterday I saw a very charming and touching small book at Margot Hausenstein's, to which you stood godfather: *Mitsou*. The little boy's ability to express his experience in drawings is wonderful and almost frightening.

I will close with many good wishes, above all that you may be able to spend early and full spring in the lovely countryside where you are now living, an incomparably splendid season there. I remain in admiration

Yours very truly,
Kurt Wolff

Heinrich Mann

Kurt Wolff to Heinrich Mann

The Balkans
February 1, 1916

Dear Mr. Mann,

I did not want to write you myself until I had received confirmation from Mr. G. H. Meyer that my great and long-standing wish to be active on your behalf as publisher of your work will actually be fulfilled, with your complete approval and that of your previous publisher. I have now received this confirmation and would like to express my great, great pleasure over the serious but gratifying responsibility that has now been placed in my hands. Our agreement and the acquisition of your work do indeed strike me as the greatest professional responsibility I have ever taken on. In the case of other authors, a small lapse on my part now and then as their business representative means some annoyance; in your case it seems to me today that it would be a crime. You have had some half a dozen publishers between Mr. Jacques a/k/a Jakobäus Hegner and Cassirer, of whom two at least made great efforts to represent you and your work. It would be in poor taste and unjust to snipe at them, but I may say this much, perhaps: one of them, in my view, was enthusiastic about your work, but he wanted to earn his money in an entirely different field, and so no advantage could accrue to you; another, who places too high a value on the Weimar classics, is devoted body and soul to authors whose copyrights have expired. As a *publisher* it is my desire not to wax enthusiastic, but to sell books; not to add your books to a collection of *objets d'art* assembled by my firm, but to add to the *cent liseurs* [hundred readers] who are already there *cent mille* [a hundred thousand] more; to make a great deal of money for you and with you. — Perhaps it is a particularly fortunate circumstance that has made me an advocate for you work, now and in the future. I am convinced that, among the writers of the generation before my own, the future belongs to only two . . . (I will also be active on behalf of the other, Karl Kraus, from now on, in a special form) and this conviction has taken such possession of me that I want to publicize it with every means at my disposal. My own activities after my return home will be devoted to this above all. I want to work like Saccard for the Universelle. And I dare to make this comparison because he and I share the same fanaticism, but the silver mines of Carmel were more imaginary, more fictitious than the figures of Violante von Assy or Claude Marehn, figures who should be hammered into the consciousness of contemporary readers until they are their most secure possessions and can be handed down to their heirs. One must just wait for "these stirring times" to be over, and for the outbreak of peace . . .

I have said nothing about your books, which I have read for the second time in the course of the past few weeks, some of them for the third. It does not seem appropriate to me for the publisher to speak about matters of art to the artist. I merely wanted to tell you of my intention to seek readers and purchasers for these books, and to seek you approval for the means by which this will be done, and for which more detailed proposals will be sent to you.

I send my regards today with my great admiration and respect, full of gratitude for your confidence in me, and as your—not eighth or ninth but now permanent—publisher,

Kurt Wolff

Hermann Hesse

Hermann Hesse to Kurt Wolff

Relief Office for German Prisoners of War
Library Dept.
Thunstraße 23
Bern
December 30, 1916

Dear Mr. Wolff:

My sincere thanks for the package of Heinrich Mann's books, with which you have done me such a favor! I own some of the earlier editions, but by no means all of them. My favorite has always been *Die kleine Stadt* [The Little Town], which I hold in very high regard; at one time I overhastily judged some of the early novels as too sensational. In any event Heinrich Mann, who was and is a talented and outstanding figure, has continued to develop in a distinct and creditable manner, avoiding the tendency our authors seem to have to lose their fire after one success and acquire the attitude of someone minding a store.

I have an intense, almost pathological longing to devote myself to beautiful things again at my leisure, to read and write and the like. For months I have been involved in an undertaking which continues to be worthwhile, but at the same time is killing me. My respect for the "real" world of businesses and organizations has not grown; art remains not merely more beautiful than all this hustle and bustle, but also more real and more serious.

I really ought to take back what I said about Scheler's war book. [1]

---

1. The philosopher Max Scheler wrote a lengthy, chauvinistic book heralding the German war effort, entitled *Der Genius des Krieges und der deutsche Krieg* [The Genius of War and

When I first read it I had not given any serious thought to his approach, and the book's own enthusiasm came into it as well. But for me none of his ideas on time and history has stood the test of reflection.

With my best regards I am

Yours very truly,
Hermann Hesse[2]

Hermann Hesse to Kurt Wolff

Relief Office for German Prisoners of War
Library Dept.
Thunstraße 23
Bern
September 19, 1917

Dear Mr. Wolff:

I have written a few lines on Heinrich Mann's *Die Armen* [The Poor] for *März*.

All the same, the book is a disappointment! You have better ones in your list.

I will say nothing about the technique, which once again is splendid, at least in part. But it is a terrible shame that, if the man is going to tackle such a clearly defined problem, he should treat it like a stage comedy, simplifying and degrading one party until it becomes ridiculous. The struggle between workers and capitalists becomes interesting and challenging only if something resembling good will is present on both sides, if the capitalist, even though he is rich, is still a decent person. If he has stolen his money, as in Mann's book, then the whole problem loses its seriousness, and a subject for real intellectual debate turns into a detective story. It is a pity, since there are

the German War]; it was published by Verlag der Weißen Bücher in 1915. Hesse reviewed it favorably in *März* 1, no. 9 (May 22, 1915): 167–68. [Editor's note]

2. The letters of December 30, 1916, September 19, 1917, August 21, 1925, November 2, 1929, June 22, 1932, March 1933, and March 12, 1959, from Hermann Hesse to Kurt Wolff are used by permission (© Suhrkamp Verlag, Frankfurt am Main 1978, 1979, 1981, 1986, 1990).

traces of greatness in the book, but solely with respect to the writing. There is no greatness in the treatment of the idea.

I have met Dr. Scheler twice and we have become good friends.

With regards,
H. Hesse

Hermann Hesse to Kurt Wolff (postcard)

Montagnola near Lugano (Switzerland)
[Date of receipt: August 21, 1925]

Dear Mr. Kurt Wolff:

Thank you for your lines (W/Ha) of August 6. The volumes of Zola you mentioned will probably reach me in the next few days; they have not arrived as yet.

I have another request! I am a great admirer of Kafka and have only his *Landarzt* and the *Strafkolonie* [In the Penal Colony]. Several of his other books were published by your firm: *Die Verwandlung, Der Heizer, Das Urteil*, and others. I would be especially grateful for them. I found the posthumous novel, which was recently brought out by a publisher in Berlin, extraordinarily enjoyable.

With cordial regards,
Hermann Hesse

Hermann Hesse to Kurt Wolff

Hotel Ochsen
Baden, Switzerland
Winter address:
Schanzengraben 31
Zurich
[Date of receipt: November 2, 1929]

Dear Mr. Kurt Wolff,

Your kind letter has reached me at the end of my cure in Baden; I shall be departing in the next few days. I shall spend the winter in

Zurich, but first be going to Württemberg for two weeks or so to visit some friends.

I was pleased to read what you wrote about Hasenclever. Among the members of my generation I find no trace of agreement with my own views, and it often strikes me as completely inconceivable that of all the German "intellectuals" between fifty and sixty I should be the only one to have experienced what I did: growing up in an apparently solid culture, seeing this culture melt away and prove to be dead as I grew older, and observing its total dissolution since 1914. It seems to me that everyone born between 1870 and 1880 *must* have experienced this and must be striving to return to the sources and outlast this era devoid of thought or conscience, so that a small minority of souls will remain in whom, over time, a new faith, a new reverence, and a new legitimacy of thought and word will become possible again.

How nice that you could spend some time with blue skies and sunshine before the winter!

With good wishes and regards,

Cordially,
H. Hesse

Hermann Hesse to Kurt Wolff (postcard)

[Postmark: June 22, 1932]

Dear Mr. Kurt Wolff:

A year ago I happened to see Mardersteig and asked after you, prompted by a feeling that these must be bad times for you; I also asked him for your address. He said little and did not give me the address, either because he forgot or wanted to spare you unnecessary correspondence. This year I insisted; I felt the need to send you something playful or a greeting, and this time I succeeded.

I am growing vegetables and flowers and my health is poor. I hope we will manage to meet again someday!

Cordially yours,
H. Hesse

The little picture shows my house, above the Casa Heise-Mardersteig.

Kurt Wolff to Hermann Hesse (draft)

July 15, 1932

My dear Hermann Hesse,

It is like magic: here I am, living tucked away in a quiet corner of southern France, and suddenly I hear my name called—and from far away words reach me, meant for me personally—

Yes, it is magic—but my present mode of life, whose direction is uncertain, has taught me the reality of magic. I have also come to understand that one never deserves the gifts one receives, but saying thank you is still allowed, I hope. My heartfelt thanks to you, the magician, who, I would have thought, could know nothing about me, not even my address, and who knows so much more than the address—

Many, many thanks—many regards from one part of the South to another and good wishes for you, your health, your work from your friend

Kurt Wolff

Kurt Wolff to Hermann Hesse (draft)

Montagnola
March 29, 1933

Dear Mr. Hermann Hesse,

Postponing the confession only makes it worse—for days now I have felt like a poacher who is hunting in your preserve.

So let me get it over with: after years of a somewhat vagabond existence we would like to settle somewhere, and have decided on Ticino; we would like Montagnola best of all. We would like to rent the little house where Mardersteig used to live and work, and to live quietly among a few books.

Whether we will actually be able to make this wish come true is still a matter of doubt, however: at the moment it appears that Switzerland, so renowned for its hospitality, makes more difficulties about granting requests for even short-term residence permits than any other European country.

But I consider it wrong, and going about it in the wrong order, to ask the authorities in Bern for permission to live in M. first and you afterwards, for the village, the region, the province in fact belong to you.

As for us, we shall do everything in our power to prevent it from coming to your notice that yet another foreign heathen has invaded your territory—and I hope that over the course of time, and in recognition of good conduct, you will be so generous as to forgive the intrusion—if it ever becomes a reality.

If, as I make plans for my future, I connect them with you and your place of residence, it is because I hope that Mr. Hesse the painter will see in the guilt-laden undersigned, as long as there is an automobile at my disposal, a potential chauffeur, who will gladly transport him to whatever sites he desires to paint . . .

With neighborly regards from us to you,

Cordially,
Kurt Wolff

Hermann Hesse to Kurt Wolff

[March, 1933]

Dear Mr. Wolff,

Thank you for your nice note! I wish every success for your plans and was pleased to hear of them, for your sake as well as ours. My wife is pleased as well.

Confined to the house by the rain, I have read a little too much and had another attack of the pain in my eyes, otherwise I would have come to pay a call on you today.

I am enclosing the newspapers. The news is sad and strange; I lay them aside and try to remain unaffected by it all. There is no front one could join; everywhere one would have to espouse a creed of cannons and terror. But there are always the "Kingdom of God" or the "universitas literarum" or the "invisible church," whose doors remain open to us.

Regards to you both,

Yours,
H. Hesse

Kurt Wolff to Hermann Hesse

Nice-Gairaut (A.M.)
"La Chiquita"
December 19, 1934

Dear Mr. Hermann Hesse,

The reprint from the *Neue Rundschau* we received has given us a great deal of pleasure. The opening pages of the *Glasperlenspiel* [*Magister Ludi*] have charmed and indeed bewitched us. With a sense of profound happiness I feel myself transported back into the magic circle of travelers to the Orient, into that enchanted twilight world composed of elements from dreams, play, and a higher level of reality and existence, through which you move with such sure steps, holding the thread of the labyrinth in your experienced hands, while the rest of us wander after you along the confusing and tortuous paths, full of curiosity, eagerness, emotion, catching glimpses of things here and there but never understanding fully, fascinated and duped at the same time . . . Indeed, reading your new work, I feel as if someone were playing melodies and harmonies for me which seem entirely familiar but which I always just fail to recognize. No doubt I shall remain a hopeless beginner in my efforts to play the glass bead game—as befits one who was so deeply immersed in the age of journalism as the undersigned—but I still look forward most eagerly to further initiation into your new world of enchantment.

May the gods bless your progress on this beautiful work! Helen and I can think of no better Christmas wish for you at the end of this year . . .

Our hope of seeing you both or Ninon alone down here has not been fulfilled so far, and now not much hope remains, for our days here are numbered. We have decided to move to Florence in the spring, or rather, to be more exact, to the countryside near Florence . . . We cannot remain here, much as we love the house and the countryside. Living here required the presence of paying guests, and although we had a steady stream of them, in the form of German friends, until the fall, the new German currency regulations have prevented them from coming since October. And so we decided to mobilize all our reserves and take advantage of the opportunity to acquire a lovely small property in Tuscany: a house with some good land that will supply us with wine, oil, grain, fruit and vegetables, as well as chickens, eggs, milk, etc. There we hope—Mr. Mussolini and the demons of politics willing—to be able to stay.

Perhaps the wish to see you both, which could not be fulfilled here, will become a reality there.

We send you both our warmest regards and good wishes, and I remain most cordially

Your old friend,
Kurt Wolff

Helen and Kurt Wolff to Hermann Hesse, Montagnola near Lugano (telegram)

JULY 2, 1957

WE ARE THINKING OF YOU MOST WARMLY ON YOUR 80TH BIRTHDAY AND HOPE THAT THE WORLD WILL EXPRESS ITS AFFECTION AND RESPECT IN SUCH A WAY AS TO GIVE PLEASURE BUT NOT EXHAUST YOU TOO MUCH FOND REGARDS TO YOU AND NINON FROM

HELEN AND KURT WOLFF

Hermann Hesse to Kurt Wolff, New York (postcard)

[Postmark: March 12, 1959]

Dear Mr. Kurt Wolff,

Today I have been reading the letter Kafka wrote to you on September 4, 1917 about A Country Doctor and the Penal Colony. Those were two of the most beautiful works you published. It made me think of you and also of the time in which that letter was written; it was the darkest in my life.

As a token of this fond reminiscence I am sending you my latest little work, four poems privately printed.

Most cordially yours,
H. Hesse

Kurt Wolff to Hermann Hesse

37 Washington Square
New York 11, N.Y.
April 4, 1959

My dear and most esteemed Mr. Hesse,

It was a very great pleasure to receive your card, which reawakened memories of Kafka in 1917, and your own four late poems.

Your greetings had an almost magical effect on me, since I was just rereading the small essay of 1954 "Über das Alter" [On Old Age], of which I am especially fond—particularly the last few pages, of course, where you speak of the joys of old age.—We hope to be in Switzerland at the end of May. Perhaps we will be able to see you and Ninon again—we shall be staying for a long time, so there is no hurry. We think of both of you often and hear news of you through mutual friends, [Winifred] Bryher in particular.

Regards and all good wishes to you and Ninon from Helen and your aging friend,

Kurt Wolff

Do you happen to have a copy of Kafka's letters at hand? Just in case you overlooked it: among the best of all is a card to Max Brod of September 6, 1923, on page 443—the story of the house of cards, and why it comes tumbling down. [3]

3. This little parable was a favorite of Kurt Wolff. It was recorded on a postcard Kafka sent to Max Brod: "Rage is something a child has when his house of cards collapses because a grown-up has shaken the table. But the house of cards didn't collapse because the table was shaken, but because it was a house of cards. A real house doesn't collapse even if the table is chopped into firewood; it doesn't need a foundation from somewhere outside. These are clear, remote, and glorious matters." Franz Kafka, *Letters to Friends, Family, and Editors*, translated by Richard and Clara Winston (New York: Schocken Books, 1977), p. 379. [Editor's note]

Thomas Mann

Thomas Mann to Kurt Wolff

740 Amalfi Drive
Pacific Palisades, California
April 21, 1941

Dear Mr. Wolff:

It is a pleasure to be able to welcome you to America. I have heard that Hans Sahl has also arrived in the meantime. We have folded our tents in Princeton and shall spend the summer here. Where we shall go after that, whether back to the East or to San Francisco, is still undecided.

Best wishes for the future!

Yours truly
Thomas Mann[1]

Thomas Mann to Kurt Wolff

Pacific Palisades, California
January 20, 1943

Dear Mr. Kurt Wolff,

The George book has reached me—a very valuable gift; please accept my sincere thanks for making me one of the first recipients of this noble first-born of your new firm.[2] I have read a great deal in it,

1. The letters of April 21, 1941, January 11, 1946, and April 6, 1947, from Thomas Mann to Kurt Wolff are used by permission of S. Fischer Verlag GmbH, Frankfurt am Main.
2. The "George book" refers to Stefan George, *Poems*, translated by Ernst Morwitz and Carol North Valhope, bilingual edition (New York: Pantheon Books, 1943).

with strangely mixed emotions. It is a peculiar and characteristic experience, one which matches our fate as a whole, to read this movingly stern legacy again in the language to which our ears and mouths must now become accustomed. Had we not been transplanted, such a book would hardly have been produced so soon; as a sincere effort to transmit German culture, it is a beautiful gift from the emigré bearers of this tradition to a world which until now has had little knowledge of this very elevated part of it. It struck me, for example, that the index of an American work on German culture of otherwise amazing scope contained not a single reference to Stefan George.

The selection of poems is excellent: felicitous, deft, accessible, I would almost say "popular." Everything loving in this proud and priestly spirit is emphasized, all the natural sweetness and feeling, yet without denying his imperious and uncompromising side. I mean the translation here, too, which conveys as much of all this as is humanly possible thanks to all the long and devoted work that has gone into it, as I well know. Of course you took a risk in presenting it side by side with the German text, a rather trusting gesture which virtually invites criticism, and here and there the urge to criticize does surface, ungenerous as that may be. For after all the parallel texts do say openly enough: "See how we must improvise and make compromises, how we cannot avoid a weak phrase here or an imprecise one there!" But the juxtaposition also reflects a justifiable pride, an awareness that these translations can hold up their heads next to the originals and truly succeed in incorporating a rare poetic sensibility into the culture of our host country. The graceful rhythms are particularly admirable. The Germans have always had a talent for absorbing foreign cultures. Now, in their diaspora, they are beginning to transmit their own culture to foreigners, and they do that well, too. One should praise them where there is something to praise.

Yours truly,
Thomas Mann[3]

3. This letter, dated January 20, 1943, from *Letters of Thomas Mann, 1889–1955* (copyright 1970) is used by permission of Alfred A. Knopf.

Thomas Mann to Kurt Wolff

1550 San Remo Drive
Pacific Palisades, California
January 11, 1946

Dear Mr. Kurt Wolff,

Many thanks for your letter, which deals with interesting enough subjects! How grateful I must also be for your confidence in me! I hope that my response will not appear all too small-minded.

Your plans are marvelous and most praiseworthy. But I cannot hold out to you the prospect of my participation, either now or in the foreseeable future. In the one instance I understand too little of poetry to feel called to the task you have proposed for me in your planned anthology. And as far as the Goethe book is concerned, for which you invite my participation with a far better claim, I simply do not feel up to it at the moment. [4] After finishing the Joseph novels, quite late, I have embarked once again on a large novel, whose inner and outer dimensions I miscalculated, as usual; I have made considerable progress on it, but it remains une mer à boire. [5] I wish to reserve all my powers (whatever that may mean these days) for this composition, which is so immensely difficult to realize—and fail, of course; you know yourself how these times and this country nip and gnaw at one. The longest interruption of this work (it will be weeks) will be for my next lecture in Washington: on Nietzsche, as I blithely announced, Nietzsche and German destiny, for better or worse. Did I say weeks? With the reading, gathering, and organizing of material it will more likely be a matter of months. If I then think of making a selection for the Goethe volume and the obligatory accompanying essay, it means in essence that I would have to abandon the novel or postpone its conclusion for an uncertain length of time—with all the mental discomfort that would involve.

---

4. The "Goethe book" was published, without the hoped-for introduction by Mann, as Goethe, *Wisdom and Experience*, edited, introduced, and translated by Hermann J. Weigand (New York: Pantheon Books, 1949). [Editor's note]

5. The "large novel" mentioned by Mann is *Doktor Faustus*, published in German in 1947. An English translation followed in 1948, published by Alfred Knopf. [Editor's note]

I must *not* think of it. One has to know what one wants and not allow oneself to become jealous of other projects, even when they seem to be made for one and leaving them to others is a difficult decision, a sacrifice. You will see from these words how clearly I recognize your right to approach me in this matter. But as long as the damned novel is weighing on me, I cannot devote myself to such a task. The worst part of it is that I cannot even recommend that you *wait* for me, since I can offer no firm assurances about *how long* you would have to wait, whether a year, or longer.

This, and no better, is unfortunately how things stand.

Who will be making the selection of German poems? I would like to see the table of contents, in fact.

Yours truly,
Thomas Mann

Kurt Wolff to Thomas Mann

January 24, 1946

Dear Thomas Mann,

Thank you very much for your letter, which was naturally a painful disappointment. But let me add at once that I completely understand and respect the reasons which make it impossible for you to make a selection of Goethe's prose for a book. Creative work must always take priority over labors in the service of others.

All the same, the kind and encouraging interest you have shown for this plan as well as for a large anthology of German poetry will prompt me to send you more precise information about both books when the time comes. Perhaps this could lead to some valuable suggestions from you.

With all good wishes for your continued health and work,

Yours very truly,
Kurt Wolff

Kurt Wolff to Thomas Mann

December 20, 1946

Dear Mr. Thomas Mann,

Oh, dear, no—how familiar and how repellent Blüher's letter is. [6] The arrogance of it, the messianic loveless tone, the disregard of customary courtesy, the sloppiness of its language, the rudeness in sending such an important letter to such an important recipient containing so many slips of the pen! "Der Gang der Ereignisse" [the course of events] not your "Rang" [rank] has placed you in the role of an arbiter.

The world has had more than its fill of this presumptuous German thinking, which is the exact counterpart of the German boot. And when I read sentences such as, "It is not a question of me personally but of my work," then "some higher force in us revolts," as Stifter says—as if a person could be separated from his work, as if we did not express our nature in our work—as if such a person could produce a work of mature richness, of insight and wisdom.

I think Blüher disqualifies himself in this letter. One should lay it aside and say no more about it. The future will presumably take shape without benefit of his theories. The Anglo-Saxon world has as yet taken no note of the work of Dilthey, Scheler, or Husserl, and hardly any of Max Weber has been translated into English. Let us leave it to the younger generation to decide whether they need Blüher.

How sorry I am, my dear Mr. Mann, that you are forced over and over again to play a public role by so many parties.

Please forgive the vehemence of my reaction.

With most sincere regards,

Yours very truly,
Kurt Wolff

Yesterday I met Erich [Kahler] and hope I did not commit an indiscretion by showing him Blüher's letter. His reaction corresponded to

6. Hans Blüher (1888–1955) had been prominent in the German youth movement, writing overblown treatises on masculinity and "aristocratic" culture. He wrote to Mann, hoping for aid in finding American publishers. [Editor's note]

mine but was mixed with Homeric laughter; he found the references to Spranger and Keyserling particularly naïve, and the table of contents gave him the impression that the new book is apparently just a summary of Blüher's earlier books, especially *Eros in der männlichen Gesellschaft* [Eros in Male Society].

Kurt Wolff to Thomas Mann

April 1, 1947

Dear Dr. Thomas Mann:

I hear that you will probably be in New York in the middle of April, but since I shall be leaving on a trip to Europe in the third week of April, it seems doubtful whether I shall have the pleasure of seeing you in New York. For that reason I have a request to make now that is very dear to my heart and which I entreat you most earnestly to grant:

Pantheon is preparing a book for the Goethe anniversary year in 1949, of selections which Ludwig Curtius has assembled in Rome over the past few years from Goethe's writings; it will be entitled something like "The Wisdom of Goethe." Curtius has collected the essential passages where Goethe expressed himself on the subjects of life and death, education, immortality, religion, history, nationalism and so on from his works, conversations, and letters, and Professor Hermann Weigand of Yale University, whom I am sure you know, has taken on the difficult task of rendering Goethe's prose into English.

For this book my dearest wish is a substantial introduction by Thomas Mann, who has a more profound familiarity with Goethe's intellectual world than anyone else alive. I see not the slightest objection to your making use, for this introduction, of material that you have written and published elsewhere in the past.

It is now spring of '47 and our book is scheduled to appear in the spring of 1949. You could therefore take your time with your contribution to this publication. If I urge you today to give your general consent, I do so from a wish to have this for me crucial question settled. Please, please do your part to make this Goethe book, for which we have found two collaborators of outstanding reputation and good will, all that we are striving for; by adding your name and introduction it can become a worthy monument in the Anglo-Saxon world to the greatest German on the two hundredth anniversary of his birth.

May this letter reach you at a propitious hour for my proposal. With all good wishes and regards to Frau Katja Mann,

Yours very truly,
Kurt Wolff

Thomas Mann to Kurt Wolff

1550 San Remo Drive
Pacific Palisades, California
April 6, 1947

Dear Mr. Kurt Wolff,

I feel on somewhat uncertain ground as to how to answer your kind letter of April 1. I cannot give you a definitive acceptance at the moment, because the Dial Press has been negotiating with me for some time now, the publishers for whom I wrote an introduction to Dostoyevsky's short novels two years ago. They also have long-standing plans for a Goethe book, for which they would like me not only to provide the introduction, but also to select the passages to be included. At the time when Dial Press first approached me about this project, I was occupied with my novel and had to request a later deadline. Recently I heard from them a second time and have had to reply that I shall be traveling from the end of this month, not only to the East coast, but also to Europe for several months, and that I am unlikely to be able to devote myself to the project during this time. I think it possible that the Press will agree to a postponement until next fall, and it seems to me it would not be fair for me to accept a similar proposal elsewhere until I have heard from them.

Incidentally I must confess that I have no practical experience in the field of editing or the technical preparation of such a volume and would prefer to limit myself to writing an introduction, as is envisioned in your case. In general your proposal has great appeal for me, of course, and if you were prepared to pay a suitable fee (the Dial Press paid me $1,000 for the Dostoyevsky introduction), I should be grateful if you could allow me some further time before I accept. My earlier pieces on Goethe are about to appear in English as part of a collection of my essays, so that I could hardly fall back on them and would have to write something new and appropriate for the contents of the volume. I would like to know what they will be in any event.

We shall not be arriving in New York until May 1 and thus shall unfortunately miss seeing you. Where will you be staying in Europe? We shall be leaving London at the beginning of June to attend the International Pen Club Congress in Zurich.

I wish you a pleasant trip and best regards to you and your wife from both of us!

Yours truly,
Thomas Mann

Kurt Wolff to Thomas Mann

April 11, 1947

Dear Dr. Thomas Mann:

Thank your for your letter of April 6. I am pleased that you are in principle willing to contribute an introduction for the Curtius-Weigand Goethe book and believe I can truthfully say that the material in the book will provide the best imaginable background for your introduction. The book will contain no excerpts from Goethe's novellas and prose works and will certainly not be a potpourri of excerpts from plays, biographical notes, and similar material; rather it will consist of a well-chosen and balanced selection presenting the essence of Goethe's thought and philosophy.

I can imagine that such a collection will provide stimulation for an essay very much along the lines of your own thinking.

It is difficult for a small press to offer the same remuneration as a large publisher such as the Dial Press, especially since our book will certainly not aim for "popularity" and is designed to appeal solely to a more intellectual readership.

I agree to your fee of $1,000 for the introduction, which will be paid to you upon receipt of the manuscript. I shall expect the manuscript by October 1, 1948 and make sure that you receive information about the contents of the book in good time. I assume that you will submit the manuscript to us in German, and I shall see to it that the best possible translation is made. The translation will be sent to you for approval before the book goes to press.

Under these conditions, I suppose I may assume that no other Goethe anthology will appear with an introduction by Thomas Mann.

In order to give you some preliminary information about the contents of Curtius's Goethe volume, I am enclosing the table of contents for eight chapters; two more are to follow, one containing his thoughts on art, and the second his thoughts on politics and government.

I am extremely sorry that I shall not be in New York during your visit, but hope very much that I shall have the pleasure of seeing you and Frau Katja Mann in Switzerland in the summer. With best regards from us to you,

Yours very truly,
Kurt Wolff

Anne Morrow Lindbergh

Anne Morrow Lindbergh to Kurt Wolff[1]

Scott's Cove, Darien
Monday, August 6, 1956

Dear Kurt,

After beginning in ink, and seeing the blotting paper effect on the paper in my little house this rainy morning, I think, if you will forgive me, I will go on in pencil. I have thought out so many letters to you since our stimulating lunch last week, that I felt I should get some of it down. Not to be answered—or perhaps even read—before you go off, but to put down some of my reactions to our talk before I forget them. First of all, after I left you on the Avenue, my immediate feeling was that I had perhaps been quite rude, carried away with my absorption on the book, I had talked too much, interrupted, hardly let you speak, not asked you about your trip and only talked about myself and my book! However, you will have to chalk that up against your being that day your most brilliant best as critic, literary mentor and midwife,—and it was impossible not to be challenged and creatively stimulated. I don't even know that I adequately thanked you. In any case, I do now, for the delightful lunch, for your creative vision of the book, for your encouragement and your criticism. I was very grateful also for your typed up suggestions and I have been studying them, arguing with them, and letting them ferment in my mind ever since they arrived.

Your criticisms are always constructive, never destructive or

1. This letter refers to Anne Morrow Lindbergh's novel in progress *Dearly Beloved*, which was published by Helen and Kurt Wolff Books in 1962. [Editor's note]

withering—and I find these last are true to form. But they are also not only revealing but somewhat appalling in what they reveal to me. I think I agree with these last comments: i.e., on what is lacking from the book, but I am not sure I am capable of doing very much about it, or at least filling the lack completely. I can do *something* but not all. I am amazed at how set the pattern of the book and the people already are in my mind. ("But there *aren't* any other members in the family," I keep protesting to myself, and "Oh no, Tim *didn't* have a good marriage.")

And then, too, how these people have hardened or firmed up since I first plotted them out, and somewhat altered from their original roles. Don was to represent the purely physical side of love, also the rebel's attitude toward marriage (*not* resigned), and Henrietta was supposed to be the possessive wife. (But I have belittled her and softened her.) And Albert was the total egocentric who really was incapable of marriage—or love. The "Happy" couple was always meant to be Beatrice and Spencer—and I had, originally, as their leit-motif "To remain in perfect love and peace together."

They have not all remained in their assigned niches and certainly don't fit your qualifications for "one couple that is not already old and whose happiness is not the result of preliminary heartbreak . . . a thoroughly compatible match" etc. "between 30 and 40." (The point of view of the desperately possessive wife does not seem to me so difficult to insert, somehow, either by playing up Henrietta or bringing in another peripheral character.) A happy marriage, though, in your sense of the word, should almost be the central pole of the book, and I do not see putting it there. In fact, I don't believe I can. It would mean a different author and a different book. I do not see it that way.

You said at lunch, "Don't you know any happy marriages?" Of course, I do, and have experienced it also for wonderful periods, but in your sense "ever to remain in perfect love and peace together" no. In the sense of a marriage which from start to finish is uniformly good, no. I have thought a good deal about this over the weekend and I have discovered some interesting sidelights. The completely happy marriages I have seen or known of fall into certain types: (1) The somewhat bucolic couple, rather simple and earthy—whose marriage does not change much from start to finish. (2) The very young or new marriage (untried by life—the honeymoon period). (3) Marriages in another generation (older) or (4) marriages in another culture. (I know one or two European couples who seemed perfectly matched and very happy.) (5) Second marriages in middle age. I know quite a few of these, and very happy ones. By far the greater number that I know, and these naturally are American, are either unhappy or have gone through quite a period of unhappiness in the middle and—the lucky ones—have come out with a good marriage—but not without some "preliminary heartbreak." (I don't think this is just my point of view or the point of view of my friends and wide because a doctor like D., who has seen many marriages, would, I believe, report about the same thing to you.) There *are* happy marriages—as you say and as you describe—but they are rare—not the usual pattern. However, it may well be,—and I suspect *is*—an American pattern. What is the matter with us? Is our definition of happiness at fault? Or our definition—and training for—marriage? Both of these are—I suspect—at fault. There are other factors, too, the changing pattern of marriage, perhaps. This, in itself, is interesting and clarifying to me, although I am not sure it gets me any nearer to filling the hole in my book. Theodore will, of course, describe a happy marriage (in another generation). And André can describe one (in another culture). But, I feel that the essential pattern of the book as originally conceived is one in which the central pole (i.e.—The ideal marriage) does not exist, at least not there in the flesh, but is looked upon by all the outsiders (Don—Deborah—Francis—Chrissie—Theodore—Aunt Harriet—André) as something they still, though perhaps reluctantly, believe in, though they haven't it now. Still, *they believe it exists.* They look on the bride and groom as its embodiment—the tangible embodiment of that belief. As weddings express the eternal hope of the human race. These people *are* outsiders—and outsiders see more clearly. The bucolic couple would see nothing. They would have no inner dialogue. ("The happiest nations have no history," etc.). (Not applicable to you and Helen!)

Alas, I agree with you, the two poles of passion—constructive and destructive—are missing. But, after all, I am not writing a treatise on marriage or a compendium. I cannot give every facet, and perhaps these particular facets are not visible to me. I see the world not in blacks and whites but in greys—all shades of greys—beautiful greys as in a Boudin seascape. It would be a better picture; it would be a better book; it would be a better life, perhaps, with the strong contrasts—but I am not sure that I have the stronger pigments to use. However, the suggestion and what it has made me analyze has been very enlightening and fruitful and it will, I am sure, germinate in me and come out in some clarification in the book. It will be a better book—if not The Perfect Book (!) for your criticism.

As for "only resignation everywhere." This has been said so often of me and my books that it must be true of my view of the world. (After all, *The Unicorn* is this). But I think it can be somewhat lightened and varied. I do basically believe in life and that it is good—not merely to be endured but to be lived joyously. I think more joy can be put into the book, and I intended to do this in the end.

How much joy there is in the Bach! That is why I love him. I played Anna Magdalena's Notebook last night—twice over—It is so beautiful. Thank you for it—and for all.

Anne

Kurt Wolff to Anne Morrow Lindbergh

August 9, 1956

Dear Anne,

Your letter of Monday came and ever since I have felt enceint by it—but it should not take nine months—not even nine days—to think out and say what it stirred up in me.

Your reaction to our discussion could not have been more alive and satisfying to your friend and midwife, though your letter made clear to me that I did not formulate my thoughts with complete felicity. But the discussion itself, verbally and by letter, and your "arguing" about it, no doubt is fruitful and good.

If you say "I am not sure I am capable of doing very much about it . . . I can do something but not all" . . . I translate this to mean: your insight, your experience, your intuition refuse what I called by the ambiguous name "happy marriage," or at least does not accept it in the form outlined by me.

My formulation was doubtless an oversimplification. Still, your letter makes clear that, *dans le fond des fonds,* we are in accord. The state of "happiness" (actually it should be the state of aliveness, of awareness, of positive relatedness) can be reached only through some kind of suffering and sacrifice—of one partner or both—through trial and error. I am deeply aware that *passio* is the Latin term for suffering. (The marriage which you call bucolic is certainly not what I had in mind.) The "happy" marriage (if we continue with this term for simplicity's sake) is most probably that relationship which has gone through the early stages of *passio,* has sublimated its self-centredness to an other-centredness, reaching a level in which tenderness continues to predominate and to prompt words and actions that lift the relationship again and again from the humdrum to an intense awareness of the other. This state of relatedness you could probably work in with the Beatrice-Spencer couple, to have a counter position to the marriage relationships that are tinged with resignation, and to the possessive kind on the other hand. As to the latter, I quite understand that you might find it relatively easy to insert this accent either in giving added sharpness and development to Henrietta, or to some other character.

You have raised the question of the European and the American pattern. That, of course, opens a wide field which one day we should have a long talk about. Here, and in relation to your book, I would say only: the main difference lies probably in the fact that Anglo-Saxons, and Americans of Anglo-Saxon background, are Puritans by tradition and education, trained to control and even suppress much of their emotional life. The Latin races, perhaps because they are so close to the ancient Mediterranean civilizations, are much less inhibited, and passionate love, going to the extreme of crimes de passion even, is an everyday occurrence. Perhaps André could have some thoughts about the European versus the American marriage. (My own impression is that, in America, women tend to be both more sensitive and more mature than men, who are so absorbed in the practical problems of life that they neglect what trains the sensibilities. Henry James has once said, and I think rightly, "In America, men provide all the canvas, and women all the embroidery.") Of course that gives to each partner a sense of isolation.

But now back to your book: of course, dear Anne, you know that nothing is further from me than to urge you to try something that goes counter to your intuition, your feelings, your nature. I would not wish to change your palette—I would consider it a "sin against the Holy Spirit." You have to follow your own law, for only then will you be able to reach, not absolute perfection, which is a myth, but your *own* perfection.

And now I wish you, with all my heart, a time of blessed creativity.

Kurt Wolff

Boris Pasternak

Kurt Wolff to Boris Pasternak

Pantheon Books, Inc.
333 Sixth Avenue
New York 14, N.Y.
February 12, 1958

Dear Mr. Pasternak:

Allow me, my dear sir, to introduce myself to you as your American publisher. I feel impelled to tell you that Pantheon Books is proud and happy to publish your great book. I have been able to read it in its entirety only in the Italian translation; at the moment we have only about half of it available in English . . . But this is enough for me to be able to say that in my opinion it is the most important novel I have had the pleasure and honor of publishing in a long professional career (from 1909 to 1929 in Germany: the Kurt Wolff Verlag), a career in which I published, among many others, all the books of my friend Franz Kafka—during his lifetime.

(I left Germany in 1929 and resumed my work as a publisher in the USA in 1941.)

Ramon Jakobson (who prepared an edition with commentary of Afanasyev's Russian folk tales in English for us) has been kind enough to supply your address, and so I hope that these greetings will reach you.

I have been eager to write to you ever since I read *Safe Conduct* and learned from this autobiographical fragment that you were a student in Marburg and loved the town and Hermann Cohen. I was a student in Marburg about a year before your time and spent an unforgettable semester reading Plato in Cohen's seminar, and your reminiscences about the town and the university reawakened my own memories of that time.

What pleasure it would give me to talk about Cohen, Natorp, and the others with you! (Perhaps you remember Theodor Birt, the professor of Latin, Johannes Weiss, the theologian and excellent pianist, Jenner, the musicologist who was also a pupil of Brahms, the Germanist Professor Vogt, and Elster.) I was on friendly terms with all of them, not because I was a brilliant student (I certainly wasn't), but because I always took my cello along when I went to call on them, and in those days I was the only decent amateur cellist in Marburg—they were all musical, and making music in their homes was an integral part of their lives. We could also talk about Rainer Maria Rilke, whom I also knew well in the years 1914–1927. It would be nice to chat about all this and more—perhaps there will be an opportunity in Stockholm toward the end of 1958.

Are there any books we could send you?

With all good wishes and thoughts,

Yours sincerely,
Kurt Wolf

[English in original]
Quote from our first announcement:
"No synopsis can do justice to the richness of this book. Not only is it a vast panorama of a country undergoing the most radical revolution in history. It also probes, with deep and desperate concern, the fundamental values of human existence. Written with the intensity of genius, it is lit again and again by images of striking force, originality, and beauty. If this book is read only for its political implications, it will be read for the wrong reasons. It deserves to be read as one of those rare masterpieces that grow out of the anguish, love, and courage of a great mind."
And that's what we sincerely believe.

Boris Pasternak to Kurt Wolff

May 12, 1958

Dear Mr. Wolff,

In haste I seize an unexpected opportunity to send a reply, through indirect channels, to your kind, warm, informative letter, which gave me so much pleasure when I received it. First and foremost: thank you, thank you, thank you for writing so simply and in such lively and concrete detail about yourself, your student years in Marburg (and much else).

Your letter reached me in the hospital in mid-March, where I was forced to spend almost three months being treated for a very painful case of neuralgia in my leg. This is the reason why my reply has been so unpardonably delayed.

I shall not be able on this occasion to respond with the same openness to your generosity and many expressions of warm feeling. The kindness with which you have overwhelmed me, the regard which I do not deserve by half, place me forever in your debt.

I shall increase this degree of indebtedness even further now by asking a favor of you.

Rumors abound that the novel has already appeared with you and with Collins.[1] I do not believe it; it is probably too early for this to be correct. If it is indeed the case, however, what a pleasure it would be for me to receive a copy from you! You have a wealth of addresses to choose from: Either in care of the Writers' Union (addressed to me) at Vorovsky Street 52, Moscow G-69. My address in town: Lavruschinsky per. 17/19 log. 72, Moscow W 17. My country house (this is best): Peredelkino near Moscow. Or, if Gerd Ruge is in Moscow, send him everything you may have to hand in the way of clippings about me, etc., with a note that he should come to see me at 2 in the afternoon on the next Sunday during the summer that is convenient. But what would make me happiest of all is another long letter from you.

I have the feeling of having said nothing except how enormously

1. The rumors were groundless: *Dr. Zhivago* was actually published in the fall of that year, September 1958. [Editor's note]

grateful I am. But this was all that was truly necessary. What you write about Stockholm will never take place, since my government will never give permission for me to accept any kind of award.

This and many other things are difficult and sad. But you will scarcely be able to imagine what a minimal role these particular signs of the times play in my life. On the other hand it is precisely these insurmountable barriers imposed by fate that give our life impetus and depth and gravity and make it quite extraordinary—joyful, magical, and real.

I wish you happiness, health, and success in all your undertakings.

Yours,
B. Pasternak[2]

Kurt Wolff to Boris Pasternak

37 Washington Square
New York 11, N.Y.
October 25, 1958

Dear friend,

I was just about to drop the enclosed letter in the mail when I received a telephone call with the news of the Nobel Prize.

I have always believed that Boris Pasternak should and would receive the Nobel Prize. (You know this from my letters.) However, we also know that sadly, sadly the right thing usually fails to happen. How nice that it has happened after all! (Your idea that the prize should have gone to Moravia I find absurd—I beg your pardon.)

At the beginning of my publishing career an author of the Kurt Wolff Verlag, Rabindranath Tagore, received the Nobel Prize. At the time my pleasure was largely the selfish one that this would be a great help to a young firm; I was pleased for the dear old Indian ascetic, to be sure, but it was not all that important, and another writer could have been chosen just as well. That was almost fifty years ago. Era un

---

2. Published by permission of the Pasternak Trust.

altro mondo. [It was another world.] Today the Nobel laureate is Boris Pasternak; it could and should be no other, and all my great, unmixed joy is for him. And it is a joy that transcends the merely personal: recognition of a writer and his work, work which has no equal in contemporary literature in the beauty of its language and the purity of its ideals.

The reaction of readers here has been a pleasant surprise for me. I will try to explain why: the ability to judge quality properly has almost been lost. Every college and university in this country offers courses in "creative writing." People are seriously convinced that creative writing can be taught and learned. Et en effet les étudiants apprennent quelque chose: le métier, the craftsmanship [And indeed the students do learn something: the craft]. Bad novels are amazingly well crafted here, fabriqué, surement, mais bien fabriqué. As a result a good craftsman is taken for a genius, and the geniuses, who are usually poor craftsmen, go unrecognized. Votre roman n'est pas fabriqué [Your novel is not manufactured]; it is "merely" a work of genius. But this time it has actually been recognized as such here. Your book is read and loved for its marvelous lyric, epic, ethical qualities. (Seventy thousand copies in six weeks—that is fantastic, and it will certainly be a hundred thousand copies by the end of the year.) But enough of my chatter. You have other, more important letters to read, other more important things to think about. Let me just add this:

Priestley: Yes, he did write enthusiastically about the book. His piece was sent off to you by air mail four days ago.

Hemingway and Faulkner: Of course we sent the book to both of them, with an accompanying letter. I will write to them both again today and enclose a copy of the letter to Hemingway. I don't know whether it will help. If it doesn't, don't be sad. Both are great writers, of course, but both are unreliable, seldom or never write letters, and both are alcoholics.

Acceptance speech, Stockholm: It has just occurred to me that both Faulkner and Camus gave very fine speeches when they received the Nobel Prize, which have both been published here. I will try to locate copies of them immediately and send them to you air mail.

Stockholm: I am making reservations at the Grand Hotel for the ninth of December, but it goes without saying that I will come to

Stockholm only if you yourself are present. And I make the reservations in the hope and expectation that you will save a day for me when IT is all over. As long as the crowds are around you, we may just shake hands, but I will not take one minute of your time. But maybe afterwards we may have a few quiet hours all to ourselves . . .

Kurt Wolff

Kurt Wolff to Boris Pasternak

37 Washington Square
New York 11, N.Y.
December 14, 1958

My dear friend,

It has been an age since you last heard from me—but I acted in the belief that not writing was the more proper and friendlier way to behave, since letters can become a burden to the recipient. Still my thoughts, concern, good wishes have never been so exclusively directed toward anyone as toward you in the weeks between October 23 and December 10. During this period you took a decisive step forward—you have moved beyond the history of literature into the history of mankind.

I doubt that you, in your present isolation, have any inkling of the worldwide fame you have achieved. Your name has become a household word throughout the world, a synonym for the man who refuses to give in, for the courage of genius. What you have done, and not done, has stirred countless people, not in the political but in the moral sense. You have set a standard, and despite many misunderstandings the essentials have come through. It is not true that your name is being misused only or primarily for a political campaign. Two brief examples to disprove this:

Time (Dec. 15): "The West certainly has no ground for claiming B. P. as a political ally, and at best will have to live up to him as a moral one. Yet *Zhivago* has become one of those portents of freedom whose ends are incalculable. For mankind Pasternak is a symbol of the 'élan to good' which he believes is the spirit of the coming age."

Text of a Chicago television station: "His message has come forth to all of us—not just Americans, not just Westerners—but to every individual human spirit who will listen.—And a lesson to us too, How quickly do we give in—to the boss, to the main chance, to the quick buck. How readily do we 'play it safe, not half safe?' What excuse do we find—in our personal life, our business life, our life as Americans not to 'rock the boat'—to relax, to conform, to play along. It took the weight of an entire oppressive system to make this brave man knuckle under. I ask myself tonight, don't you, how long would I have held out. At what point would I finally have said: 'I am in earnest . . . I will not equivocate . . . I will not excuse . . . I will not retreat a single inch' . . . And I will be heard."

There is not one individual in this country, whether child or adult, who does not know the doctor's name—look at the enclosed child's drawing, which is one example of many.

There is something else, more exciting, more a portent of the future: you have exposed, just as if you had a divining rod, a subterranean current, the dawning of a new spirituality, the longing for what is simple and good, for what can truly bring people together—in a time of opposing enemy camps, of political division.

To be sure, you have paid a price for it, and your countless friends around the world have been in fear for you and suffered with you. But if immortality means "ourselves in others," as you put it so well, dear friend, then you most certainly have achieved the greatest immortality in the hearts, spirit, feelings of many nations. You have changed the world. I don't believe there has been any "affair" in the world since the Affaire Dreyfus that has so moved people as yours has, with the difference that in this case the figure at the center is no mere chance actor, no hapless obscure captain, but rather a man *à la hauteur de son grand destin* [at the height of his great destiny].— These are not just grandiose words or exaggerations, but facts that have become history.

I mentioned *my* thoughts, concerns, and wishes above—for this please read *"our."* Your intuition has surely already told you that Helen and I form a "we," united in our profession (which we love), united in our thoughts, concerns, and wishes to the degree that is humanly possible. We have taken you into our hearts, we press the hand that has become dear to us . . .

Kurt Wolff

Günter Grass

Günter Grass to Kurt Wolff

Karlsbaderstraße 16
Berlin-Grunewald
March 29, 1960

Dear Mr. Wolff,

You have had no sign of life from me for a long time, but moving the whole household has hardly provided an opportunity. Now, however, I am sitting in a spacious old apartment in Berlin, thinking about my next opus and letting Oskar work for me. On the side, with my left hand in a manner of speaking, I have been drawing a lot, since in the fall I want to publish a volume of poems with illustrations. (Only so that I can then go to the Book Fair and say hello to you.)

Dr. Schöffler wrote me about the difficulties you are having in finding a translator.

A suggestion from me would be Jerome Rothenberg—in New York—who edited a collection of German poets for City Lights Books and translated several of my own poems, too. "New Young German Poets."—Whether Mr. Rothenberg is a diligent enough worker to be able to translate prose I don't know.

I will certainly be in Switzerland again at the end of August and remain in Ticino until October. Will you be staying at the Hotel Dolder again, looking down upon Zurich? Or could it happen that some good fairy will put it into your head to come visit Berlin, and us?

Our best regards to you and you wife.

Yours truly,
Günter Grass

Günter Grass to Kurt Wolff

Berlin
December 29, 1960

Dear Mr. Wolff,

Before this year is over we want to send you and you wife our best wishes for the coming year. As experienced residents of Ticino we particularly wish you a summer with a humanly tolerable amount of rain.

Progress on my novel is uneven; and actually my desire to have something to show you in a year is a particular help in dry patches. When this year gives up the ghost my wife and I will drink to your health and to a meeting, wherever it may be.

Yours truly,
Günter Grass

Kurt Wolff to Günter Grass

Hotel Locarno
April 4, 1961

Dear Günter Grass,

The translator of the *Blechtrommel* [*The Tin Drum*] has asked us what the expression "zwei Angströhren" [literally, "two fear tubes"] on page 196 means. The only significance I know for the word "Angströhre" is "top hat," but this makes no sense at all in the context. And I can't begin to imagine what two "Angströhren" mean.

Please be so good as to tell me what the sentence means on a postcard, so that Ralph Manheim can find a corresponding English phrase.

When are the two of you coming to Ticino?
Warm regards from us to you,

Kurt Wolff

Günter Grass to Kurt Wolff (postcard)

Berlin
April 10, 1961

Dear Mr. Wolff,

On people with thin necks you often see two clearly defined muscles running from the uppermost neck vertebra to the back of the head—or "Angströhren," as I call them.—

This summer we will be going to Denmark and not to Ticino. But on June 25 I will give a reading in Zurich, at the Schauspielhaus. Perhaps you and your wife will be somewhere nearby at that time.

We send our warm regards,

Günter Grass

Günter Grass to Kurt Wolff

Brunsby, Samsø
July 16, 1961

Dear Mr. Wolff,

We have come here to pleasantly boring Denmark with our sons and are becoming increasingly addicted to Danish cooking; good weather is our only concern.

I wish I could send you my novel in the form of a presentable manuscript, but the permanent nightmare is going to last another good two years; everything is still in flux, and the fragment I read in Zurich—and which was printed in *Akzente*—has already been changed again.

In compensation, however, Luchterhand Verlag will soon be sending you the page proofs of my novella *Katz und Maus* [*Cat and Mouse*], written last winter. Perhaps you will enjoy these 170 pages. The material for it emerged as I was working on the novel and had to be written down at once, since it was in the way.

We will not be back in Ticino until next summer, but I read that you will be staying in Berlin during and on account of the festival. There will be discussions, about art, of course, and I have agreed to join in since the invitation said you would be participating.

I am sure you know how pleased we would be if we could have you and you wife here as our guests.

Our regards to you and your wife.

Sincerely,
Günter Grass

Günter and Anna Grass to Kurt and Helen Wolff

[End of December, 1961]

Dear Mr. and Mrs. Wolff,

All over our house trains are going up and down the tracks and cars are having accidents; it is even possible—as my sons have shown—to construct the Berlin Wall out of blocks. In a nutshell: we are in the throes of a family Christmas. Yesterday—just for example—our dried out Advent wreath went up in flames and gave father an opportunity, amid terrible shrieks, to display his paternal courage by dousing the blaze. So you see that the two bottles you were kind enough to send us are being put to good use: the exhausted parents revive, swig by swig. But we hope to save the remainder for New Year's Eve, so that we will be well supplied to drink your health.

Yours,
Günter and Anna Grass

Günter Grass to Kurt Wolff

Berlin
March 16, 1962

Dear Mr. Wolff,

Thank you very much for your letter. I am too deeply mired in my dog story to be able to give you an answer on the spot. [1] I think *Cat*

---

1. Grass's reference to his "dog story" refers to *Hundejahre* [*Dog Years*], published by Luchterhand in 1963. It was published in 1965 by Helen and Kurt Wolff Books, in a translation by Ralph Manheim. [Editor's note]

and Mouse ought to come out six months, or perhaps even a whole year after *The Tin Drum.* I came to this agreement with Mr. Schabert in Frankfurt. I am very eager to see the American edition. I read a fragment of the translation in the *Evergreen Review* and liked it very much.—Here winter is going on too long. In mid-June we will be in Ticino, all five of us.

We look forward to seeing you and your dear wife.

Cordially yours,
Günter Grass

Laudatio

On Cantate Sunday, May 15, 1960,
Kurt Wolff was awarded the Medal of Honor
of the German Booksellers Association, which is given
to outstanding foreign publishers in recognition
of their work. On the face of the medal a quotation
from Petrarch is engraved: "Libri medullitus
delectant, colloquuntur, consulunt, et viva quadam nobis
atque arguta familiaritate iunguntur [Books delight to the marrow,
converse, advise, and in a kind of vital,
acute intimacy are united with us].
On the reverse
is engraved the name of the recipient
and the seal of the German
Booksellers Association.

LAUDATIO

by Lambert Schneider

AT THEIR MEETING in February of this year the executive committee of the German Booksellers Association, in conjunction with the awards committee, voted to present you with the Association's Medal of Honor on Cantate Sunday, 1960.

I was somewhat surprised to learn that the executive committee had chosen me to deliver the laudation, since I do not know you well personally (although we met in 1947). But I do know your work, your achievements.

When I learned from the minutes of the committee's meeting that I had been given this assignment, I at first felt some alarm, since I am not much of a public speaker and have no gift for resounding official phrases. But then I thought of what your publishing house and your work meant to me in my youth, and of what I owe to you as a reader with a thirst for literature. How pleasant, at my age and on such an occasion, to be able to make good the omissions of one's youth and express my appreciation and regard! It is with genuine pleasure that I carry out today the commission entrusted to me.

Fortunately my library shelves still contain many books from your active years in Germany, including almanacs and catalogues. Leafing through them to refresh my memory, I was startled to see the profusion of authors of note, some of whose names I would like to mention here: Franz Kafka, Georg Trakl, Franz Werfel, Heinrich Mann, Gottfried Benn, Else Lasker-Schüler, Georg Heym, Hasenclever, Zuckmayer, Edschmid, Iwan Goll, Carl Hauptmann, Kokoschka, Meyrink, Max Pulver, Ringelnatz, Schickele, Sternheim, Ernst Toller, Fritz von Unruh, Paul Zech, Arnold Zweig. And there were young French writers, too, whose names and work are still familiar to us today, such as Paul Claudel, Francis Jammes, and Charles Péguy.

In those days young readers were particularly attracted by your series *Der jüngste Tag*, those slim volumes with their black covers that introduced us to the newest contemporary writing. The announcement of the forthcoming series contained the following passage: "*Der jüngste Tag* will present a series of shorter works by authors of the younger generation, which may be considered characteristic of our times and as pointing the way to the future. True to its name, *Der jüngste Tag* will attempt to gather together works which, while drawing their strength from their roots in the present, show promise of lasting life."

The names of the authors mentioned above prove that the undertaking lived up to this proudly and boldly announced aim. To be sure, Herr Hitler and his cohorts had no use for them. Their books were burned and banned, the authors driven into obscurity, but there can be no doubt that German Expressionist literature is returning to new life. Dissertations exploring it are being written at German universities. The older publishers among us are familiar with these writers, just as we are with the name of Kurt Wolff, their publisher, and the younger generation would do well to seek out copies of the Kurt Wolff Verlag's publications in libraries and secondhand book stores. The education of every friend of German literature—and this should apply to all publishers—is incomplete without them.

At the beginning of this century the German book market for belles lettres was dominated by a profusion of outstanding publishers, on whom we look back today with amazement and admiration: Eugen Diederichs, Samuel Fischer, Anton Kippenberg, Georg Müller, Bruno and Paul Cassirer, Albert Langen, and Reinhard Piper, to name just some of the most important. A notable group, who performed an incalculable service to German and world literature, and furthermore gave German books an exceptionally handsome appearance, by commissioning painters and graphic artists to design and illustrate them.

At the age of twenty-one, my dear Kurt Wolff, you entered the publishing arena to compete for authors who all seemed to be claimed already by the great princes of the publishing industry. A bold venture, but a new generation of poets and writers had grown up with you, so that as a publisher you became the mediator and in fact the champion of this young generation. Your name has become permanently linked with the history of German Expressionism.

It cannot be my task here to summarize your development as a publisher. Karl H. Salzmann did just that in the *Archiv für Geschichte des Buchwesens* [Archive for the History of Book Publishing], and every bookseller can read it in the *Börsenblatt* [Newsletter of the German Booksellers Association] of December 22, 1958.

You, my dear Kurt Wolff, must have been a restless spirit in your youth, with a passion for founding firms. I was amazed to learn from Salzmann's essay that you either founded or took over the following presses. He writes: "In the beginning there was the first 'Ernst Rowohlt Verlag' in 1908, originally founded together with Rowohlt and which later became the Kurt Wolff Verlag. Beginning in 1914 the firm (KWV) acquired Erik-Ernst Schwabach's Verlag der Weißen Bücher. In 1916 Wolff created the Verlag der Schriften von Karl Kraus (Kurt Wolff). Then in 1918, together with Peter Reinhold and Curt Thesing, Wolff founded the firm Der Neue Geist [The New Spirit]. In 1921 Kurt Wolff acquired the Hyperion Verlag, and in 1924 the Pantheon Casa Editrice was founded in Florence.

An extensive empire with many provinces, in which you could enjoy pursuing your intellectual ambitions. Art books of high quality at the Pantheon Verlag or sociology and the humanities at the Verlag Der Neue Geist. During this period of your publishing empire, before 1930, authors and publishers exchanged the many anecdotes in circulation about Kurt Wolff. The man who could have collected them, and who in fact created many of them out of a mixture of fact and fiction, your friend and colleague Georg Heinrich Meyer, has been dead for thirty years.

This oversize publishing empire could not withstand the stormy economic crisis of the late nineteen twenties. It collapsed. Salzmann summarized the later fate of the presses named above in his *Archiv* article.

In 1931 Kurt Wolff turned his back on Germany and withdrew like a deposed sovereign after a revolution—or so it seemed to those of us in the trade at the time—to the shores of the Mediterranean. You were only forty-four years old at the time. Did you have a premonition of what was to take hold of Germany two years later? Did you foresee the spirit which would take control and make independent publishing impossible—unless one retreated into a ghetto or into the catacombs of a literature written in secret code? I do not know, and it is just as well, for everyone has the right to his privacy.

Kurt Wolff the publisher disappeared from view for more than a decade—but even if he had not, we would not have been able to see and hear him, for we Germans, we who wanted to conquer the world and remake it in our "image," were trapped behind a frontier of barbed wire that a maniac forced us to extend ever farther into other countries and nations, "no matter what the cost," in his monstrous phrase.

You, Kurt Wolff, fled before German expansion from Southern France to America in 1941, and in 1942, at the age of fifty-five, founded Pantheon Books in New York. You quietly set about investing all your skill as a publisher, all the experience acquired in a full life into this new firm, and the result was a long list of precious books, precious for both their content and form. You refused to be affected by your competitors, the mammoth American publishing houses which produce new books daily and spend vast sums to advertise them; this is clearly evidenced by your books, which bear no resemblance to the average American product. You have had the courage to offer a reading public with a reputation for conformity a new type of work, to carry on the best English and German traditions in book publishing from the turn of the century, and the effort it must have cost has been rewarded by the friends, readers, and customers you gained. You have published German writers such as Hermann Broch, Stefan George, Robert Musil, Theodor Haecker, Josef Pieper, and Romano Guardini in English translation and introduced these names into American intellectual circles. In the midst of the Second World War you prepared complete English-language editions of Jacob Burckhardt, Gustav Schwab, and Grimms' fairy tales, and your many bilingual editions created a spiritual bridge between the somewhat rough-hewn but vigorous new world and an old and tired, thoroughly battered postwar Europe, an achievement which cannot be praised too highly.

I should like to interject a personal comment here, dear Kurt Wolff, for I admire publishers who dare to indulge in literary activities themselves now and then. I am very fond of your anthology *Tausend Jahre deutscher Dichtung* [Anthology of German Verse], which you edited in 1949 in collaboration with Curt von Faber du Faur, and I also admire your debut as an editor, with Joh. Heinrich Merck's *Schriften und Briefwechsel* [Writings and Correspondence] in 1909 and Klinger's *Dramatische Jugendwerke* [Early Dramatic Works] in 1912.

In these remarks I have attempted to give an appreciation of a German, a European publisher, who was forced to seek refuge across the Atlantic, a fate imposed by this century, which saw a destructive and evil power arise in the heart of Europe, in our beloved Germany. Kurt Wolff suffered under this demonic force, but his spirit remained indomitable. Again and again, with wisdom, generosity, and patience, he sought out the forces of good and let them speak through his books, finding a new audience for them in a foreign land, his adopted country. For this we German publishers and booksellers owe him a debt of gratitude.

ACCEPTANCE SPEECH

by Kurt Wolff

I SHOULD LIKE to express my sincere thanks for the award which you have bestowed on me, and particularly to Lambert Schneider for his undeservedly kind words of praise. There are many publishers, I believe, in Paris and Milan, in New York, London, and elsewhere, whose merits in the service of literature outshine my own, but as we know, medals and awards are not always given to the most deserving. History books contain many accounts of victors in battles that may have been won by others. Such is the way of the world, however, and it remains for me to thank you humbly for this honor.

It is a pleasure, a great pleasure indeed, to be here today among colleagues to whom I feel strong ties, none stronger than the love we share for a marvelous profession. It is a profession that demands courage and faith, to be sure, but one in which miracles also occur again and again, for authors and readers are unpredictable, thank God, and nothing resists statistics with more success than creative ability and the response it calls forth, or fails to, in the reading public. In the last analysis readers are as diverse as publishers and booksellers. We would all like to think that our opinions are correct, and that the only true good taste is our own. So be it. It gives our profession its color and variety, and in the end history will have the final say on judgment and taste—history, and not the present time. For if immediate success were decisive, then publishing Kafka would be one of the greatest errors I ever made. But it is gratifying, after all, and a particular pleasure, to have one's judgment confirmed after decades and to see these long-neglected works recognized and appreciated throughout the world.

A marvelous profession, as I said, one that is rewarding and exciting. Who would become a publisher or bookseller if he were not a passionately enthusiastic reader? And so you know what I mean when I speak of the excitement of publishing, the intensity with which we await the new book of an author in whom we believe and the reaction of the critics whom we respect. I assure you that I read the first few pages of a manuscript sent to me by an unknown young writer in 1960 with the same sense of excitement, curiosity, and anticipation as I did in, let us say, the year 1910.

A marvelous profession, unique in its dependence on individuals, on individual personalities and initiative. I know of no publishing house that was created by shareholders. A publishing firm's development can always be traced back to the temperament of its founder. Lambert Schneider has mentioned a number of such outstanding personalities. In the early days in Germany my own activities and interests led me to be especially aware of Rowohlt, S. Fischer, Diederichs, and Piper. These men gave their own stamp to all their firms; as publishers they were more than faceless businessmen, and to this list I should add other names, names from other countries, a few at least such as Gallimard in Paris, Victor Gollancz in London, Alfred Knopf in New York, and one could mention many, many more. All had their unique character and passed it on to their firms, an essential part of it being their commitment to something perhaps only their children and grandchildren will come to understand and love. An essential part of it is the courage to strike out on new paths, even if they prove to be detours or dead ends. An essential part of it is a willingness to involve oneself with more than just sales figures and production costs. In the beginning was the word, not the number. And thus what I, an old man, wish for my young colleagues in the profession, those of you I know and those who are strangers, is courage for the future.

I would like to close with a line from a poet very dear to me:

"Creation's work is self-surrender."

I thank you.

KURT WOLFF
BIBLIOGRAPHY

"Drei ungedruckte Briefe von Ludwig Tieck an Jean Paul Richter."
Mitgeteilt von Kurt Wolff. Beilage der *Münchner Neuesten
Nachrichten*, July 12, 1908.

Johann Heinrich Merck, Schriften und Briefwechsel. In Auswahl
herausgegeben von Kurt Wolff. Leipzig, 1909.

Adele Schopenhauer, Tagebücher. Zum ersten Male nach der Hand-
schrift herausgegeben von Kurt Wolff. Leipzig, 1909.

"Zur Goethe-Bibliographie." In: *Zeitschrift für Bücherfreunde* NF 1
(1909/10) Beibl. p. 156.

Briefe und Verse aus Goethes Zeit. Herausgegeben von Kurt Wolff.
Privatdruck, 1910.

"Von einem Exemplar des ersten 'Werther.' " In: *Zeitschrift für
Bücherfreunde* NF 2 (1910/11) pp. 231 f.

"Emil Preetorius." In: *Zeitschrift für Bücherfreunde* NF 2 (1910/11)
pp. 373 ff.

"J. H. Mercks Briefe." [Review of *Johann Heinrich Merck, Briefe an
die Herzogin-Mutter Anna Amalia und an den Herzog Carl August von Sachsen-Weimar*. Herausgegeben von H. R. Gräf.
Leipzig, 1911.] *Darmstädter Tageblatt*, March 4, 1911.

Goethe. Götter, Helden und Wieland. Herausgegeben und mit
Nachwort versehen von Kurt Wolff. Leipzig, 1911.

"Intime Bücher." In: *Zeitschrift für Bücherfreunde* NF 3 (1911/12)
pp. 232 ff.

"Fritz Schlossers Bibliothek." In: *Zeitschrift für Bücherfreunde* NF 3
(1911/12) pp. 58 ff.

"Vorwort." In: Deutsche Literatur des 18. und 19. Jahrhunderts. Bibliothek Kurt Wolff. Versteigerungskatalog Joseph Baer. Frankfurt
am Main, 1912, pp. III f.

"Der Dramatiker Herbert Eulenberg." In: *Mitteilungen der Lite-rarhistorischen Gesellschaft*. Bonn. 1912, Heft I.

"Eulenberg." In: *Die Schaubühne*. 1912, Heft 8.

Friedrich Maxmilian Klinger, Dramatische Jugendwerke. In drei Bänden herausgegeben und mit einem Nachwort versehen von Kurt Wolff und Hans Berendt. 3 Bände. Leipzig, 1912/13.

"On Franz Kafka." In: *Twice a Year*. 1942, Nr. 8/9.

Tausend Jahre deutscher Dichtung [Anthology of German Verse]. Herausgegeben von Curt von Faber du Faur und Kurt Wolff. Pantheon Books Inc. New York, 1949.

"Begegnung mit dem Absoluten. Erinnerungen an Karl Kraus." In: *Forum.* June, 1956.

"Walter Hasenclever." In: *Blätter des Deutschen Theaters in Göt-tingen*. Spielzeit 1957/58. Heft 115.

"Worte des Dankes." [Acceptance speech for the Medal of Honor of the German Bookseller's Association]. In: *Börsenblatt für den Deutschen Buchhandel*, Frankfurter Ausgabe. May 20, 1960.

"KURT WOLFF UND HERBERT G. GÖPPERT: *Porträt der Zeit im Zwiegespräch*" [Interview]. In: *Börsenblatt für den Deutschen Buchhandel* 20 (1964), pp. 2053–2067.

Autoren, Bücher, Abenteuer. Betrachtungen und Erinnerungen eines Verlegers. Berlin: Wagenbach [1965]. 117 S. (Quarthefte I.)

Kurt Wolff. Briefwechsel eines Verlegers 1911–1963. Herausgegeben von Bernhard Zeller und Ellen Otten. Verlag Heinrich Scheffler. Frankfurt am Main, 1966.

SELECTED TITLES FROM
THE PUBLISHING HOUSES
OF KURT WOLFF

1913 Max Brod, *Arkadia: Ein Jahrbuch für Dichtkunst* [anthology]
     Walter Hasenclever, *Der Jüngling* [poems]
     Georg Heym, *Der Dieb: Ein Novellenbuch*
     Kurt Hiller, *Die Weisheit der Langenweile*
     Francis Jammes, *Die Gebete der Demut* [translated into German by Ernst Stadler]
     Franz Kafka, *Der Heizer: Ein Fragment*
     Philipp Keller, *Gemischte Gefühle* [novel]
     Oskar Kokoschka, *Dramen und Bilder*
     Else Lasker-Schüler, *Gesichte* [essays]
     Ludwig Rubiner, *Kriminalsonette*
     Georg Trakl, *Gedichte*
     Robert Walser, *Aufsätze*
     Franz Werfel, *Wir sind: Neue Gedichte*
1914 Paul Boldt, *Junge Pferde! Junge Pferde!* [poems]
     Walter Hasenclever, *Der Sohn* [play]
     Carl Hauptmann, *Krieg: Ein Tedeum*
     Karl Kraus, *Die chinesische Mauer* [with lithographs by Oskar Kokoschka]
     Kurt Pinthus, *Das Kinobuch: Kinodramen* [anthology]
     Marcel Schwob, *Der Kinderkreuzzug*
     Carl Sternheim, *Busekow: Eine Novelle*
     Robert Walser, *Geschichten*
     Robert Walser, *Kleine Dichtungen*
1915 Ernst Blass, *Die Gedichte von Trennung und Licht*
     Max Brod, *Tycho Brahes Weg zu Gott: Ein Roman*
     Franz Blei, *Über Wedekind, Sternheim und das Theater*
     Kasimir Edschmid, *Die sechs Mündungen: Novellen*

Franz Kafka, *Die Verwandlung*
Gustav Meyrink, *Der Golem: Roman*
René Schickele, *Aïssé: Novelle*
Carl Sternheim, *1913: Ein Schauspiel*
Carl Sternheim, *Napoleon: Eine Novelle*
Carl Sternheim, *Schuhlin: Eine Erzählung*
Georg Trakl, *Sebastian im Traum: Gedichte und Prosa*
Franz Werfel, *Die Troerinnen des Euripides*

1916 Johannes R. Becher, *Verbrüderung: Gedichte*
Gottfried Benn, *Gehirne: Novellen*
Albert Ehrenstein, *Der Mensch schreit: Gedichte*
Kurt Hiller, *Das Ziel: Jahrbücher für geistige Politik* [to 1919]
Franz Kafka, *Das Urteil: Eine Geschichte*
Karl Kraus, *Worte in Versen I*
Gustav Meyrink, *Das grüne Gesicht: Roman*
Arnold Zweig, *Geschichtenbuch*

1917 Oskar Maurus Fontana, *Erweckung: Ein Roman*
Walter Hasenclever, *Tod und Auferstehung: Neue Gedichte*
Oskar Kokoschka, *Der brennende Dornbusch / Mörder,
Hoffnung der Frauen: Zwei Schauspiele*
Karl Kraus, *Worte in Versen II*
Heinrich Mann, *Die Armen: Roman*
Gustav Meyrink, *Walpurgisnacht: Roman*
Ottomar Starke, *Schippeliana: Ein bürgerliches Bilderbuch*
Carl Sternheim, *Ulrike: Erzählung*
Fritz von Unruh, *Ein Geschlecht: Tragödie*

1918 Johannes R. Becher, *Päan gegen die Zeit: Gedichte*
Karel Čapek, *Kreuzwege: Novellen*
Iwan Goll, *Dithyramben*
Carl Hauptmann, *Einhart der Lächler: Roman*
Karl Kraus, *Nachts*
Karl Kraus, *Worte in Versen III*
Heinrich Mann, *Der Untertan: Roman*
Ludwig Meidner, *Im Nacken das Sternenmeer*
Karl Otten, *Der Sprung aus dem Fenster: Erzählungen*

1919 Francis Jammes, *Das Paradies: Geschichten und Betrachtungen*

Franz Janowitz, *Auf der Erde: Gedichte*
Franz Kafka, *In der Strafkolonie*
Franz Kafka, *Ein Landarzt: Kleine Erzählungen*
Karl Kraus, *Pro Domo et Mundo*
Karl Kraus, *Weltgericht*
Karl Kraus, *Worte in Versen IV*
Heinrich Mann, *Macht und Mensch: Essays*
Mynona, *Die Bank der Spötter: Ein Unroman*
Carl Sternheim, *Europa: Roman*
Franz Werfel, *Der Gerichtstag: Gedichte*
1920 Otokar Brežina, *Winde von Mittag nach Mitternacht: Gedichte*
Alfred Brust, *Spiele*
Karl Kraus, *Ausgewählte Gedichte*
Karl Kraus, *Worte in Versen V*
Frans Masereel, *Mein Stundenbuch*
Erich Mühsam, *Brennende Erde: Verse eines Kämpfers*
Mynona, *Der Schöpfer: Phantasie*
Carl Sternheim, *Bürger Schippel: Komödie*
Fritz von Unruh, *Platz: Ein Spiel*
Voltaire, *Candide oder die beste Welt* [with drawings by Paul Klee]
Franz Werfel, *Der Spiegelmensch: Magische Trilogie*
Paul Zech, *Das Terzett der Sterne*
1921 Ferdinand Hardekopf, *Privatgedichte*
Wilhelm Hausenstein, *Kairuan oder Eine Geschichte vom Maler Klee und von der Kunst dieses Zeitalters*
Richard Huelsenbeck, *Doctor Billig am Ende: Ein Roman* [with drawings by George Grosz]
Frans Masereel, *Die Passion eines Menschen: Holzschnitte*
Frans Masereel, *Die Sonne: Holzschnitte*
Walter Mehring, *Das Ketzerbrevier: Ein Kabarettprogramm*
Mynona, *Mein Papa und die Jungfrau von Orleans: Grotesken*
Rabindranath Tagore, *Gesammelte Werke*
Ernst Toller, *Gedichte der Gefangenen: Ein Sonettenkreis*
Franz Werfel, *Bocksgesang: Schauspiel*
Carl Zuckmayer, *Kreuzweg: Drama*

1922 Kurt Hiller, *Der Aufbruch zum Paradies: Sätze*
Fritz von Unruh, *Stürme: Ein Schauspiel*
Ernst Weiss, *Nahar: Roman*
1923 Alfred Brust, *Himmelsstraßen*
Adolf Feulner, *Bayerisches Rokoko*
Hans Reimann, *Von Karl May bis Max Pallenberg in 60 Minuten*
Joachim Ringelnatz, *Kuttel Daddeldu* [poems with drawings by Karl Arnold]
Ernst Weiss, *Atua: Drei Erzählungen*
Emile Zola, *Die Rougon-Macquart*
1924 Alfred Brust, *Die Würmer: Tragödie im Feuerofen*
Leo Frobenius, *Der Kopf als Schicksal*
Georg Heym, *Umbra vitae* [with woodcuts by E. L. Kirchner]
Erwin Panofsky, *Die deutsche Plastik des 11. bis 13. Jahrhunderts*
Wilhelm Pinder, *Die deutsche Plastik des 14. und 15. Jahrhunderts*
1925 Max Brod, *Rëubeni, Fürst der Juden: Ein Renaissanceroman*
René Schickele, *Ein Erbe am Rhein: Roman*
Emile Zola, *Werke*
1926 Charles de Coster, *Die Geschichte von Ulenspiegel und Lamme Goedzak* [translated into German by Karl Wolfskehl; woodcuts by Frans Masereel]
Adolf Feulner, *Die deutsche Plastik des 16. und 17. Jahrhunderts*
Rudolf Fuchs, *Ein Erntekranz aus hundert Jahren tschechischer Dichtung*
Will Grohmann, *Das Werk Ernst Ludwig Kirchners*
Franz Kafka, *Das Schloß: Roman*
Max Sauerlandt, *Die deutsche Plastik des 18. Jahrhunderts*
1927 Franz Kafka, *Amerika: Roman*
Joseph Roth, *Die Flucht ohne Ende: Ein Bericht*
René Schickele, *Blick auf die Vogesen: Roman*
Adolfo Venturi, *Giovanni Pisano: Sein Leben und Werk*
1928 Adolph Goldschmidt, *Die deutsche Buchmalerei*
Frans Masereel, *Das Werk: Holzschnitte*

Joseph Roth, *Zipper und sein Vater: Roman*
1943 Jacob Burckhardt, *Force and Freedom: Reflections on History*
Stefan George, *Poems* [bilingual edition]
Charles Péguy, *Basic Verities* [bilingual edition]
1944 Hermann Broch, *The Death of Virgil; Der Tod des Vergil*
Grimms' Fairy Tales
1945 Joseph Bédier, *The Romance of Tristan and Iseult*
Adalbert Stifter, *Rock Crystal*
1946 Georges Bernanos, *Joy*
Gustav Schwab, *Gods and Heroes: Myths and Epics of Ancient Greece*
1947 Hermann Broch, *The Sleepwalkers*
Eduard Mörike, *Mozart on the Way to Prague*
1948 C. F. Ramuz, *What Is Man*
Paul Valéry, *Reflections on the World Today*
1949 Marc Chagall, *Arabian Nights* [lithographs]
Curt von Faber du Faur and Kurt Wolff, *Anthology of German Verse*
André Gide, *Anthology of French Verse*
1950 Riccardo Bacchelli, *The Mill on the Po; Pascal's Pensées* [bilingual edition]
1951 Flann O'Brien, *At Swim-Two-Birds*
Josef Pieper, *Leisure: The Basis of Culture*
1952 *The Correspondence between Paul Claudel and André Gide*
Werner Heisenberg, *Philosophic Problems of Nuclear Science*
1953 Friedrich Hölderlin, *Poems* [bilingual edition]
Marcel Jouhandeau, *Marcel and Elise*
1954 *The Letters of Jacob Burckhardt*
1955 Anne Morrow Lindbergh, *Gift from the Sea*
Robert Musil, *Young Törless*
1956 Hellmuth Gollwitzer, Reinhold Schneider, and Käthe Kuhn, *Dying We Live* [documents of the German Resistance]
1957 Plotinus, *The Enneads*
Alan W. Watts, *The Way of Zen*
1958 Boris Pasternak, *Doctor Zhivago*
1959 Boris Pasternak, *I Remember*
1960 Giuseppe di Lampedusa, *The Leopard*

1961 Joy Adamson, *Living Free*
1962 Karl Jaspers, *The Great Philosophers*
      Anne Morrow Lindbergh, *Dearly Beloved*
1963 Günter Grass, *Cat and Mouse*
      Bernard Berenson, *Sunset and Twilight*

It would be arbitrary to close with 1963, the year of Wolff's death, since many books that he originated and contracted for appeared in later years. Several works—*Man and the Living World* by the Austrian zoologist Karl von Frisch, *Images and Shadows*, the memoirs of Iris Origo, and *Memories, Dreams, Reflections* by Carl Gustav Jung—were elicited by Kurt Wolff in talks with the authors. [Editor's note]

GLOSSARY OF SELECTED
NAMES

Altenberg, Peter (1859–1919). Viennese master of short prose; major promoter in pre-WW I literary scene of Central Europe.

Andreas-Salomé, Lou (1861–1937). Writer and friend of Nietzsche, Rilke, Freud. Published short epistolary work with KWV in 1917.

Bahr, Hermann (1863–1934). Austrian playwright and influential critic.

Ball, Hugo (1886–1927). Dramatist and cofounder of Dada in Zurich 1916.

Becher, Johannes R. (1891–1958). Expressionist and later socialist poet. Minister of Culture in GDR.

Benjamin, Walter (1892–1940). Influential cultural critic and philosopher, linked to Frankfurt School of critical Marxism.

Benn, Gottfried (1886–1956). Lyrical poet and essayist. Early Expressionist roots. KWV published the novellas *Gehirne* in 1916.

Björnson, Björn (1859–1942). Stage actor and dramatist.

Blass, Ernst (1890–1939). Berlin poet and editor of *Die Argonauten*. Published with KWV during WW I.

Blei, Franz (1871–1942). Biographer, cultural historian, and translator. Founder of many periodicals.

Bonsels, Waldemar (1880–1952). Poet and writer, also published in Munich.

Brandes, Georg (1842–1927). Very influential Danish writer, literary critic, and historian. Defined much of Central European cultural "modernism."

Broch, Hermann (1886–1951). Austrian novelist and essayist. Author of *The Sleepwalkers* (1947 with Pantheon) and *The Death of Virgil*.

Brod, Max (1884–1968). Prague novelist, critic, and poet. Friend and patron of Kafka. Published with KWV.

Bryher, Winifred (1894–1983). British author of historical novels published by Pantheon and Harcourt Brace Jovanovich. Daughter of financier Sir John Ellerman and mutual friend of the Wolffs and Hermann and Ninon Hesse.

Buber, Martin (1878–1965). Jewish philosopher and social thinker. Author of *I and Thou*.

Burckhardt, Jacob (1818–1897). Eminent Swiss cultural historian. Published by Pantheon.

Cassirer Verlag. Publisher of fine art books.

Cohen, Hermann (1842–1918). Neo-Kantian philosopher at Marburg University.

Cotta Verlag. Venerable German publishing house; publisher of Goethe and German classical authors.

Dauthendey, Max (1867–1918). Turn-of-century Impressionist poet and dramatist.

Delbrück, Hans (1848–1929). German political and social historian at Berlin.

Dilthey, Wilhelm (1833–1911). German philosopher of "life," of history, and of the humane disciplines.

Döblin, Alfred (1878–1957). Poet and novelist (*Berlin Alexanderplatz*, 1929). Early protagonist, later antagonist of Expressionism. Not a KWV author.

Drugulin Druckerei. Famous Leipzig printing firm. Printer for KWV.

Edschmid, Kasimir (1890–1966). Early Expressionist work appeared with KWV.

Ehrenstein, Albert (1886–1950). Expressionist poet and prose writer. Author of *Tubutsch*, with drawings by Kokoschka. Published by KWV.

Einstein, Carl (1885–1940). Art critic and prose writer. Great influence upon Expressionist generation.

Eulenberg, Herbert (1876–1949). Neo-Romantic poet, dramatist, and novelist. "House author" of Rowohlt Verlag and later for KWV.

Faber du Faur, Curt von (1890–1966). Emigré German bibliophile and collector specializing in Baroque literature. Instrumental in the founding of Pantheon Books.

Ficker, Ludwig von (1880–1967). Long-time editor of Austrian literary journal *Der Brenner*. Friend of Trakl and Kraus.

Fischer, Samuel (1839–1934). Founder of Fischer Verlag and arbiter of literary scene at turn of the century.

Frank, Leonhard (1882–1961). Prose writer and dramatist. Winner of Fontane Prize in 1914.

Frobenius, Leo (1873–1938). Ethnologist of Africa. Published with KWV.

George, Stefan (1868–1933). Influential German "pure" poet and center of far-reaching literary circle.

Gerlach, Helmut von (1866–1935). Pacifist, Christian Socialist, and editor of *Die Welt am Montag* in Berlin.

Gide, André (1869–1951). French writer, essayist, and poet. Nobel Prize in 1947.

Grass, Günter (1927–). Major post-war German novelist. *The Tin Drum* (1962) and *Dog Years* (1965) published in translation with Panthcon Books and Helen and Kurt Wolff Books.

Green, Julien (1900–). French writer of American origin. Diaries and novels published by Pantheon and Helen and Kurt Wolff Books, Harcourt Brace Jovanovich.

Grohmann, Will (1887–1972). Very influential art critic and historian. Promoter of modern art.

Grossmann, Stefan (1875–1935). Coeditor of the Berlin periodical *Das Tagebuch*.

Grosz, George (1893–1959). Satirical painter and graphic artist. Known for his savage depictions of the Weimar establishment.

Gruppe 47. Signal post-WW II literary group of major German writers, including Heinrich Böll, Günter Grass, Johnson, Hans Werner Richter. Held annual gathering.

Guardini, Romano (1885–1968). Catholic religious philosopher at Munich.

Gundolf, Friedrich (1880–1931). Member of George Circle and literary historian at Heidelberg. Wrote heroizing works on German historical figures.

Haas, Willy (1891–1973). Writer and critic. Editor at KWV and of *Literarische Welt*.

Hamsun, Knut (1859–1952). Norwegian novelist. Nobel Prize in 1920.

Hasenclever, Walter (1890–1940). Expressionist writer and dramatist. His early drama *Der Sohn* (1914) was extremely popular. Author and editor at KWV.

Hauptmann, Gerhart (1862–1946). Renowned German dramatist and writer of many stylistic directions. Nobel Prize in 1912. Not a KWV author.

Hebel, Johann Peter (1760–1826). Celebrated for his mastery of German prose.

Heise, Carl Georg (1890–1978). Art historian, museum director (Kunsthalle Hamburg) and promoter of Expressionist painters.

Heller, Erich (1911–1990). Emigré and later German professor at Northwestern University.

Hesse, Hermann (1887–1962). German writer of world renown (*Demian, Steppenwolf, The Glass Bead Game*). Nobel Prize in 1946. Not a KW author.

Heym, Georg (1887–1912). Early Expressionist poet.

Hiller, Kurt (1885–1972). Writer, publicist, and Social Democratic activist. Published with KWV before and after WW I.

Hofmannsthal, Hugo von (1874–1929). Austrian poet, dramatist, and writer. Wrote the libretti for several Richard Strauss operas. With Max Reinhardt founded the Salzburg Festival. Towering figure in modern literature.

Huelsenbeck, Richard (1892–1974). Psychiatrist and writer. Founder of Dada movement.

Husserl, Edmund (1859–1938). German philosopher and founder of phenomenology.

Jung, Carl Gustav (1875–1961). Swiss psychiatrist, cofounder with Freud of analytic depth psychology, and philosopher of culture: Published by KW.

Kafka, Franz (1883–1924). Poet and novelist of unique power and influence. Published by KWV.

Kahler, Erich von (1885–1970). Austrian cultural philosopher critic. Published *Man the Measure* with Pantheon Books in 1943.

Kaiser, Georg (1878–1945). Influential Expressionist dramatist.

Kerr, Alfred (1867–1948). Giant of Berlin theater criticism. Editor of *Pan*.

Kestenberg, Leo (1892–1962). Musical director, professor, and critic.

Keyserling, Hermann Graf von (1880–1946). German cultural philosopher.

Kierkegaard, Søren (1813–1855). Danish philosopher and religious thinker. Precursor of later Existentialist movement.

Kippenberg, Anton (1874–1950). Publisher and director of Insel Verlag.

Kirchner, Ernst Ludwig (1880–1938). Expressionist painter and founder of the artists' group known as "Die Brücke" of Dresden.

Klee, Paul (1879–1940). A great twentieth-century Swiss painter. Associated with the Bauhaus.

Kokoschka, Oskar (1886–1980). Austrian painter, graphic artist, and poet. Author and illustrator for KWV. A leading Expressionist artist.

Kollwitz, Käthe (1867–1945). Berlin graphic artist of social pathos.

Kraus, Karl (1874–1935). Viennese writer, critic, and poet. Editor of the influential review *Die Fackel*.

Kubin, Alfred (1877–1959). Austrian artist, illustrator, and writer.

Lasker-Schüler, Else (1869–1945). Influential poet and supporter of new talent. Published with KWV.

Leonhard, Rudolf (1889–1953). Poet and aphorist published by KWV.

Lichnowsky, Princess Mechtilde (1879–1958). Poet, playwright, and novelist. Published with KWV.

Loos, Adolf (1870–1938). Influential Viennese architect of strong modernist leanings.

Ludwig, Emil (1881–1948). Prolific biographer and writer.

Madelung, Aage (1872–1949). Danish writer. The novel *Zirkus Mensch* appeared with KWV in 1918.

Maeterlinck, Maurice (1862–1949). Belgian Symbolist poet and dramatist. Nobel Prize in 1911.

Mahler, Alma (1879–1965). Wife and muse of Gustav Mahler, Walter Gropius, and Franz Werfel. Renowned for her relationships with these and other outstanding men of her epoch.

Mann, Heinrich (1871–1950). Major political German novelist, essayist, and dramatist. A pacifist and socialist, much admired by Expressionists. Brother of Thomas Mann. Published with KWV after 1916.

Mann, Thomas (1875–1956). The greatest German novelist of the twentieth century. Nobel Prize in 1929.

Manheim, Ralph (1907–   ). Well-known American translator.

Mardersteig, Hans, later Giovanni (1882–1977). Typographer, printer, and advisor to KWV.

Masereel, Frans (1889–1972). Belgian painter and graphic artist of social-critical bent.

Meyrink, Gustav (1868–1932). German writer of the fantastic. Author of *Der Golem* (1915).

Mühsam, Erich (1878–1934). Socialist writer and activist. Published poetry with KWV in 1920.

Musil, Robert (1880–1942). Major Austrian writer and thinker. Author of *The Man without Qualities*.

Natorp, Paul (1845–1927). Neo-Kantian philosopher at Marburg University.

Nolde, Emil (1867–1956). Expressionist painter and member of "Die Brücke."

Pacquet, Alfons (1881–1944). Travel-writer and essayist. Published by KWV.

Pasternak, Boris (1890–1960). Russian poet and novelist (*Dr.*

Zhivago 1958). Awarded the Nobel Prize in 1958 but declined under government pressure. Published with Pantheon Books.

Péguy, Charles (1873–1914). French writer, publicist, and poet of "Catholic Renewal."

Pieper, Josef (1904–   ). Catholic philosopher, Thomist.

Pinthus, Kurt (1886–1975). Writer and editor with KWV. Important critic and anthologist.

Preetorius, Emil (1885–?). Scenic designer, graphic artist, and illustrator. Designer of KWV signet.

Pritzel, Lotte (1887–1926). Well-known puppeteer in Munich.

Pulver, Max (1889–1952). Swiss poet, dramatist, and editor at Insel Verlag. Published dramas and poetry with KWV.

Radek, Karl (1885–1939). Polish, German, and Russian publicist and revolutionary socialist activist. Disappeared in USSR.

Rée, Paul (1849–1901). Philosopher and close friend of Nietzsche and Lou Andreas-Salomé.

Reinhardt, Max (1873–1943). Director of Deutsches Theater in Berlin, producer of Salzburg Festspiele. One of the great figures in twentieth-century theater.

Rilke, Rainer Maria (1875–1926). Lyric poet and novelist of enormous influence in the twentieth century. Rilke did not publish with KWV.

Rolland, Romain (1866–1944). Eminent French dramatist, novelist, and biographer. Published in translation with KWV. Won Nobel Prize in 1915.

Roth, Joseph (1894–1939). Austrian novelist and prose writer.

Rowohlt, Ernst (1887–1960). Major German publisher and interpreter of modern literature. Collaborated with KW before WW I.

Salten, Felix (1869–1947). Austrian writer and theater critic.

Schaeffer, Albrecht (1885–1958). Formalist poet not associated with Expressionism.

Scheerbart, Paul (1863–1915). Neo-Romantic writer of fantastic tales. Influence on early Expressionists.

Scheler, Max (1874–1928). German philosopher and social thinker. Called the "Catholic Nietzsche."

Schickele, René (1883–1940). Pacifist writer, poet, and editor of the antiwar periodical *Die Weissen Blätter.*

Schiffrin, Jacques (1883–1950). Founder of Les Editions de la Pléiade (later absorbed by Gallimard). Partner of KW at Pantheon.

Schmidt-Rottluff, Karl (1884–1976). Expressionist painter and member of "Die Brücke."

Seewald, Richard (1889–1974). Painter, designer, and writer. Began as an Expressionist.

Simmel, Georg (1858–1918). German philosopher and sociocultural thinker of great importance.

Spengler, Oswald (1880–1936). Controversial German cultural historian and commentator, most famous for his book *The Decline of the West.*

Spranger, Eduard (1882–1963). German psychologist, philosopher, and pedagogue. Close to Dilthey and phenomenology.

Stadler, Ernst (1883–1914). Early Expressionist poet and literary historian. Translator for KWV.

Sternheim, Carl (1878–1942). Powerful German dramatist and prose stylist. KWV author.

Strindberg, August (1849–1912). Swedish Naturalistic writer who exerted great influence upon German literature.

Suhrkamp, Peter (1891–1959). Well-known German publisher and essayist.

Tagore, Rabindranath (1861–1941). Indian poet and philosopher. Nobel Prize in 1913. Published with KWV.

Trakl, Georg (1887–1914). Austrian Expressionist poet of great power.

Tucholsky, Kurt (1890–1935). Prolific writer, publicist, and biting satirist. Editor of *Weltbühne* after 1926.

Tzara, Tristan (1896–1963). Rumanian writer and founder of Dada. Moved to Surrealism.

Unruh, Fritz von (1885–1970). Expressionist dramatist and prose writer. Major voice in Weimar Republic. Dramatic works published by KWV.

Valéry, Paul (1871–1945). French poet and philosophical essayist. Published by Pantheon and later in the Bollingen Series.

Viertel, Berthold (1885–1953). Austrian writer, theater and film producer. Close to Expressionism in early period.

Walser, Robert (1887–1956). Swiss writer and poet. Published by KWV long before his later fame.

Weber, Max (1864–1920). Preeminent German sociologist and economist.

Wedekind, Frank (1864–1918). Controversial German poet and dramatist at the turn of the century. Influenced Expressionism.

Werfel, Franz (1890–1945). Early Austrian Expressionist poet, dramatist, and later best-selling novelist. Published and collaborated with KWV.

Zech, Paul (1881–1946). Expressionist poet and storyteller.

Zuckmayer, Carl (1896–1977). Major German dramatist and writer. One drama, *Kreuzweg*, with KWV in 1921.

INDEX

INDEX

INDEX

INDEX

Kafka, Franz (*continued*)
60; "Der plötzliche Spaziergang," 63,
65; *Das Schloß*, x, 59; "Das Urteil,"
59–60, 67; *Das Urteil und andere
Erzählungen*, 53, 153; *Die
Verwandlung*, 67, 153; Wolff as
publisher of, vii, x, xi
Kahler, Erich, 165–66
Kaiser, Georg, 20
Katz und Maus (Grass), 185
Kerr, Alfred, 28–30, 110
Kestenberg, Leo, 33
Keyserling, Hermann, 121–23
Kierkegaard, Søren, 19
"Kinder auf der Landstraß" (Kafka), 65
Kippenberg, Anton, ix, 24, 26, 192
Kirchner, Ernst Ludwig, xi
Klee, Paul, xi, 68
Kleine Stadt, Die (Mann), 26, 151
Knaur's Kleines Lexikon, 13–14
Kokoschka, Oskar, xi, 15, 33, 72, 191;
Dramen und Bilder, 15; and Kraus, 83,
84, 90, 92, 97, 114
Kollwitz, Käthe, 68
Kösel Verlag, 82
Kraft, Werner, 82
Kraus, Karl, ix, xix, 150; *Ausgewählte
Gedichte*, 95; *Die chinesische Mauer*,
84, 92, 95, 108, 114; "Dorten," 102,
107; "Elysisches, Melancholie an Kurt
Wolff," 98–102; essay on, 82–108; and
Expressionism, 20; *Heine und die
Folgen*, 95; *Kultur und Presse*, 88;
letters, 108–15; *Die letzten Tage der
Menschkeit*, 97–98; *Literatur oder man
wird doch sehn*, 105; *Literatur und
Lüge*, 97; *Nachts*, 95; *Nestroy und die
Nachwelt*, 95–96; *Pro domo et mundo*,
95; *Sittlichkeit und Kriminalität*, 95;
Die Sprache, 82, 94; *Sprüche und
Widersprüche*, 95; *Untergang der Welt
durch schwarze Magie*, 112, 114; "The
Violation of Pandora," 94; "Wiese im
Park," 84; *Worte in Versen*, 84, 92, 95
Kreuzweg (Zuckmayer), 22
Kubin, Alfred, xi
Kultur und Presse (Kraus), 88

Kunst, Die (Rodin), 15
Kunst und Religion (Hartlaub), 15
Kurt Wolff Verlag, vii, viii, 5–6;
acquisition of authors by, 10–18; and
Andreas-Salomé, 136; and
correspondence between Kaiser
Wilhelm and Czar Nicholas, 42–45;
and Expressionism, 18–20; and
Gauguin, 37–42; and Hasenclever, 32–
34; and Hauptmann, 26–28; history of,
ix–xii, xix–xxiv, 192–93; and Joyce,
45–46; and Kafka, 53–60; and Kerr,
28–30; and Kraus, 82–115; and "luring
away" of authors, 21–36; and Munthe,
46–47; and Rilke, 23–26; and
Spengler, 47–50; and Tagore, 116–18,
128; and Werfel, 32, 34–36, 69–70,
74–81

Lampedusa, Giuseppe di, xiii
Landarzt, Ein (Kafka), 59, 153, 159
Langen, Albert, ix, 26, 85, 93, 192
Lao-tsu, 127
Lasker-Schüler, Else, 191
Lebensrückblick (Pfeiffer), 136
Leopard, The (Lampedusa), xiii
Letzten Tage der Menschkeit, Die (Kraus),
97–98
Lewis, Sinclair, x
Lichnowsky, Princess Mechtilde, 14, 31, 97,
144
Lindbergh, Anne Morrow, xiii, xxvii; *Dearly
Beloved*, 170n; *Gift from the Sea*, xiii,
xvii; letters, 170–75
Literarische Welt, Die (Haas), 96–98
Literatur oder man wird doch da sehn
(Kraus), 105
Literatur und Lüge (Kraus), 97
L'Offrande lyrique (Tagore), 128
Loos, Adolf, 83, 84, 90
Ludwig, Emil, 31

Macmillan Co., 116
Madelung, Aage, 25, 28
Maeterlinck, Maurice, 117
Mahler, Alma, 35–36, 71–74
Mahler, Gustav, 36

INDEX

INDEX